Organisational Learning in the Automotive Sector

This book examines the concepts of organisational learning and the 'learning organisation' and their take-up in four contemporary work organisations in the European automotive sector. This sector is renowned for continuous change and innovation in work organisation and employment practices. In this dynamic environment, the pursuit and implementation of approaches that encourage individuals to learn and challenge existing orthodoxy are now dominant on the management agenda. Using a case-study approach, Penny West critically evaluates changes to processes, structures, cultures, and the employment relationship *per se* in this seemingly more inclusive and participatory arrangement.

Key issues and themes explored in the book include:

- organisational learning and change in the automotive sector, historical and contemporary developments;
- conceptual foundations of organisational learning;
- learning in organisations, theory, practice and barriers;
- the relationship between learning, development and change;
- case studies of the Rover Group, Volvo, XZZ Components and Creative Engineering.

Written for professionals such as managers and human resource developers, as well as for students of business and management completing courses in management education, organisational behaviour and learning, this book will provide an essential practical/theoretical framework to underpin the processes of learning and change in contemporary business.

Penny West is Senior Lecturer and Undergraduate Programmes Manager in the Centre for Business and Management Studies at the Edge Hill College of Higher Education, Lancashire.

Routledge Advances in Management and Business Studies

Organisational Learning in the Automotive Sector

Penny West

London and New York

First published 2000
by Routledge
11 New Fetter Lane, London EC4P 4EE

Simultaneously published in the USA and Canada
by Routledge
29 West 35th Street, New York, NY 10001

Routledge is an imprint of the Taylor & Francis Group

© 2000 Penny West

Typeset in Baskerville by Steven Gardiner Ltd, Cambridge
Printed and bound in Great Britain by
St Edmundsbury Press, Bury St Edmunds, Suffolk

British Library Cataloguing in Publication Data
A catalogue record for this book is available from the British Library

Library of Congress Cataloging in Publication Data
West, Penny, 1951–
Organisational learning in the automotive sector / Penny West.
     p. cm. – (Routledge advances in management and business studies)
Includes bibliographical references and index.
ISBN 0-415-21986-8 (alk. paper)
1. Automobile industry and trade – Management – Case studies. 2. Organizational
learning – Case studies. 3. Comparative management. I. Title. II. Series.
HD9710.A2 W47 2000
629.2′068 – dc21   00-22535

ISBN 0 415 21986 8

To Mark, Kate, Emily, Luke and Daniel

Contents

Tables

Acknowledgements

I would like to thank Dr Bernard Burnes of Manchester School of Management, University of Manchester Institute of Science and Technology for his guidance, support and encouragement throughout my research. I am indebted to all those who allowed access to the organisations and who took part in the interviews. People at the research sites gave their time and their views in spite of hectic schedules and demanding production targets and I thank them for their honesty and willingness to participate. As Silverman (1993) and many others suggest, interviewees construct not just narratives but social worlds and the approach to research I chose to pursue meant I needed to capture authentic insights into people's experiences of their work and life in organisations. In recording and analysing the data collected in these social worlds I entered, my concern throughout was to respect confidentiality, to represent people's views fairly, and to portray them consistently with their meanings. If there are misinterpretations or misunderstandings then the responsibility is mine and mine alone.

Colleagues, friends and students in the Centre for Business and Management Studies at Edge Hill, Ormskirk, UK contribute to a stimulating and intellectually challenging environment and I thank them for their support and interest in the project. Finally, I am grateful to Mark Oakley, my family and my daughters Kate and Emily for continued encouragement and understanding.

Introduction

Change and how it can be managed effectively has always preoccupied managers but most particularly since the 1950s. Commentators such as Drucker (1959) and Toffler (1971, 1981) articulated the necessity of coping with change but only in the last twenty years when change has come to seem more complex, rapid and urgent has it become a key theme on the management agenda. This concern has been fuelled by the popularity of texts offering benchmarks and best practices for every aspect of the organisational and managerial landscape. Indeed, how to deal with change has become both a serious preoccupation for employers and a healthy revenue stream for management consultants and theorists.

Added to this, we now find that developing organisational learning capability has become an equally dominant and linked theme for management at the turn of the new century. Indeed, the 'learning organisation' is a concept that has attracted widespread attention, particularly since the publication of Senge's *The Fifth Discipline: The Art and Practice of the Learning Organisation* in 1990. Subsequently, a number of prescriptive texts emerged to ensure that most managers knew at least what a learning organisation was, if not how to encourage their own companies to learn. Since then, many writers have tended to neglect the analytical and conceptual foundations from which the ideas of organisational learning are derived. These aspects seemed somewhat irrelevant given the urgency of supplying the ultimate 'recipes for success' (albeit very often lacking solid empirical foundations) to a very receptive and growing market place.

But at the beginning of a new century researchers and practitioners are growing more and more disillusioned with a series of management 'fads', which promise much but deliver comparatively little in terms of fundamental improvement to and understanding of the nature of work and organisational life. This book therefore offers a small contribution towards redressing the balance. It explores some of the theoretical foundations that underpin learning and change and connects these with practical contemporary contexts. Case-study research was undertaken between 1994 and 1997 in four organisations in the automotive sector that are recognised as having transformed themselves – the Rover Group, Volvo, Creative Engineering, and XZZ Components. The automotive sector is particularly relevant to the organisational learning/learning organisation debate because it is characterised by globalisation, aggressive competition, innovative work practices and hence a drive for continuous improvement and change. How far the learning organisation and organisational learning are robust concepts in both theoretical and practical terms were therefore explored in this context by observing and interviewing samples of people at different organisational levels. Some of their main observations and concerns are identified, together with what they consider to be the significant issues to do with how the nature and terms of the employment relationship are affected through the promotion of individual and organisational learning. This has particular relevance to the question of how far learning assists (or inhibits?) the process of change, its applicability and usefulness to the automotive sector (and perhaps beyond), and why players in the industry think developing their organisational capacity to learn is important.

Chapter one discusses the development of the automotive sector from the beginning of the twentieth century and explores the nature of change in work arrangements and their effect upon organisational life. In this environment characterised by change and increased competition, individuals must be proactive and engage in continuous learning and development if they are to cope. Chapter two then looks at the literature on organisational learning and examines contemporary concepts underpinning redefined approaches to work organisation that involve a learning approach to environmental change.

Chapter three considers the theoretical and practical perspectives associated with developing receptivity to organisational learning. An analysis of learning as an individual, group and organisational activity is undertaken, identifying the levels of learning and their implications for the development of people and their subsequent contribution to the organisation. Barriers to learning are noted, in the course of an exploration of practical approaches that may provide appropriate contexts for learning and change to occur. Chapter four examines traditional and contemporary perspectives on the management of change and identifies parallel learning themes. Organisational approaches to learning and change are then explored, taking internal and external factors into consideration, with particular reference to the implications of resistance, power and control.

Chapter five reports four case studies of international organisations in the automotive sector that acknowledge they are in the process of promoting organisational, group and individual learning. The chapter explores the approaches of each organisation and suggests that while they share the generic goal of striving for continuous improvement through learning and change, their performance and effectiveness is specific and reflects their development and the nature of factors manifest in their internal and external environments.

Chapter six revisits the main themes examined in the literature in order to provide a foundation for the analysis of the issues that arise from the research findings, discussed in Chapters seven and eight. These themes are identified as first, the ability of senior managers to understand and articulate the nature of environmental change; second, the involvement and contribution of individuals and teams so that existing orthodoxy is challenged and innovative strategies may emerge; third, the development of cultures that support this phenomenon; and finally, the relevance of the learning and development of individuals so they have the skills and knowledge to meet new challenges.

Chapter seven explores how far the evidence gathered during the research on the Rover Group and Volvo reflects or challenges the theoretical perspectives examined in earlier chapters. It identifies approaches of the organisations that involve developing individual and organisational learning to manage change. In the Rover Group there are clear indications that such approaches are enabling the organisation to move into a transitional phase, with individuals prepared to take an increasing role in identifying and addressing their own development needs. In Volvo, the approaches seem well-established and strategically connected with organisational culture and systems. It would appear that the emphasis here is on a process whereby individuals are placed in an environment that encourages them to learn how to learn (double-loop learning), rather than focusing solely on skills and knowledge acquisition and application.

Chapter eight moves to the analysis of the component suppliers Creative Engineering and XZZ Components and shows that the companies are pragmatic in their approaches to development. It is suggested that training and development in Creative Engineering assumes a higher profile, with more encouragement of interventions that promote creativity and problem solving. In XZZ Components, in which there remain people with traditional conceptions of the employment relationship, team and individual learning is beginning to complement the more structured training interventions. The chapter reaches the conclusion that new (and future) manufacturing methods need to be accompanied by complementary human resource management approaches that encourage integrative double- and treble-loop learning, so that individuals are equipped with the skills and abilities to manage future change.

Chapter nine summarises the literature and research findings with respect to the key themes. Effective management of change is dependent upon organisational learning that challenges the status quo. This requires:

- an understanding of the nature of change in the external environment and the ability of senior management to communicate this to the organisation;
- strategies that emerge through the contribution of individuals and teams;
- a dominant culture that encourages individuals and teams to challenge established norms;
- promoting individual learning and involvement in the organisation so people are equipped to meet new challenges.

The study concludes that whilst the organisational environment is characterised by change, uncertainty and instability, there is much that managers can do to exercise choice and control in that environment to influence future survival and success. However, the form of control is more subtle than that evident in traditional work arrangements and represents a new employment relationship that is more participatory and inclusive. Parameters of the relationship, however, remain defined and controlled by management, and this in turn influences the depth and extent of individual and organisational learning that can or is likely to occur. In organisations where traditional approaches to managing people remain dominant, opportunities for transferring learning in the organisation are limited and perhaps precluded by failure fully to exploit the process. The chapter nevertheless concludes that promoting learning is important in assisting the change process. It can occur at different levels and at identifiable stages in the life cycle of the organisations, and management can employ deliberate strategies and interventions to encourage – or discourage – the process.

1 Organisational learning and change in the automotive sector

Summary

This chapter outlines the context of the empirical research and provides an historical background to the nature of work and organisational life in contemporary organisations operating in the automotive sector. It identifies the distinct phases related to the employment relationship and work organisation that characterise the development of the sector, drawing upon the approaches adopted by producers in the United States and Europe. The entry of Japan as a leading agent of change to work practices in both Europe and the United States is discussed, in terms of the influence and transferability of its 'lean' approaches. In tandem with that, the simultaneous effects of the global nature of change characterised by flexibility, human resource management and excellence, are considered. The chapter continues with an exploration of what might be termed 'post-lean' developments, together with the future of the automotive sector itself, clearly increasingly operating within a global environment that is characterised by market saturation, mergers, alliances and new producers emerging from Eastern Europe and the Asia–Pacific region. In view of such increased competition and globalisation, it is clear that managing change and continuous improvement will be key issues, essential to ensure survival for contemporary organisations in the sector. The chapter concludes that the organisations most likely to survive will be those that engage the commitment of people to learn and innovate, thereby ensuring continuous improvement – provided that appropriate systems, structures and processes are in place for this to occur.

Background

Automobile production is the largest manufacturing activity in the world. It has a turnover of over a trillion dollars and employs ten million people; it is estimated that in 2000 the industry has the capacity to produce twenty-two million more vehicles than the world population wants or needs (*The Economist*, 10 May 1997). The industry has traditionally been at the forefront of innovation in work organisation and it continues to be the lead sector for the advancement of new work practices and organisational forms. The trigger for profound change in

Western companies was the threat of their own collapse due to market maturity, over-capacity and the increasing penetration of established markets by Japanese producers during the 1960s, 1970s and 1980s. Whilst Japanese approaches to work organisation evolved over time, this precipitated a major crisis for Western companies in the sector that forced them to re-invent themselves in order to remain competitive.

This faced companies with two key challenges if they were to survive. First, they needed to learn new skills associated with new organisational forms developed in Japan incorporating 'lean' approaches. Whilst they appeared enlightened they also posed a threat to established Western organisation and management systems. Second, they had to ensure that people would embrace and adopt the changes. The key for success in this environment is seen as the ability to learn and change continuously; the key approach for achieving this is the creation of what some theorists and practitioners describe as 'learning organisations' that are capable of continuously transforming themselves to meet the challenge of change.

The emergence of Fordism: the first phase

The shift to mass production in the early part of the twentieth century characterised the first significant watershed in the development of work and organisational activity for society. Henry Ford established a system of vehicle production that was to be copied throughout the Western world in a variety of manufacturing settings. Again, after World War Two a second change occurred within the automobile industry that was to culminate in the development of 'lean' manufacturing, pioneered by Eiji Toyoda at the Toyota Motor company in Japan. As before, the impact and implications of the processes involved have spread far beyond the automobile industry. Indeed Womack *et al.* (1990) observe that the two changes within the industry during the century have led to fundamental changes within society itself.

Thus it is acknowledged that the development of the automobile has had a profound impact upon the social fabric of society. It changed the way people lived, worked, occupied their leisure time, and the nature of social interaction. To explore the past, present and potential impact of the automobile industry, an initial analysis therefore needs to be located in the development of organisations, together with associated work practices and management approaches. Thompson and McHugh (1995: 23, citing Goldman and Van Houten 1980: 108) suggest that from the beginning of the twentieth century business organisations were beginning to be 'transformed from chaotic and *ad hoc* factories to rationalised, well-ordered manufacturing settings.'

The emergence of mass production – defined by Piore and Sabel (1984) as long runs of standardised products made on dedicated special purpose equipment by Taylorised, semi-skilled workers – characterised the shift from traditional, skilled craftsmen controlling the manner and pace in which work was executed. Mass production created a system that was dictated by the employer and was essentially outside the discretion of those at the point of production. It therefore not only required the establishment of a structural framework within organisations, but also required that a complementary management approach had to be developed. Thompson and McHugh (*op. cit.*) consider that changes involved systematising and stabilising both the practices of management and the organisation of the employment relationship. This resulted in hierarchies, division of labour, and new work patterns with a greater emphasis on supervision, measurement and reward.

The creation and manifestation of these changes have been well documented insofar as they emerged in the early part of the twentieth century as part of the classical approach to organisational design and management. Key contributors included Frederick Taylor (1856–1915), Henri Fayol (1841–1945) and Max Weber (1864–1920) and their ideas soon became apparent within the fast-developing automobile industry founded in the early part of the twentieth century in the United States of America by Henry Ford and William C. Durant. Burnes (1996) suggests that the American approach to industrial development owed much to individual entrepreneurship. Leaders such as William C. Durant of General Motors Company and Henry Ford played a significant role in establishing both the foundations for future practice throughout the world and the consumer society that was to become the expanding market for products. In 1908, when the automobile was priced out of the mass market, Durant anticipated one-million-car sales in the coming year (Sloan 1986). Similarly, Henry Ford's intention was to create a car for rural America that was affordable to as many people as possible (Hodgson 1995).

The visions of both leaders clearly meant that the way cars were traditionally built, and the way workers built them, had to undergo profound change. What followed was the emergence of mass production and Fordism, with the moving assembly line transforming the daily lives of those involved in the processes. Moreover, the major impact of the assembly line and the key to mass production, Womack *et al.* (*op. cit.*) believe, was the complete interchangeability of parts and the fact that they could be simply and quickly attached to each other. The structural characteristics that emerged within organisations from the development of mass production meant that work had to be strictly controlled and monitored within clearly established parameters of authority, as Weber (1947) identified. The organisation of people on a moving assembly line meant that work tasks had to be closely co-ordinated, giving rise to the 'scientific, rational' approach to work and management pioneered by Taylor (1911).

Morgan (1986: 32) suggests that the notion of separating the planning and design of work from its execution was the most destructive aspect of Taylor's approach, as it essentially advocated the separation of hand and brain. He quotes Taylor's often repeated phrase 'you are not supposed to think, there are other people paid for thinking around here' to demonstrate that men were employed only to provide the energy for production and profit. The Fordist approach not only promoted the development of the interchangeable part but also the interchangeable worker by taking the idea of the division and separation of labour to its ultimate extreme (Womack *et al. op. cit.*). Workers performed only one or two tasks and required the minimum of training, often just a few minutes in duration. Their pace of work was controlled by the speed of the line and if performance was not acceptable, people were easily, and quickly, replaced. In terms of motivating workers, it was considered that money and material incentives were the only means to encourage people to work purposefully. Indeed, the strategy of better pay for Ford workers in Detroit in the 1920s (five dollars per day) ensured a plentiful supply of labour and the rapid establishment of a consumer society that was willing to purchase the finished goods. Beyond this, however, was recognition that a systematic approach to the organisation of work also demanded an approach to managing change that would encourage workers to 'accept rather than reject or resist the introduction of new methods, techniques and technologies.' (Burnes *op. cit.*: 25)

Within the context of the classical approach and the emergence of mass production, there was also acknowledgement by Fayol of the need to train and educate managers in order that they could prevent industrial unrest through fairer and more consistent management methods. In view of what would inevitably lead to the emergence of an increasingly divided labour force, this would prove to become an essential factor. As the manufacturing system produced workers who were narrowly skilled, so the roles of quality inspector, repair and rework specialists and industrial engineer, appeared on the factory floor. Additionally, sub-specialist roles also began to emerge within these groups. Hence, workforces became more divided within and between groups.

In terms of career progression, opportunities and scope for involvement were limited for the shop-floor worker in the Fordist regime. Neither were they encouraged to volunteer information concerning malfunctions or how operating processes could be improved. Nevertheless, over time, and with the emergence of specialist roles, those who developed skills in product and manufacturing engineering became the newly emerging professionals who could advance within their own specialist areas. As the automobile became more complicated in its design and manufacture, however, the division of labour within the engineering professions also became more pronounced (Womack *et al. op. cit.*).

In the automobile industry in the United States, huge gains in productivity were made in the first quarter of the twentieth century and the entrance of General Motors, and later Chrysler, saw the differentiation of products to serve different parts of the market. It seemed that Henry Ford was not only responsible for diffusing the manufacturing approaches he had developed, but also for providing a classical management model for other entrepreneurs to follow. Thompson and McHugh (*op. cit.*), however, consider that the focus on organisational design, strategy and structure offered by the classical theorists is valuable but partial. They contend that the approach neglects the informal dimensions of organisational life, increasingly addressed by the emergent band of social scientists and industrial psychologists after the First World War.

The Human Relations approach

The Human Relations school developed in response to studies on work fatigue (Burnes *op. cit.*) and was fuelled by the wave of hostility generated among workers by Scientific Management. Over time it seemed to erode skills and demand a faster work pace through time and motion studies (Thompson and McHugh *op. cit.*). The philosophy of 'one best way' was criticised on the basis that human behaviour and industrial conditions generated their own complexity that also entered into the equation of the organisation and management of people. In tandem was the view that while 'the growth of bureaucracy was gathering pace, so too was people's antagonism towards faceless machine-like organisations where employees and 'customers alike lost their individuality and became numbers' (Burnes *op. cit.*: 46). In the United States, a drift towards 'welfarism' was apparent to combat these feelings, particularly in those organisations that provided houses, schools, medical facilities, shops and personnel departments for employees, in return for their loyalty and hard work. In Ford, there was limited provision of this nature, but considerable potential for its development through the 'Sociological Department' and the 'Plant Protection Service'. These groups employed investigators who were able to visit homes to check on absenteeism and monitor families' values and habits. In tandem were profit sharing schemes that were offered to those employees who were found to be 'suitable.' This interest was not philanthropic, Thompson and McHugh (*op. cit.*: 46) argue; rather it arose 'from attempts to grapple with the recruitment and motivation problems deriving from the increasing size of the labour force and a new industrial relations situation shaped by declining loyalty and rising unrest.'

At this time, theorists were beginning to reject the notion that employees were motivated by financial incentives alone. The most significant research was that associated with Elton Mayo (1880–1949) and the experiments conducted in the Western Electric Company's Hawthorne Plant in Chicago in the 1920s and 1930s. Despite contemporary criticisms, the results at that time indicated that it was not money alone that motivated individuals, but social relationships and positive interaction in the workplace were also significant issues. As Burnes (*op. cit.*: 49) comments 'the focus of good management practice would shift to the importance of leadership and communication in order to win over employees.'

From the 1930s onwards, other researchers contributed to, and enriched, these findings. Chester Barnard (1938) identified the importance of recognising the organic nature of formal and informal relationships in organisational life and advanced the need for co-operative activity between managers and employees. Similarly, Douglas McGregor (1906–1964) illuminated an approach to management that was based upon positive (Y) and negative (X) assumptions of human nature. He advocated management adoption of the positive approach towards workers in order to achieve a response that encouraged identification with, and commitment to, organisational goals.

By the 1930s, corporate America was besieged by legislation that allowed greater control over markets and pricing. In return, there was acceptance of minimum wage and maximum hour codes, together with guarantees of union membership and collective bargaining rights. Organisations such as General Motors looked to the ideology of human relations as an approach to management that would support these changes. Ford, however, resisted their adoption for as long as was possible, maintaining the traditional approaches that promoted a reputation for 'plant brutality for which the company had become infamous' (Abodaher 1986: 72). It was not until 1946 that change occurred, when Henry Ford II 'made it clear that while the Ford Motor Company had operated on, and exploited, the fear of its workers during the past twenty years, those days were gone' (Abodaher *op. cit.*). He continued 'cars could not be built as cheaply as when good human relations existed inside the company.' Womack *et al.* (*op. cit.*) describe 1955 as the pinnacle of success for the American automobile industry with Ford, General Motors and Chrysler accounting for 95 per cent of all sales, and six models accounting for 80 per cent of all cars sold. They add, however, that all traces of craft production had disappeared in the United States by this time. Significantly, 1955 also marked the decline of the domination of the United States in the market, the main reason being that mass production had become common-place throughout the world. European producers Volkswagen, Fiat and Renault were producing at a comparable scale to Detroit's facilities. Womack *et al.* (*op. cit.*) confirm that European craft-producers such as Daimler-Benz had also made the transition to mass production.

The automobile industry: a second phase

Jones (1981) identifies a second phase in the global automobile industry that began in 1955. He sees it as characterised by incremental technical change, leading to a standardised product design and the refinement of the organisation of production on a large scale. In the United States, he suggests, the overall product design was stabilised by 1960 and this was accompanied by a slowing down in the rate of product innovation. This was not, though, the case in Europe, where market conditions were favourable and new innovations, including front-wheel drive and disc brakes, continued to be introduced throughout this period. Jones (*op. cit.*) suggests that from this time, car design in North America was not destined to be the dominant design world-wide. Indeed, from a global perspective, the centre of innovation moved from the United States to Europe and later Japan.

In terms of organisational design, by the 1960s the accepted view was that bureaucracy was being replaced with an approach that was more flexible and people-centred, although the development of a generic approach to managing was acknowledged to be piecemeal. Thompson and McHugh (*op. cit.*: 75) justifiably point out that 'management is caught in the contradiction of needing to exert control and authority over labour to secure profitability in competitive conditions, while requiring workers to be motivated and co-operative.' Using the motor industry as an example, they suggest that during the 1940s and early 1950s, most workers were treated as core, they were part of powerful trade unions and they were essentially co-operative with management due to post-war recovery conditions. The intensification of competition, however, provoked management to challenge wage systems, work group practices and staffing levels. Intense struggles between unions and management within Ford, Chrysler and Leyland in Europe and the United States throughout the 1960s signified a shift in power relations, with more direct controls exerted by management.

Increased managerial control led to growing unrest in the automobile industry in Europe. During the early post-war years, large numbers of immigrants were employed in European factories operated by Fiat, Renault and Volkswagen. Whilst some returned home, others stayed, only to be joined by returning indigenous workers. As Womack *et al.* (*op. cit.*: 47) remark

> The workers in Turin, Paris and Wolfsburg realised that mass production was not a way station to self-employment back home; it was, instead, their life's work. Suddenly the inter-changeable, dead-end monotony of mass production plants began to seem unbearable. A wave of unrest followed.

As a result, organisational ideology increasingly focused on the need to provide employees with opportunities for personal growth and development in order to compensate for the alienation experienced. Theorist Warren Bennis, for example, argued that the conditions that created the need for adjustments in approach included rapid and unexpected change in the environment. Added to this was the diversity of skills increasingly needed to maintain organisational effectiveness. Growth in size of organisations and a subsequent change in managerial behaviour that leaned towards McGregor's theory Y assumption of human nature also provoked change (Burnes *op. cit.*).

In terms of practical demonstrations of the human relations approach, it was not until workers and managers began to challenge the Tayloristic basis of work organisation and job design that significant change occurred. Organisational psychologists such as Argyris and Herzberg argued that the alienation experienced by workers could be reduced if attention was paid to their 'higher level needs' (Maslow 1943). Morgan (*op. cit.*: 42) suggests that this was appealing to managers 'as it offered the possibility of motivating employees without paying them any more money.' Womack *et al.* (*op. cit.*: 47) argue, however, that, in reality 'the European mass-production systems were patched up in the 1970s by increasing wages and steadily decreasing the weekly hours of work.'

Nevertheless, in the 1960s and 1970s management focused on redesigning work and implementing work humanisation schemes through job enrichment, job enlargement and granting more autonomy to the individual and group. But changes to work organisation and design, advocated by the human relations approach, were, according to Womack *et al.* (*op. cit.*), only palliatives for the majority employed in the sector. In an economic environment which reduced worker expectations and employment alternatives, they suggest that in the 1980s European workers continued to find mass production systems so unpleasant that the first priority in any negotiations between management and unions continued to be reducing hours spent in the plant.

Volvo's approach

An exception was the Volvo plant in Kalmar, Sweden, in which management chose to address the problems of labour turnover and absenteeism by attempting to make work more varied and attractive. At the same time, Volvo was conscious of its image as one of Sweden's leading employers and it gained much publicity through the reintroduction of craft techniques by giving small groups of workers responsibility for assembling a whole vehicle. The view portrayed was that if Volvo workers were motivated and happy in their work, then this would help them (and the organisation) produce higher quality vehicles (Morgan *op. cit.*).

Volvo was able to devote attention to innovative work practices because labour market conditions in Sweden at this time were different to the rest of Europe and were such that unemployment remained low and wage differentials between different sectors and companies small. Companies in the automotive sector therefore could not compensate for poor working environments with high wages and other benefits (Berggren 1992). Also, the interest and influence of trade unions in work environments and organisation increased, and legislation in 1976 (the Swedish Co-determination Law) meant that companies were legally obliged to involve unions in any proposed changes. This resulted in the creation of new production systems that were more adapted to human demands.

The automobile industry in the United States

Throughout the 1960s and 1970s, the global automobile industry was preoccupied with innovation and higher productivity in order to remain competitive. Jones (*op. cit.*) suggests that American manufacturers were able to concentrate on the latter at the expense of the former. He adds that the development of more sophisticated production techniques and competition in increasingly similar products, together with depressed market conditions and the oil crisis of 1973, were responsible for the squeezing out of the smaller producers and assisting Japanese manufacturers to gain advantage. Indeed, the cars selling best at this time were made by Japanese manufacturers Honda, Toyota and Datsun and were characterised by their small size and low fuel consumption, unlike those models produced by American companies (Abodaher *op. cit.*). A climate of economic crisis in the United States continued and, by March 1975, this meant that 135,000 General Motors workers and over 120,000 at Ford and Chrysler (the three main employers in the United States industry), were laid off. It therefore became apparent that the entire American automotive sector found itself in need of a fundamental change in direction if it were to survive.

The automobile industry: phase three

Clearly, the crisis that was becoming evident in Europe and the United States was exacerbated by the successful penetration of the established markets by Japanese manufacturers who by 1979 had overtaken the United States as the world's leading automobile manufacturer. As a result, it was clear that the global automotive sector would need to undergo profound change if it were to remain intact

(Abodaher *op. cit.*, Sloan *op. cit.*, Womack *et al. op. cit.*). Economic and labour market conditions, the amalgamation of markets through European integration, lower tariff barriers and increased imports of smaller cars in the United States and European markets from Japan meant that manufacturers and suppliers had to adapt in terms of both product output and geographical presence. Additionally, the industry witnessed slower growth and instability as established markets reached maturity. As a result, the automobile sector was almost at a state of collapse with General Motors, Chrysler, Ford and British Leyland amongst those severely affected. Indeed, British Leyland (subsequently the Rover Group) was only saved when it was nationalised by the Labour Government of 1975.

It was the entry of Japanese producers as strong competitors in the global automotive sector that provoked most interest and played a significant role in creating the impetus for change in the nature of work and organisational design in Western industry. Unlike previous initiatives that might be considered merely attempts to rejuvenate stagnant mass production systems, what the Japanese seemed to offer was an entirely new approach to manufacturing. Its significance was that it also appeared to require a revised approach to human resource management and organisation that seemed to offer a radical solution to the problems encountered by the traditional approaches within the Western automotive sector. Nevertheless, the adoption of Japanese systems was not destined to be an easy solution and has therefore attracted debate in terms of its implications for Western industry.

The rise of Japan as an economic power has been well documented (Horsley and Buckley 1990, Thurow 1993, Vogel 1979, Whitehill 1991) but its ascendancy as a major player in the automobile industry continues to be a key source of interest and debate. Concomitant with this is the explicit influence that Japanese organisations have had on the West by means of direct investment, for example Nissan locating vehicle production in the north east of England (Crowther and Garrahan 1988). Smith (1988), therefore, considers that two aspects of 'Japanisation' have co-existed in recent years that focus on joint ventures and management and organisational practices. He cites as an example the partnership between Honda and Rover (formerly British Leyland), developed from 1978, together with the new management style introduced by Rover in 1986 (then Austin Rover) which appeared to incorporate Japanese characteristics.

As discussed, it would seem that the nature of any innovative change in work organisation in the automobile industry is that it is high-profile. From both academic and practical perspectives, therefore, it quickly becomes significant to other sectors. For this reason, an analysis of Japanese lean approaches and an examination of theoretical perspectives surrounding the 'Japanisation' of Western industry would appear relevant to the enquiry and the case studies examined later in the text. This involves an exploration of how players in the automotive industry in the West have had to learn and change as a result of increasing competition following Japan's overtaking of the United States as the world's leading automobile manufacturer in 1979.

The 'Japanisation' debate

The late 1980s and into the 1990s have seen an increasing interest in Japan and the 'Japanisation' of industry in the West has attracted the attention of theorists and practitioners alike (Ackroyd *et al.* 1987, Bratton 1992). Oliver and Wilkinson (1992: 5) remark upon 'a sense of evangelism . . . which as the 1980s drew to a close . . . appeared to be on the decline, as the difficulty in implementing these practices began to be appreciated.' Interest, they consider, was revived with the publication of *The Machine that Changed the World* (Womack *et al. op. cit.*) which reported a five-year research project undertaken by the Massachusetts Institute of Technology (MIT) International Motor Vehicle Programme. Its purpose was to research into productivity and management practices in the global automotive industry. The main finding, Oliver and Wilkinson (*op. cit.*: 6) contend was

> one model of production organisation . . . lean production . . . was systematically related to superior productivity and quality. The study indicated that lean production was the dominant form of production used by vehicle producers in Japan, but that the methods were apparently transferable to locations outside Japan.

The effect of these findings was significant. It not only reinforced Western awareness of Japanese manufacturing methods but also highlighted the size of the productivity and quality differentials apparent in the global automobile industry. Furthermore, it gave an indication that there was some hope for recovery for those companies that were prepared to adopt lean manufacturing techniques. Significantly, research indicated that the productivity and quality of Japanese transplants in North America came 'close to equalling those of Japanese plants in Japan itself' (Oliver and Wilkinson *op. cit.*: 9). Other comparative studies in the automobile industry followed. Clark and Fujimoto (1991) compared product development performance within American, Japanese and European manufacturers and found the Japanese to be superior in productivity, lead times and quality by their use of lean production methods.

Lean production

Lean production emerged from the ideas of Eiji Toyoda and Taiichi Ohno in the Toyota automobile plant in Nagoya. After years of studying American techniques for car manufacture, Ohno concluded that mass production would not succeed in Japan for social and economic reasons. Similarly, craft production would not allow the manufacture of sufficient volume to enable entry into mass markets. The alternative system he devised was lean production, described by Oliver and Wilkinson (*op. cit.*) as an interrelated and mutually supportive set of manufacturing practices. It is characterised by short lead times and reduced set-up times, inventory reduction through just-in-time (JIT) systems, together with a high concern for quality and continuous improvement (*kaizen*). In order for the system to work efficiently, however, Womack *et al.* (*op. cit.*) claim that it requires an extremely skilled and highly motivated workforce that can anticipate problems before they occur by using their knowledge and initiative to devise solutions.

Lean production is therefore dependent upon the flexibility of both workers and the manufacturing system itself (Boer 1994). Workers are grouped into teams or cells and given the opportunity to work together to achieve the best methods of performance. Members of the cell are responsible for housekeeping and for contributing suggestions for improvements to the system. In contrast to mass production and in order to improve quality on an ongoing basis, each member of the work station is able to stop the assembly line if a problem is detected which cannot be rectified. This places responsibility for quality with those at the immediate point of production and has shown dramatically reduced rework and rectification problems at the end of the process (Womack *et al. op. cit.*).

Lean production and JIT are dependent upon integrated buyer–supplier relationships between organisations involved in production and assembly. In terms of the development of close buyer–supplier relationships and sub-contracting, the Japanese approach has been extolled by Smitka (1991) and Nishiguchi (1994) as the model for the rest of the world to achieve. Berggren (1995: 54) cites Nishiguchi's (1994: 214) basic argument:

> The Japanese sub-contracting system has undergone a long evolutionary process. The result is a distinctive mechanism in which the problem-solving orientated commitments by customer and sub-contractor are reinforced from within by means of institutional arrangements that promote the continuous and flexible output of high-quality, low-cost products.

Japanese buyer–supplier systems are based upon close relationships throughout the production process within a JIT framework. Initially, Toyota organised its suppliers into functional tiers with first-tier suppliers responsible for working as an integral part of the product development team (Womack *et al. op. cit.*). It is likely that suppliers and buyers will have close association at the design and assembly stage and will be involved in joint training and development needs identification and delivery. Preferred supplier status grants an element of security to the supplier in the relationship, as it signifies that the buyer is satisfied with levels of quality and performance and is confident of the organisations' commitment to continuous improvement. The buyer, however, assumes a dominant role in the relationship and can exert considerable controls over the supplier, particularly in terms of monitoring, performance, delivery and pricing. Kenney and Florida (1993) comment on the significance of the development of supplier complexes in the West. They state that just as General Motors and Ford were significant in transferring Fordist techniques to Europe, they consider that the transplant supplier complexes are proving to be important for the transfer and implantation of the Japanese model in the United States and elsewhere.

They further assert that the creation of an integrated just-in-time supplier complex may well represent a new mode of organising industry. Using the

American automobile industry as the example, Kenney and Florida (*op. cit.*: 154) consider that large manufacturers such as Toyota, Honda, Nissan and Mazda have used their resources and power to construct JIT complexes that have become a source of discipline and structure for the network of producers. They continue:

> The Japanese model represents a distinct path, one that is better suited to the demands of advanced industrial production than either the earlier model of fordist mass production or the utopian formulation of flexible specialisation. . . . The automobile supplier complex that is emerging . . . provides striking evidence of the transfer and generalisability of the Japanese model of production both inside and outside the corporation.

The implications of the viability of transference of practices are therefore far-reaching in terms of the automobile industry in general. In his analysis of lean production, Harrison (1994) suggests that the competitive advantages of lean manufacturers who can offer low-cost, high-quality products with short order-to-delivery times can be devastating in the marketplace.

Theorists, nevertheless, continue to debate the feasibility of the transference of Japanese lean approaches to Western manufacturing environments. Oliver and Wilkinson (*op. cit.*) consider that Japanese production methods have been viewed from three main perspectives that they categorise as being the technological/rational, the social/political and the philosophical/ideological. The techno-logical/rational approach (Kenney and Florida *op. cit.*, Voss and Robinson 1987, Schonberger 1982, Womack *et al. op. cit.*) essentially suggests that practices such as lean production are transferable and can achieve the same results anywhere in the world, provided the systems are accurately executed. Kenney and Florida (*op. cit.*: 302) explored the transferability and generalisability of what they term 'innovation-mediated production' and found that 'the heavy industries grouped around automobile production have actively and, in large measure, successfully transferred the new system to the United States.'

The social/political perspective is considered by Oliver and Wilkinson (*op. cit.*: 10) to be diverse, but a recognisable position is that taken from a critical, social science standpoint. They cite Briggs (1988), Crowther and Garrahan (1988), together with Turnbull (1988), whose predominant argument is that Japanese manufacturing methods lead to work intensification, and that the social organis-ation of production relies more heavily upon managerial control and exploitation of the workforce than in previous manufacturing regimes. Similarly, Delbridge, Turnbull and Wilkinson (1992: 102) argue that Japanese approaches increase the monitoring and surveillance of shopfloor workers, intensify work pressures and reduce, rather than increase, autonomy. They further contend that the system produces a 'highly regulated and regimented labour process with many of the characteristics of bureaucratic control' seen in traditional regimes.

In terms of the philosophical/ideological perspective, this represents what might be termed a paradigm shift (Kuhn 1962) towards a 'new approach' to the nature of work, emanating from Japan. A converse strand to this argument, however, is the 'diluting' of Japanese approaches to 'fit' Western organisations so that their interpretation is superficial and unrepresentative of a new paradigm. Graham (1988), for example, suggests that many of the Japanese methods are not novel to the West but their introduction to Western organisations has been legitimised by their association with Japan. The Japanese identity links them to competitiveness and success and provides a persuasive reason for profound organisational change. So, the impact of Japan's emergence as a major force in the automotive sector clearly provides a platform for debate. Nevertheless, consideration must also be given to concomitant influences on work organisation that would appear to have been instrumental in changing Western approaches in the automotive sector.

Simultaneous influences on work organisation

In terms of the ideologies underpinning contemporary manufacturing and production processes, together with the management of people, Wood (1991) remarks that terms such as Japanisation and Toyotaism have taken on an increasing theoretical significance over time. Bratton (*op. cit.*), however, indicates that Japanisation is only one of a number of approaches that have been influential in contributing to the process of industrial change in the West. It is important, therefore, to examine the variety of changes in the task and contextual environments in order to explore the range of theoretical perspectives that attempt to analyse and explain the development of contemporary practice in the auto-mobile industry. In agreement, Oliver and Wilkinson (*op. cit.*: 12) suggest

> the term Japanisation is just one of a number of labels current in the late 1980s and early 1990s attached to models developed and promoted by various movements in management thinking that purport to explain changes in the way in which Western industry organises and manages its production processes.

They discuss flexible specialisation (Piore and Sabel 1984), the flexible firm (Atkinson 1987) and the 'excellence movement' (Peters and Waterman 1982) and indicate that, in common with Japanisation, they all 'encompass clusters of management practices that apparently share many elements in common' (Oliver and Wilkinson *op. cit.*: 13). In tandem, debates surrounding the emergence of human resource management clearly have implications for all perspectives (Legge 1995). Wood (*op. cit.*) also acknowledges the diversity of drivers for change in the industrial process. He cites these as being technology, internationalisation and increased democratisation in society. He stresses that Japanisation may be an important factor in the analysis of contemporary transformations of work, particularly for the auto industry where Japanese manufacturers tend to dominate in terms of innovative practices.

As with all 'labels', however, they attempt to describe the depth and extent of changes occurring within the nature of work and organisational life. It is worth noting the divergence of views on the concept of 'Japanisation' itself which range from its existence as nothing more than a conceptual framework for change (Wood *op. cit.*), to a perspective that industry may be changing but not necessarily towards a Japanese model (Marchington and Parker 1988). Included in the continuum is the view that 'Japanisation' is too simplistic an interpretation and is unrepresentative of the complexity of incremental industrial change that has, and is continually, occurring globally (Elger 1990). In support of this, Williams *et al.* (1992), in their analysis of the manufacturing achievements of Ford, comment that the moving assembly line centred view of Ford is unreasonable. They suggest that the company's approach was not only to mechanise handling but also to eliminate transfer and movement by re-designing layouts so that work in progress travelled shorter and more direct routes. This would seem to be a clear demonstration of an evolving just-in-time approach.

They go on to suggest that Ford's machinery was flexible and they made use of 'pace-setters' who demonstrated how work could be done faster and more efficiently. Drawing on the work of Sorensen (1956), they indicate that Ford was an organisation that was continuously experimenting and improvising to achieve better production. Significantly, Williams *et al.* (*op. cit.*) assert that Ford in the 1910s discovered the many of the benefits of 'lean' production, which they consider is falsely assumed to have been first invented by Toyota in the 1950s. Sandkull (1996) also suggests that lean production is a myth and that the production system reflects a number of Tayloristic principles that include dedicated technology, horizontal division of labour, with strict specialisation and a hierarchy of control. He further suggests that the lean production system is firmly embedded in a particular societal setting, stating that the system is not lean to the individuals involved and their ability to influence events is restricted to the point of production.

Wood (1989), however, argues that Japanese manufacturing techniques represent a departure from Fordism by utilising the tacit skills of workers at the point of production. The implications are that 'Japanisation' in the automobile industry represents not only a technical system but also a social dimension, re-defining the responsibilities of the individual in a way that has considerable implications for management practices and the development of the automobile industry itself. One aspect that is considered highly relevant is the use of teams within the contemporary manufacturing environment.

The emphasis on teamwork among line workers is considered by Womack *et al.* (*op. cit.*: 99) to be at the core of modern production processes in the automobile industry. They comment:

> Building these efficient teams is not simple. First, workers need to be taught a wide variety of skills . . . they need to acquire additional skills. Then they need encouragement to think actively, indeed proactively, so they can devise solutions before problems become serious.

The implications for management in a manufacturing environment are therefore significant. If continuous improvement is to be a realistic goal there needs to be a sense of reciprocal obligation, in which workers respond if they feel that management values their skills, will endeavour to retain them and will delegate responsibility to the team. Sandkull (*op. cit.*: 76), however, warns 'because lean production at present is in the form of an ideology, it is being introduced with little reference to the reality of particular cases. It readily becomes managerial rhetoric, a device to maintain established power structures, the inertia of which precludes learning.' Clearly, there will continue to be debate surrounding the nature of change in production and manufacturing processes within the automobile industry. The preoccupation for continuous improvement so sought after in the major producers and suppliers will inevitably generate new methods that may be interpreted as parallel and/or post-lean dimensions. An example is that of reflective production, developed by Volvo at its plant at Uddevalla, together with refinements to lean systems adopted by Japanese manufacturers.

Parallel and post-lean approaches

Ellegard *et al.* (cited in Harrison 1994) have proposed that the Volvo approach instigated at Uddevalla together with the developments that the company has since employed, have considerable advantages over lean production methods. They describe the approach as 'reflective production' and suggest that 'principles of learning rest on man's natural way of thinking.' When the system was first introduced at Uddevalla, cars were assembled in quiet rooms by separate teams overlooking a fjord. Other characteristics of the process include parallel material flows that enable autonomous work teams to assemble vehicles independently of each other. In addition, work tasks comprised a larger number of operations and required longer work cycles – usually two hours or more. The Uddevalla plant has been closed for production and there is no evidence to indicate whether this human centred, socio-technical approach leads to improved productivity and/or quality.

Significantly, however, this development has provided theorists with a 'post-lean' or 'post-Toyotaism' avenue to explore, particularly those whose empirical research concluded that lean processes were negative and stressful (Fucini and Fucini 1990, Garrahan and Stewart 1992, Parker and Slaughter 1988). Benders (1995) however, indicates that elements of the process have indeed been incorporated into lean approaches. Citing Jurgens (1992: 33) he suggests that the Uddevalla factory had been a 'partial example' for a new Honda factory in Japan producing the NSX sports car, in so far as the utilisation of the conveyor belt was questioned. Similarly, Rehder (1992: 68) is quoted as stating 'the NSX . . . is being built in a new factory by teams without an assembly line or moving conveyor system.' Benders (*op. cit.*) also suggests that Japanese automobile manufacturers, specifically Toyota, have modified their automation policies to incorporate simpler and cheaper equipment that will support rather than eliminate, human effort.

As a result, some 'worker friendly' changes have been instigated which focus on ergonomic measures (noise reduction, improved lighting, etc.) and the development of an assembly automation line where people rather than machines play the main role (Niimi 1993). Benders (*op. cit.*) also comments upon Toyota representatives visiting Volkswagen assembly lines in Germany. From this, their new concept 'More Human, Easy-to-Work Production Lines' emerged. Developments include the segmentation of large line structures into smaller mini-lines and is, according to Benders, typical of Dutch and Swedish socio-technical design. Similarly, General Motors has experimented with 'agile manufacturing' which according to Taylor (1994) embodies a shift from muscle power to intellectual power. The agile concept depends upon highly flexible production facilities, constantly shifting alliances among suppliers, producers and customers, and direct communication of sales information into the factories.

Whether such changes indicate the emergence of a 'post-lean' era, however, are debatable. Sandkull (*op. cit.*) suggests that any contemporary production system reflects both techno-economic logic and human logic, which is based on the actions and communication between human beings. Techno-economic logic inevitably dominates. What is important, therefore, is that in an industry that so publicly upholds the concept of continuous improvement, the cross-fertilisation of new ideas and innovative work practices are continually monitored and critically analysed. This should allow consideration of not only potential for improved levels of productivity, quality and cost reduction, but also the impact upon those people most affected.

The future?

The global automobile industry has undergone rapid and profound change over the past fifteen years with many companies having been forced to re-invent themselves. This has been characterised by globalisation strategies and mergers by existing players, changes in consumer demand and the explosive entry of Asia–Pacific region manufacturers into established markets, each displaying its own organisational and management practices (Chen 1995). Indeed, the Asia–Pacific region was the world's biggest producer in 1999 and it is anticipated that the increasing globalisation of the industry will lead to significant change.

Whilst there was an increasing trend towards automation throughout the industry at the start of the 1980s, coupled with the adoption and refinement of Japanese approaches in systems and processes, problems remain. These are associated with the legacy of growth in the industry in the second half of the 1980s, when demand grew at 4.5 per cent a year to a manufacturing capacity in the peak years of 1991–2 of 13.5 million cars. At this time, new and more efficient plants were opened in Europe, but old and inefficient ones were not closed. The result has been a global surplus manufacturing capacity. Added to this has been the increased production of Japanese transplants in the United Kingdom whose strategy is to manufacture one million cars per year by the end of the 1990s. In 1999 Japan is to be allowed to abandon the 'voluntary' limits capping the number of cars it can sell in the European Union. In mature markets that are characterised by slow growth, there is evidence to suggest that profound change and rationalisation is taking place.

In Europe, adaptation as the industry matures is therefore a significant issue. There is increasing pressure on manufacturers to compete on price alone as mass-market vehicles become more alike. The industry is also characterised by a fragmented supplier network although the emerging trend for suppliers in the latter part of the 1990s increasingly is to consolidate in order to gain critical mass, expertise and global reach. Industry wide, there also appears to have been reluctance to close out-dated factories to maintain employment levels. Nevertheless, in order to solve the problem of over capacity, the industry is now characterised by mergers and rationalisation. Existing companies have closed their less productive plants, engaged in more collaborative alliances and used flexible production methods to raise profitability. These combined factors have occurred largely due to the industry being heavily guided by political intervention to uphold national economic and labour market interests. For example, the merger between BMW and Rover in 1994 has been assisted and sustained by state aid from the British Government of £200 million in 1999. Volkswagen has reduced its workforce and embarked upon changes to work practices, recruitment strategies and production systems and Ford has taken over Volvo. Industry analysts indicate that the European market shows a high level of saturation and while 1998 might have been a good year for car production, profit margins would be under severe pressure from increased global competition in the future.

In the United States, evidence that automobile manufacturing is declining in national economic importance as a competitive factor is revealed in a study from the MIT International Motor Vehicle Programme. Taylor (*op. cit.*) quotes Daniel Roos, one of the original leaders of the MIT research, who states that Ford, Chrysler and General Motors have considerably narrowed the differences between the United States and Japan in terms of quality and productivity. Predictions for the future suggest that the role of the manufacturer will increasingly move towards the co-ordination of highly involved and integrated suppliers; the role will be one of the integration of the vehicle in a 'virtual factory.' It is also possible that suppliers themselves will assume a more dominant role in their relationships with producers (Taylor *op. cit.*).

Nevertheless, the contemporary situation in the United States is less optimistic. Despite manufacturers having increased productivity and quality, the automobile industry is experiencing slower growth. This is due to reduced consumer demand for new products, high vehicle prices and the availability of reliable, used cars in the market. It is predicted that any future growth will be derived from foreign producers such as Honda and Toyota, BMW and Mercedes-Benz who have located in the United States. Inevitably, whilst they will create employment, profits eventually return to the country of origin of the producers.

Despite their current financial and economic challenges, the potential of the emerging markets in the Asia–Pacific region will prove a volatile environment for all competitors, particularly those traditionally established in the automobile industry. The entry of South Korean automobile producers who are building production capacity at five times their projected domestic market into what appears to be an already overcrowded arena has created an additional threat for established global manufacturers. Whilst Hyundai, Kia and Daewoo aim to increase sales in the United States of America and Europe, their overall strategy is also to penetrate newly emerging markets in India, China, Russia, Latin America and the Middle East with low priced vehicles. In order to achieve this, they are establishing assembly operations in Egypt, Botswana, Vietnam and Uzbekistan. Within this changing context, Chen (*op. cit.*: 298) observes that management systems in the East and West have their own unique competitive advantages and critical weaknesses. It is therefore he says 'better to borrow the strong points of the others to supplement one's own system than to abandon one's own system' altogether. Accordingly, the automotive sector is increasingly characterised by partnership and joint venture activity in research, design and production and displays a continuously developing approach to work practices.

Conclusion

The future of the automobile industry appears characterised by uncertainty, continuous change and innovation in technology, work practices and markets. Kenney and Florida (*op. cit.*: 324) suggest 'the advanced capitalist world has crossed a historic turning point . . . a whole new model for organising technology, production, work and industry has emerged.' The model, however, continues to evolve with the central focus of attention shifting from the 'abstract mass' of systems and structures typified in the Fordist regime, to the creative processes associated with the development of the individual and the group within a 'leaner' environment. These issues have become increasingly prevalent in contemporary approaches to work organisation in the sector (Bratton *op. cit.*, Nonaka 1988, Zuboff 1988). Whether this indicates that the automotive industry has become sympathetic to Legge's (*op. cit.*: 67) suggestion that 'employees are proactive rather than passive inputs into the production process; they are capable of development, worthy of trust and collaboration, to be achieved through participation and informed choice' will continue to provoke debate. Clearly, managing change effectively by encouraging innovation, learning and continuous improvement are now purported to be the key issues that are essential in order to ensure survival for contemporary organisations in the sector. Some companies go so far as to espouse that their goal is to become a 'learning organisation' with their commitment to this end actively demonstrated both internally and externally. But it is only by engaging the commitment of the people to such principles that their energy can be harnessed for the benefit of the organisation. Thus, a framework that supports individual and organisational learning as an effective platform for change management would need to be constructed and those involved must believe that such activities will lead to a better state. Indeed, the case study organisations examined in later chapters are convinced that the pursuit of organisational learning potential is a priority objective that must be achieved to ensure future survival. Chapter two will therefore explore the historical and theoretical foundations of the 'learning organisation' and organisational learning, concepts that would appear to underpin and pre-occupy contemporary approaches to managing change in the automotive sector.

2 The learning organisation
Historical and conceptual foundations

Summary

The chapter will examine the emergence and development of the 'learning organisation' and organisational learning as viable concepts to assist contemporary companies to manage change and environmental instability. It explores how the approach has developed in response to both the nature of environmental change and the evolutionary process within organisations. The range of definitions that theorists advance, together with the framework that underpins the concept of organisational learning are considered, in order to identify the reciprocal connection with the process of change. On this basis, the chapter continues with an examination of contemporary concepts that explain the need for redefined approaches to work organisation that incorporate a learning approach to environmental change. It concludes that traditional systems, structures, processes and attitudes may need to be realigned in order to maximise the contribution of the individual in this new employment relationship.

Organisational learning

The term 'learning organisation' is a comparatively new addition to management vocabulary (probably mid-1980s). Academic interest in 'organisational learning', however, appears to have evolved in response to the continual and changing demands thrust upon business and has emerged from required behavioural, cultural and structural realignments to these demands. Most significant is the requirement that contemporary organisations are not only able to initiate, manage and sustain the process of change, but also, as Legge (1995: 14) suggests, 'are able to deal with the major contradiction in capitalist systems – the need to achieve both the control and consent of employees.'

Accordingly, Garratt (1995) considers that the concept of the learning organisation has essentially gained wide acceptance in the 1990s as a result of the recession and aggressive competition from East Asia. This has forced companies to confront the reality that many organisations do not survive beyond the age of forty (Senge 1990). Consequently, managers have looked for solutions that increasingly focus on 'breaking free of traditional modes of operation to enhance continuous learning' (Morgan 1997: 90) at the individual, group and organisational levels. To position the learning organisation in its historical and evolutionary context, early writers in the field, Pedler, Burgoyne and Boydell (1991), consider that this can be broadly perceived within distinct stages emanating from the 'training process' that are identified and discussed below.

The systematic approach

The systematic approach, which evolved during the 1950s in Europe and the United States due to problems of skill shortage was, and still is within some organisations, task analysis leading to formal training plans in which operations and learning are separate. For most of its history, the training field has considered the individual learner to be the passive unit of analysis (Wood 1988). The approach is rational, static and essentially conformist, with the assumption that any training intervention is completed at the end of the programme.

Ashton and Felstead (1995), however, suggest that during the twentieth century occupational labour markets were gradually undermined as the basis of skill acquisition because mass production systems gave management greater control of the production process at the expense of the worker. Additionally, the economic base of skilled work shrank with the decline of the manufacturing sector, while the growth occupations in the service sector were essentially outside the control of unions. They suggest that these factors gave management greater control over the skill-formation process. As a result, companies exercised significant control over the amount and levels of training interventions offered.

Nevertheless, after the Second World War, politicians and some business leaders expressed concerns regarding the threat of foreign competitors overtaking the United Kingdom. The national position regarding skill levels was therefore examined. It was considered that the availability and quality of training was too important an issue to be left to individual, and often reluctant, employers. The result was the 1964 Training Act, seen as an attempt to put pressure on employers to enhance the training they provided. In essence, this represented a shift from a voluntaristic to an interventionist strategy on the part of government (Ashton and Felstead *op. cit.*). Nevertheless, by the late 1960s and early 1970s, as line managers slowly began to play a part in identifying training needs, the issue emerged of the gap between skills development on a training course and improved job performance – the 'transfer of training' issue.

Organisational development and change

Improved organisational performance became paramount for survival during the 1970s following the oil price wars and rampant inflation. In response to this crisis, work tasks began to be used as the primary learning vehicle. Personnel departments appeared pre-occupied with methods to improve performance and instigated briefing groups, joint productivity planning committees and later, with the influence of Japan's success, quality circles. Ideas of worker participation emerged, with work 'humanisation' schemes focusing on improving the quality of working life; responsible autonomy and collective innovation were promoted to increase productivity and to encourage employees to be more responsive to change.

The adoption of 'organisational development' (OD) activities aimed to improve confidence and participation at all levels in the organisation. Burnes (1996: 180) cites the following definition of OD offered by Cummings and Huse (1989: 1).

> A systemwide application of behavioural science knowledge to the planned development and reinforcement of organizational strategies, structures and processes for improving an organization's effectiveness.

Development rather than training therefore became a more appropriate description for the process, on the grounds that it was attempting to address the individual's capacity for growth, and the values of openness, trust and creativity (Pedler *et al. op. cit.*). 'Training' interventions became increasingly more strategic, particularly with the increased pace of technological change during the late 1970s and 1980s. OD programmes, for example, appeared to be concerned with adjusting employees to the goals and structures in change processes. Fast communications and new equipment demanded that people could learn on the job and quickly, often without any recourse to formal training plans or programmes. Some organisations provided learning resources, encouraged action learning sets and promoted self development as a feasible concept, initially for managers, but soon advocating 'employee development' for the whole company. The more innovative organisations established the function of human resource management (HRM) and integrated this within the overall business objectives to display their broad commitment to the simultaneous development of people and work. Keep (1992), for example, identifies a number of organisations in the automotive sector including Jaguar Cars and Lucas whom he considered to be prominent in the Human Resources Management (HRM) movement at this time, and who had successfully managed to integrate training and development into their wider business planning.

The flexible firm

In terms of company-wide integration of training and development within an ideological framework of HRM, the emergence of debates surrounding upskilling/deskilling and the 'flexible firm' offer relevant perspectives that are worthy of further exploration at this point. Ashton and Felstead (*op. cit.*: 242) suggest 'the debate surrounding the long-term trajectory of skills – downward or upward – has raged for decades'. They argue that if technological change is considered to have increased the complexity of work tasks and skills to carry them out, then the implication for work organisation is that emphasis must be placed on nurturing employee initiative and providing greater discretion at work. The perspective of upskilling therefore fits within the HRM framework in so far as employees are seen as assets to the organisation as opposed to costs. If, however, management use technological change to routinise jobs, to remove discretion and to make it easy to substitute one employee for another, then this represents a tightening of control to raise productivity and profits. Deskilling occurs which contradicts the idealised HRM scenario (Braverman 1974).

The debate surrounding the flexible firm (Atkinson 1984, Atkinson and Meager 1986) has direct implications for HRM in so far as it identifies considerations for organisational design in terms of decentralisation and de-layering. It also raises the issue of alleged changes in employer strategies in terms of dividing workers into core and peripheral groupings. This represents a two-tier employment structure that separates a full-time core group from those who work under non-conventional employment contracts (part-time, sub-contracting, temporary/home work, self-employment etc.). Indeed, small business creation in the United Kingdom from 1979 to 1989 has increased by 66 per cent (Daley and McCann 1992).

The implications of the flexible firm and levels of training and development in this environment continue to attract debate (Marginson 1989, Pollert 1988). Ashton and Felstead (*op. cit.*: 244–5) indicate

> It is undeniable that non-standard forms of employment have grown rapidly during the last decade. It is among these workers that the training incidence is lowest and that the emphasis on labour as a cost to be minimised is greatest. . . . HRM may fail to touch this growing army of 'peripheral' workers; if HRM is to be found anywhere, it will be among a narrow band of 'core' workers.

Nevertheless, evidence from the Employment in Britain survey (Gallie and White 1995) suggests that higher level qualifications are now required for the jobs respondents currently perform compared to what was required in 1986. In addition, 63 per cent of the respondents considered that they had experienced an increase in their skills since 1986. Most significant were findings that more people are now being trained, more want to be trained and more are willing to pay for it themselves. From the 1980s onwards, it is possible, therefore, that interest in the promotion of self-development initiatives addresses the issue of the increasing numbers of people who are likely to fall outside mainstream organisational training and development intervention strategies, yet must still maintain their ability to be employable.

The emergence of 'excellence'

Self-development and action-learning strategies gained ground as a result of the work of Revans (1982) and OD proponents. Japan's success during the 1980s was also influential insofar as it indicated that poor performance in the West was attributable to the lack of 'fit' between previous training initiatives and the structural and cultural constraints placed upon individuals in traditional organisations and work arrangements. It was argued that excessive control mechanisms and bureaucratic regimes tended to block any learning efforts so that the organisation failed to maximise the potential of both the individual and the company.

In this context, the impact of Japan's economic success was attributed at this time to the high degree of commitment of their employees, which seemed to be achieved through shared beliefs and strong corporate cultures. This influenced management interest and thinking in the West, particularly after the publication of Peters and Waterman's *In Search Of Excellence* (1982), in which top-performing companies were identified, all appearing to display strong cultures and identities, and a pre-occupation with employee empowerment and involvement.

Debate continues on the research findings, together with the centrality of the relationship between corporate culture and its impact on organisational perform-ance (Denison 1990, Guest 1992, Wilson 1992). Additional perspectives concerning the success of Japanese companies that have emerged (other than manufacturing and production practices) are that they are not only able to adapt quickly to changes in their environments but also that they create knowledge and learn rapidly from their experiences (Nonaka and Johanssen 1985, Pedlar 1991). In addition, it is suggested that Japanese employers start from a higher base-level of skills in their labour force and are also subject to government pressure/support that facilitates learning at work (Ashton and Felstead *op. cit.*).

Concomitant with such approaches can be seen the emergence of what some theorists describe as a post-Fordist or neo-Taylorist phase, which sees self-directed, action and experiential learning as vital in maximising the potential of the individual and in coping with organisational change. In this environment, decentralised organisations and team-based structures allow individuals to discover and learn together, generating knowledge, innovation and entre-preneurialism. The enlightened corporate development interventions have increasingly become 'workshops' and 'team-building experiences' rather than 'training courses' (Wood *op. cit.*) and would appear to signify a shift from training to learning (see Table 2.1). Such developments have evolved from dominant paradigms that have emerged over the last decade, which broadly encompass learning from and adopting 'best practice' or global benchmarking, especially that evident in North America and Japan.

Additionally, the ideological intensity of the 'enterprise culture' and the weight attached to the contribution of management consultants, change agents and 'gurus' of organisational change have intensified the transference of knowledge and practices between organisations and have provided a platform for new approaches to emerge (Wilson *op. cit.*). In this context, a further consideration can therefore be identified as that of HRM, seen by some managers and academics as a viable construct that supports and encourages organisational learning.

Developments in human resource management

Keep (1992) suggests that the increasing interest in HRM by academics and large organisations, and the degree to which this interest is translated into action, has

Table 2.1 Characteristics of learning and training (adapted from Pearn *et al.* 1995)

	Training	Learning
Origins	Planned	Organic
Timeframe	Sporadic	Continuous
Control	Trainer	Learner
Energy flow	Trainer to trainee	From learner
Motivation	Unclear to learner	Usually clear
Roles	Learner is passive	Learner active
Costs	Add-on costs	Integral to work
Focus	Activities and delivery mechanisms	Processes inside the individual

been significant in promoting organisational learning. But whether this merely represents a change in the vocabulary of management as suggested by Legge (1995) continues to be debated. Keep (*op. cit.*: 334) argues that training and development 'are activities central to the reality of anything that can meaningfully be termed human resource management'. This being so, any widespread commitment to this end should ensure that skills training and knowledge acquisition are secured and promoted both internally and externally by developing relationships with associated organisations.

Notwithstanding this observation, it would seem that genuine HRM policies appear to be confined to a limited group of large companies competing in international markets (Keep *op. cit.*). Despite indications of increased perceptions of upskilling and values attached to training at the individual level as discussed earlier, little evidence is available concerning the volume of organisation-wide training employers are prepared to undertake. Indeed, Ashton and Felstead (*op. cit.*: 248) assert that employers are increasingly left to decide upon what level of training they are prepared to invest in. They consider that there is 'certainly no systematic evidence to suggest that there has been a conversion to human resource management which is producing a transformation in training activity at the company level.' Gill (1995) indicates that while contemporary companies are less preoccupied about training activities and more concerned about solving perform-ance problems, most HRM professionals still spend the bulk of their time in the design and delivery of classroom-based training events. He goes on to suggest that even in high-performance organisations, the profession has not transformed itself to meet learning needs.

Contemporary developments in the field of training and development in the United Kingdom include the Government-inspired National Vocational Qualifications (NVQ) and Management Charter Initiative (MCI). These are considered to be 'more geared to job performance in specific functions and to developing national standards of performance expressed in terms of outputs rather than inputs' (Iles and Salaman 1995: 216). Competence is defined generically as the ability to perform activities within an occupation, to standards defined and expected in that occupation.

Iles and Salaman (*op. cit.*: 216) cite four main strands of criticism that have been directed towards such models which include the ambiguity between performance and competence, the second, the generic nature of the competency models,

> . . . particular sectors, industries and organisational cultures require much more organisation specific sets of competences, in part to ensure that employees can identify with the language of the model used, and to generate greater commitment and ownership.

Third, they suggest that such models are often present- or past-focused, relying on what has achieved successful performance in the past, rather than on what might be needed in the future. A final criticism is that existing competence models give insufficient emphasis to key managerial activities and 'soft' skills that are traditionally hard to measure, such as creativity, communication and sensitivity.

Hence, if the NVQ system is viewed within the HRM ideology, it is clear that the two concepts do not sit comfortably together. HRM attempts to move training and development to a level beyond the measurement of present competencies in order to take a proactive stance regarding the process of change. The issue that many people and organisations face is not only what skills do they need now, but also what will they need to assist in the future survival of the organisation and to sustain their own employability? Clearly, the current models only partially address this issue. Added to this, there is evidence to suggest that the competence model itself lacks clarity and coherence. A recent survey (*Training* April 1996) indicates that under a quarter of employers fully understand how the United Kingdom's system of NVQs works, 18 per cent have no understanding and more than 20 per cent of private sector employers said they did not understand thesystem.

Within this structured framework of individual development, there also appears to be confusion surrounding the term 'learning organisation' and what it implies. The survey also showed that less than 60 per cent of respondents had only a vague notion of what the term 'learning organisation' meant, yet one third stated that they would describe their own employer as a learning organisation. The results also confirmed that most members of the HRM profession were striving to be seen as committed to the approach but each had a different interpretation of its meaning.

The adoption of specific management ideologies, models and practices for organisational effectiveness therefore, particularly apparent from 1950 to the present day, continues to attract debate. Pascale (1993: 13) has remarked that management have been 'caught up in a kind of fads industry' for the past two decades and that instead, they should be looking for a paradigm shift in their underlying culture and beliefs in terms of the contribution of the individual to the organisation. He suggests a departure from fads that focus on 'doing' towards the more Eastern concept of 'being', implying that more attention needs to be directed towards organisational processes and cultures rather than purely skills acquisition.

Kramlinger (1992) says that this demands a change in direction towards a different level of complexity – culture change and corporate alignment by which the whole organisation, rather than the individual, becomes the unit of analysis for learning, transferring knowledge and skills. Hendry (1996) however, believes that it is the group, or linked 'communities of practice', that are most powerful in terms of generating and transferring learning within the organisation. Indeed, this is supported by the previously cited survey which showed that employers rate the ability to communicate and to work effectively as part of a team as the two most essential core skills (*Training* April 1996). In order to consider the projected evolution of being, or aspiring to become, a learning organisation and to achieve a deeper understanding of the concept, it is, therefore, important to explore some of the contexts and evolutionary processes influencing the receptivity of the individual and group to learn and develop.

The evolutionary process in organisations

From the late 1980s and early 1990s, it would appear that two strands of organisational response in terms of learning and development have emerged. The influence of organisational development (OD) has resulted in organisational transformation (OT) while the themes of self-development and action-learning have enabled the concept of the learning organisation to gain ground. Owen's (1987) work on OT defines organisational transformation as essentially an ongoing, evolutionary process in the life span of an organisation. Lessem (1989) suggests that the convergence of the two themes of OT and the idea of the 'learning company' indicates that an increasing number of organisations might now be faced with a 'bureaucratic crisis phase' in their development (Greiner 1972).

Tensions, conflict, individualistic and job specific orientations result and an inward-looking mentality emerges which tends to disregard the customer, so that people become progressively less aware of the needs of the external stakeholders. In response, bureaucracies may attempt to involve members by promoting opportunities for self-development. Frequently this may be seen as being somewhat divisive with certain members uninterested in, or excluded from, pursuing such approaches. Initiatives may also have little real connection or co-ordination with wider organisational goals and objectives.

Although such responses promise minimal long-term advantages for the organisation, Lessem (*op. cit.*) suggests that they may be useful, if not essential, to enable the organisation to move into the developmental phase in its evolution. He considers that the ideology now emerging as a 'way forward' is an approach of continuous corporate improvement that promotes and integrates workplace learning and self-development. Learning is required at all levels of organisations in order to cope with change, uncertainty and increased competition. The priority is placed on human resource development which, ideally, is integrated with overall business planning and employee participation.

Garratt (1987) suggests that the concept would appear to embody a shift in emphasis over the past fifty years from stability to dynamism, from systemisation to creativity and from teaching to learning. While research is still limited in this area, within this phase the organisation also begins to display evidence of integration between people and functions. It is this phase which embodies the concept of the learning organisation and in which its associated principles are essentially able to develop and exist. Lessem (*op. cit.*) considers that this is also the phase in which the Total Quality Management (TQM) ideas of Deming might emerge, whereby systems and procedures based on quality and transparency are integrated within a wider chain of customers and suppliers. Moss Kanter (1989) describes this as becoming PALs – pooling, allying and linking across companies by developing open relationships in which organisations can learn from each other. People within the network are responsible for their own actions and decisions; cultures within the organisations display high trust, with management acting as facilitators and enablers. By such means, boundary management is relaxed and favours collaboration rather than competition. Handy (1989) for example, depicts this as a shamrock whereby the organisation is based around a core of essential executives and workers supported by outside contractors and part-time help, whose services can be bought in as, and when, required. Pedler *et al.* (*op. cit.*: 31) describe their idea of the learning company as essentially about 'energy flow' within and between individuals and the organisation, a view which is supported by Tosey (from Burgoyne, Pedler and Boydell 1994).

From such perspectives, it appears that organisational learning aspires to move companies to a level beyond the developmental, integrated phase. But generating a learning climate would appear to be individual, group and organisational processes that are both evolutionary in nature and complex to sustain in the long-term, unless and until, as Huber (1991) suggests, they become embedded in organisational identity, culture and memory. In order to explore and analyse the factors that generate and promote organisational learning, we will move on to examine some of the contributions from the literature. These attempt to identify what a learning organisation purports to be and why theorists and practitioners suggest that contemporary organisations should aspire to achieve the state.

Organisational learning defined

There are a number of interpretations of organisational learning (see Table 2.2.) although a clear definition continues to prove elusive. Perhaps the most concise and simple assessment is that which suggests that learning means getting everyone in the organisation to accept change (Stata 1989). Whilst organisational theorists have studied learning over a long period, the variety of existing definitions suggests that there is still a large degree of disagreement. Most theorists seem to view organisational learning as a process that unfolds over time, and link it with knowledge acquisition and improved performance (Garvin 1993).

Nevertheless, they appear to differ on a range of significant issues. For example, Fiol and Lyles (1985: 803) consider that 'organisational learning means the process of improving actions through better knowledge and understanding' while Argyris (1977) suggests that it is a process of detecting and correcting error. Huber (*op. cit.*:

Table 2.2 Organisational learning: some key issues

Name	Key issues for organisational learning
Argyris (1957, 1977, 1995)	Detecting and correcting error
Stata (1989)	Everyone accepts change; shared insights, mental models, behaviour change
Huber (1991)	Behaviour change through information processing
Burgoyne (1992, 1995)	Organisational transformation linked to the development of people
Garvin (1993)	Organisation creates, acquires and transfers knowledge; people modify behaviour to reflect new insights
Fiol and Lyles (1985)	Improving actions through better knowledge and understanding
Garratt (1987, 1990)	People learn naturally but the organisation should develop systems to ensure it becomes effective and transformative
Tsang (1997)	A learning organisation is one which is good at organisational learning but there is confusion over the learning process *per se*

89) takes a systemic approach by stating that 'an entity learns, if, through its processing of information, the range of its potential behaviours is changed.' Stata (*op. cit.*: 64) considers that organisational learning occurs 'through shared insights, knowledge and mental models and builds on past knowledge and experience, that is, on memory'.

From the variety of perspectives quoted, some theorists consider that behavioural change is required for learning, while others suggest that new ways of thinking are sufficient. Some indicate information processing as the mechanism by which learning occurs, while shared insights and organisational memory are prioritised by others. Garvin (*op. cit.*), however, indicates that whilst these may be triggers that contribute to the learning process, the essential issue is that unless there are changes to the way work is organised and performed, significant improvement or double-loop learning is unlikely to occur (Morgan 1997, Senge *op. cit.*).

In this context, Garratt (1995) indicates four key conditions that can be stated for sustained organisational learning:

(1) People are naturally learning while working, but they need help to learn both regularly and rigorously from their work.
(2) Such learning needs both robust organisational systems and a positive organisational climate to move the learning to where it is needed.
(3) Learning is valued by the organisation in achieving its objectives.
(4) The organisation is so designed as to be able to transform itself continuously through its learning to the benefit of its stakeholders.

Garvin (*op. cit.*: 80) presents the following definition, acknowledging that new ideas are an essential starting point if organisational learning is to occur:

A learning organisation is an organisation skilled at creating, acquiring and transferring knowledge, and at modifying its behaviour to reflect new knowledge and insights.

New knowledge creation can occur as a result of insight or inspiration from within the organisation; additionally it can also be provoked from external influences. Whatever their source, such new ideas form the foundation for organisational improvement and learning. They alone cannot create a learning organisation, however, unless there are accompanying changes to the manner in which the organisation performs. In other words, Garvin (*op. cit.*) indicates that while many organisations can develop skills in acquiring and creating knowledge, few are successful in applying that knowledge to their own activities and behaviour. This would appear to confirm the view that for learning to be of relevance to the organisation, there have to be changes to structures, systems and behaviours. The key focus identified by Burgoyne (1992) is 'organisational transformation', suggesting the importance of understanding processes by which the organisation can develop itself rather than being changed by outside intervention. The inference is that if the organisation is recognised as an open system operating in a dynamic environment, it also has a degree of control over its own destiny (Morgan 1986, Stacey 1996).

Moss-Jones (1993) suggests that the development of a learning organisation essentially requires agreement on some basic assumptions. These recognise that learning is of value and that whilst learning happens all the time, the quantity and quality of learning can be increased if it is done deliberately rather than by being left to chance. Moreover, that learning is a continuous process with no beginning and no end; and that shared learning with other people is easiest to sustain. Moss-Jones argues that the core features involved in generating and sustaining a learning organisation include a clear commitment to the development of all people and a coherent vision and future orientation which is communicated to all. Furthermore, there is a deep commitment to continual improvement in individual and organisational performance through continual learning and organisational change. In agreement with Burgoyne (1992) the organisation is continually transforming itself while maintaining or increasing its effectiveness by challenging and adapting its operating norms. Finally, high transparency throughout the organisation and beyond is established by effective communication both internally and externally.

On a more practical level, Garvin (*op. cit.*) argues that learning organisations are basically skilled at five main activities that enable them to manage and integrate their learning more effectively. He identifies them as:

(1) Systematic problem solving, which underlies much of the total quality movement (TQM), in so far as it promotes reliance on scientific method, data analyses and statistical tools, all of which are essential for learning because they continually place new demands upon those involved. While such methods are comparatively easily communicated, Garvin states that achieving the necessary mental outlook and approach is more difficult to establish. It requires that people develop a more

disciplined attention to detail, that they must continually look beyond the adequate to strive for the excellent. In support of this, Deming (from Pedlar 1991) suggests that many organisations fail to maximise the potential of TQM, only interpreting it within narrow confines of tangible work processes that stop people from thinking and learning. He stresses that TQM is essentially focused on transformation in management and about the profound knowledge needed for the transformation.

(2) Experimentation – learning organisations actively seek and test new knowledge, often motivated by opportunity, elements of risk and expanding horizons rather than by current problems.

(3) Past experience – by reviewing and reflecting on past successes and failures and by communicating them to employees, managers can access valuable knowledge for the future.

(4) Learning from others – while reflection and self-analysis are vital to the learning process, much can be gained from looking outside the immediate environment. Enlightened companies are those which engage in using others for inspiration and creativity, with 'enthusiastic borrowing' and benchmarking replacing the 'not invented here syndrome'. Customers should also be included in the process.

(5) Communication – for learning to be transferred throughout the organisation, knowledge must spread quickly and efficiently via effective communication flows.

Many of the perspectives on receptivity to organisational learning appear to involve profound implications for the culture and ideology of organisations. Often this may be dependent upon specific and individual 'starting points' for individual companies. Some may be broadly sympathetic to the basic philosophy of the learning organisation, while for others this may represent a radical shift in culture and management approach.

Using Pedler *et al.*'s (1987/8) framework to identify key attributes, it would appear that a learning organisation requires:

(1) Management must be committed to generating and sustaining a climate in which individuals are encouraged to learn and to develop to their full potential. People perform beyond competence and take initiatives. They are assisted in taking responsibility for their own self-development.

(2) The boundaries of the organisation should be relaxed or eliminated to enable responsiveness and flexibility. A learning culture is extended to include customers, suppliers and other stakeholders.

(3) Human resource strategy is central to, and integrated with, the business objectives. Knowledge creation, individual and organisational learning become central business activities.

(4) A continuous process of organisational transformation is tolerated which is harnessed to make changes to goals, assumptions, norms and procedures. On this basis, the drive towards self-direction is internally generated rather than imposed during moments of crisis as a reaction to external pressures.

(5) There are successful attempts at power-sharing and involvement of all

stakeholders in decision-making and problem-solving. This encompasses attempts to democratise policy-making within a climate of constructive conflict and debate, whilst at the same time such activities are structured and developed as learning processes.

Group interaction and learning

Criticism, however, has been directed at those theorists who have neglected an analysis of the significance and contribution of the interaction of groups in terms of the organisational learning process (Hendry, Arthur and Jones 1995). In view of the increasing significance of teams, particularly within the automotive sector, it would appear relevant to explore the contribution of this issue to the debate. Hendry *et al.* (*op. cit.*) draw upon March and Olsen's (1975) model which describes three themes that contribute to the analysis of learning in terms of the individual, the organisation and the environment.

Theme one

Individual learning occurs in successive foundation, formation and continuation stages. The foundation stage is concerned with basic readiness to learn, the skills needed to achieve learning, together with the experience of success and self-confidence through learning activities.

Theme two

The formation stage focuses on the wider issues of self-development, independent learning and an understanding of role interdependence and teamwork.

Theme three

The continuation stage is displayed by self-motivation and independence as a learner, the development of a questioning approach and an increasing level of autonomy on a group and individual level.

Hendry *et al.* (*op. cit.*) continue their analysis by drawing a matching frame of reference at the level of the organisation (see Table 2.3.). They see this as involving dependency, transitional and independency phases.

- The dependency phase responds to people at the foundation learning stage by means of formal job training, remedial education together with a basic introduction to teamwork.
- The transitional phase attempts to respond to individuals at the formation learning stage by offering wider opportunities for job rotation and shadowing, wider industry training together with increased opportunities for teamwork and experiential learning.
- The independency phase responds to the continuation learning stage by

Table 2.3 Individual readiness to learn and the organisational response

Individual learning ability	Organisational response
Continuation stage The individual is self-motivated; has achieved independence as a learner; has developed a questioning approach; demonstrates autonomy at a group and individual level	Independency Organisation offers linked career planning; shared responsibility for production and investment goals; broad commitment to work group autonomy
Formation stage Self-development; independent learning; role interdependence; interest in team work	Transitional The organisation offers job rotation and shadowing; wider industry training; opportunities for team work; experiential learning
Foundation stage The individual is ready to learn; shows interest in acquiring the skills to learn; involvement in learning activities	Dependency The organisation offers formal job training; remedial education; introduction to team work

offering linked career planning, shared responsibility for production and investment goals and broad commitment to work group autonomy. Hendry *et al.* (*op. cit.*) suggest that activities such as working in teams, job shadowing, experiential learning, and an emphasis on group responsibility indicate the importance of a company's internal learning processes.

They indicate, however, that for organisational learning to occur much is dependent upon individual readiness to learn and eagerness to join in shared learning efforts. The manner by which this team learning is translated into organisational learning is analysed in terms of the management of 'routines' – the translation of 'learning by doing' to 'remembering by doing' (Hendry *et al. op. cit.*: 184). These findings would appear to connect with Huber's (*op. cit.*) analysis surrounding organisational identity and memory and Zemke and Zemke's (1995) suggestion that adults are pragmatic in their approach to learning and do so only when it is in their own interests. These perspectives are discussed in more depth in the following chapters.

Organisational learning: an ongoing process of change

The concept of organisational learning has achieved a high profile over recent years and many managers have been persuaded to re-examine their traditional values in order to attempt the deliberate encouragement of the approach. The implication may be that within some organisations existing hierarchies and cultures are fundamentally challenged, which may cause both internal and external dissonance. Whilst behaviour may be changed, deeply entrenched attitudes and cultural norms are likely to be more difficult to modify.

Organisations, however, are highly individualistic and will be driven by their own interpretation of the meaning of what it is to be a learning organisation. This will not be static but will continuously adapt and evolve over time and as a result of experience. As has been suggested by Burdett (1993), the learning organisation is a journey rather than a destination, implying that there cannot be a standard or prescriptive formula that will guarantee success, but merely a consciousness and meaning prevalent within the company to move learning higher on the organisational agenda.

In order to accomplish this, there is growing recognition amongst theorists that changes to the core paradigms of organisations may be required. McGill and Slocum (1993) suggest that managers have been frustrated by changes that have produced little real improvement. Increasingly they have been drawn to the concept of organisational learning. They indicate, moreover, that while every organisation is afforded rich learning experiences from its interaction with the internal and external environment, few benefit from them, and it is this failure that needs to be addressed. Those that do manage to develop the capacity for learning also develop the ability to usefully process both the experience and the way the organisation experiences it.

Hodgetts, Lufthans and Lee (1994) suggest that this is achieved through the development of effective dialogue within and between the various sub-cultures, teams, departments, etc. in the organisation, in order to recognise and remove their basic differences in order to achieve greater learning and collaboration. Thomas (1994) considers that concomitant with dialogue is scenario analysis, through which the gap between the reality of today and the critical success factors of the future results in creative learning tension for the organisation. He suggests that this enables organisations to prepare for responses under different possible future scenarios. Burdett (1994) warns, however, that despite attention to processes, a learning organisation may only emerge if multidimensional alignment is an underlying theme, enabling groups within the organisation to develop balanced skills and competences. Also, in agreement with Hendry *et al.* (*op. cit.*) and Brown and Duguid (1991), they can become 'learning communities of practice' by promoting mutually supportive groups with a common sense of purpose to achieve shared goals through common commitment.

In support of these points, Hendry (1996) develops the argument by identifying change as a crucial element of learning and vice versa. He suggests that attention should be given to the development of a culture in which learning and change are integrated to promote the success of both processes. As Vince (1996: 111) confirms 'the starting point of . . . analysis is an acknowledgement of the relationship between learning and change, whichever way round you look at them.' Until recently, it would appear that this interrelationship between learning and change has been neglected in both practice and academic debate. It is intended therefore, that the connection is explored in more depth by examining the conceptual framework that would appear to underpin and inform an understanding of contemporary approaches to organisational learning.

Organisational learning: a conceptual framework

It is apparent that the philosophy of organisational learning transcends the definition of a company that provides a high degree of training. Essentially, there are priority objectives of developing all human resources, enhancing skills and then being responsive to learning from those people regarding how the organisation can be changed and improved. In this way, the essence of learning and its transference within the company is that it is a cyclical, ongoing process that results in organisational change and effectiveness.

How organisations are able to learn and adapt to change in the collective sense continues to be a topic of debate. Indeed, it could be argued that as organisations are essentially 'constructions' they cannot 'learn' within the confines of our present limited understanding of the term (Huber *op. cit.*). Similarly, if learning is seen as purely an individual phenomenon, this indicates a very haphazard occurrence. As individuals leave, the implication is that they take their learning away and there is no benefit to the organisation. Similarly, people must also be encouraged to share their learning so that it can make a positive contribution to the pursuit of the organisation's goals and effectiveness. In this context, a further suggestion regarding how organisations learn concerns the systematisation of knowledge into practices, procedures and processes, that is, the 'routinisation' of knowledge embedded within organisational memory (Huber *op. cit.*).

Learning may also occur by absorbing other organisations through merger or acquisition, leading to the transference of knowledge (Clegg and Palmer 1996, Quinn Mills and Friesen 1992). In this instance, however, risks surround the organisation's collection of unwanted practices, procedures and behaviours that may disrupt established norms, or that there will be an inherent resistance and lack of co-operation as a result. Additionally, to consider organisational learning as a naturally occurring and intentional phenomenon, directed essentially at improving effectiveness, inevitably misses much of the complexity of the processes involved. Indeed, Huber (*op. cit.*: 89) considers 'learning need not be conscious or intentional . . . it does not always increase the learner's effectiveness or even potential effectiveness. Learning does not always lead to veridical knowledge'.

He describes four key steps in the organisational learning process that encompass knowledge acquisition, information distribution, information interpretation, and organisational memory – when knowledge becomes institutionally available, as opposed to the property of select groups. Nevis *et al.* (1995) however warn that learning does not occur in a linear progression but can take place in planned and informal, intentional and unintentional, ways. Moreover, Nystrom and Starbuck (1984) indicate that in order for organisations to move forward they must first 'unlearn' past behaviours and processes with which they have become familiar, in order to change established patterns. It is important also to consider that learning need not result in observable changes in behaviour. As Friedlander (1983: 194) explains

Learning may result in new and significant insights and awareness that dictate no behavioural change. In this sense the crucial element in learning is that the organism is consciously aware of differences and alternatives and have consciously chosen one of these alternatives. The choice may not be to reconstruct behaviour but, rather, to change one's cognitive maps or understandings.

The notion that 'choice' is and can be exercised, however, is debatable. Burnes (1996) indicates that although the potential for choice exists, many managers prefer not to exercise it and tend to continue with tried and tested approaches, regardless of their suitability to contemporary events. So, whilst the variety of contributions to the debate indicates that developing organisational learning is both complex and problematic, a more textured understanding of the quantity and quality of learning potential may be achieved by establishing the contextual and conceptual frameworks that underpin the approach.

Organisations and the environment

Over time, theories have been postulated to assist managers in their pursuit of effectiveness, many focusing on adaptability through learning and change. Contingency theorists such as Emery (1969) considered that essentially, individuals, groups, societies and organisations are organisms consisting of interdependent parts interacting with an environment, where there is an exchange of energy, information or materials across the boundaries. Consequently, if organisations are continually influenced by, and can influence their environment, the future of an organisation cannot be predicted by knowing its present state, but can only be determined by how effectively the component parts are integrated to respond to change.

Burns and Stalker's (1961) analysis of the link between the environment and organisational structure indicated that a stable environment dictated a mechanistic, bureaucratic structure whilst an unstable, turbulent environment called for a more organic, flexible approach that would enable organisations to respond to change. In this context, Emery and Trist (1965) explored the implications of different types of uncertainty in organisational environments in terms of the skills and attributes that managers needed to operate effectively. They described the 'turbulent field' of technological and market developments, in which management had little or no control in the traditional sense. In support of this, Lawrence and Lorsch (1967) considered that different kinds of structures and approaches were needed to deal with different markets and technology. They also suggested that a turbulent, unstable environment required a higher degree of internal differentiation that was flexible and responsive to environmental change. Integration by way of established hierarchical patterns needed to be replaced with a more flexible approach, incorporating the development of multi-disciplined project teams comprising people skilled in co-ordination and conflict resolution.

Thompson (1967) expanded these theories and used open systems analysis to emphasise environmental uncertainty. He stated that this could be addressed by means of co-ordination (managers see their role as one of co-ordination rather than of control, encouraging participation, empowerment and team building) and systematic organisational intelligence involving information exchange and cybernetics which promotes learning to learn, questioning and double-loop learning. Bateson's (1972) work in cybernetics emphasises the importance of remaining open to changes in the environment and challenging existing operating assumptions in a fundamental way so that double-loop learning and change can occur. Open-systems analysis therefore emphasises that companies should organise with the task and contextual environments in mind. They should develop an organisational capacity to scan and sense changes, to bridge and manage critical boundaries and areas of interdependence and to be able to develop appropriate strategic change and learning responses.

An opposing perspective to that of organisations as open systems is captured within the ideas of Maturana and Varela (from Morgan 1986), who have challenged the view that learning and change are factors that emanate from the environment. They argue that organisations are not open systems interacting with the environment, but are closed, autonomous systems of interactions, making reference only to themselves. They suggest that this autonomy, circularity and self-reference allows living systems to self-renew, using the word 'autopoesis' for the process.

According to this view, the identity of the company is its most important product and should be used to its advantage to sustain its ability to learn and change. The impact of this hypothesis is that rather than the organisation being subject to the environment, the environment is seen as a reflection of, and is part of, the organisation. In this way, a company produces itself and its own environment as part of that production. The environment is part of its inner identity. Moreover, Maturana and Varela suggest that if there is to be an understanding of the environment, there must first be an understanding of the organisation itself. Also, that the organisation is only one part of the environment which must be understood in terms of the larger 'whole'.

Logics of change

To resolve the tension between the hypotheses of open and closed systems, Morgan (1986: 233) describes a view of organisational evolution, learning and change in which flux and transformation are continuous processes. He considers that change can therefore be explored through three different images that he sees as methods of explaining how the reality of an organisation is embedded in the logic of change itself. First, the biological context of Maturana and Varela previously discussed acknowledges organisations as self-producing systems that have the capacity to create their own environments. This view links to the ideas of learning organisations having the potential to impact upon their environmental contexts by enrichment and development, rather than by interpreting the world as a force with which to be reconciled.

Second, Morgan uses cybernetic ideas to suggest that the logic of change is contained within a network of mutual causality shaped by positive and negative feedback. He cites the term 'systemic wisdom' (Bateson *op. cit.*) to indicate the need to find interventions which attempt to influence the patterns of relations defining a system, rather than trying to manipulate 'causes' and 'effects'. The implication is that organisations must be able to develop a capacity for learning, to learn to change with change 'influencing and shaping the process when possible, but being sensitive to the idea that in changing times, new forms of system organisation must be allowed to emerge' (Morgan *op. cit.*: 254).

Third, Morgan discusses dialectical change or the study of opposites, in which he cites examples from Taoist philosophy (the dynamic interplay of yin and yang), crystallising the notion that all life is shaped by coming and going, growth and decay, everything in the process of becoming something else. Such dialectical views have influenced the works of Hegel, Mao Tse-Tung and Karl Marx, who have considered that the world evolves as a result of change and internal tensions between opposites. Marx, for example, revealed how economic and social contradictions within a society provide a basis for its self-transformation. In his detailed analysis in *Capital*, he places much emphasis on the relationship between opposing forces, encouraging a view that all change is the product of such tension (Morgan *op. cit.*: 257).

Hence, the use of dialectical analysis demonstrates that the management of organisations continuously involves the management of contradiction, change and crisis situations in which problems emerge. If problems are formulated on the basis of opposing interests, it is likely that solutions will focus on win/lose formulae. If, however, problems are understood in terms of the logics that produce them, this may result in double-loop learning and change to the logic of the system itself, together with a realignment of the relations between those involved. It is significant that 'crisis and contradiction remove the comfortable patterns of acting, perceiving and coping with the world. In so doing, they provide a platform that initiates a new cycle of learning' (Tosey 1994: 21). The linkage with the concept of the learning organisation is that there can be a proactive, rather than reactive, relationship with the environment, in which opportunities for transformational learning are the focus of existence. By gaining a full understanding of the wider context in which they operate, learning organisations should be able to be proactive in a systemic sense, to construct their environments and develop their learning in tandem with their own identities.

Re-defining organisational approaches to change

If continued organisational effectiveness in an uncertain environment appears dependent upon developing systems and processes that foster learning and sharing information, there are considerable implications for organisations. Drucker (1989) for example, suggests that this represents a shift from a mechanical world view to a biological approach to management in which it is the perception of the whole that is critical. More significantly, he suggests that while matter is the foundation for mechanistic organisations, it is information that is the basic biological element. As information has no boundaries, it will also serve to form the basis for newly interactive communities of people. On this assumption, it seems that the terms upon which change is accepted and accomplished must be re-defined. Maturana and Varela (from Morgan *op. cit.*) acknowledge organisations as self-producing systems that have the capacity to create their own environments. This view links with the ideas of learning organisations having the potential to impact upon their environmental contexts by enrichment and development, rather than by interpreting the world as a force with which to be reconciled. Tosey (*op. cit.*: 76), for example, suggests that newer perspectives on organisations share an understanding based on the 'human experience of energy and flow and that relating direct, sensed experience to organisational processes offers considerable potential for understanding learning and change'.

If this is to occur, a learning orientation must be instilled and the role of management must shift from a process of control to one of interpretation (Vicere 1991). An emphasis on co-ordination rather than control provides a basis to increase the compatibility of individual and organisational learning by way of participation, team building, empowerment, self-awareness and reflection. Systems and procedures should essentially assist in learning from the consequences of actions and decisions. Characteristics of learning organisations identified by commentators above clearly mean that companies are required to develop a greater self-awareness of the issues and variables influencing organisational behaviour, together with collective and individual learning. If organisational learning is to occur, this necessitates transformation of basic assumptions and operating norms, together with the development of high levels of trust and commitment towards shared objectives. It could be argued, therefore, that the quest to develop organisational learning might be hampered by conventional structures and processes together with embedded attitudes and cultural dimensions that contradict the philosophy. To develop a learning approach to change, therefore, it is clear that both the traditional impression of the employment relationship and the basis on which work is organised must be revised.

A learning approach to work organisation

The development of organisational learning internalises the key to shaping business performance by placing responsibility for anticipating and dealing with environmental instability within the company. Pascale (1990) considers that this involves toleration of diversity within the organisation because if variety is reduced inside a system it is unable to cope with variety outside. In this way, the organisation is able proactively to transform or develop itself rather than being changed by outside forces. Ideally, this should enable organisations to be better equipped to be responsive and able to deal with what for many organisations is a dynamic and constantly changing environment in which uncertainty predominates. They may also avoid situations in which they are forced to embark on reactive change programmes, often commenced in an atmosphere of crisis, and usually offering minimal potential for lasting success.

Most typical were those companies in the automotive sector, which, in the late 1970s and 1980s, responded to Japanese competition by attempting to 'Japanise' their own organisations with little knowledge or understanding of the fundamental cultural implications of such change (Ackroyd *et al.* 1988). In agreement with this view, Jones (1992) argues that the organisational capability to learn and change demonstrated within the larger Japanese companies succeeds because it appeals to a deeper level of shared assumptions and beliefs. Successful culture change that promotes such learning often continues to elude Western companies because the most important skills are hidden in behaviours that are difficult to reconcile with Western beliefs and norms. Indeed, Jones (*op. cit.*: 56) suggests that the few companies that have developed strategic learning 'have not tried to do it by making one large, sudden jump'. Instead, they have recognised 'the great difficulty of connecting such learning with the realities of . . . culture [and] they have focused on building bridges . . . that lead to the gradual emergence of a hybrid, shared culture'.

Nevertheless, the concept of the learning organisation clearly involves more than the adoption of tactics and reformulation of structures and cultures in response to current crises. It presents a radical formula to drive a new approach to management thinking about the contribution of individuals and the relationship between organisations and their boundaries. To this end, theorists (Gleick 1988, Morgan 1997, Stacey 1996) have identified the relevance of chaos theory to construct a holistic understanding of the processes of learning and change in contemporary organisations.

Chaos and complexity

If the organisation is recognised as a learning organism, this implies that perception and understanding must transcend the classical scientific analysis, what Stacey (*op. cit.*) describes as the stable equilibrium paradigm, and perhaps ally more towards complexity science and chaos theory (Gleick *op. cit.*). The stable equilibrium paradigm suggests that managers can control and predict the long-term future of an organisation because cause and effect are linear and directly linked. Chaos theory, however, recognises that organisations are complex and non-linear and they are characterised

> . . . by systems of interaction that are both ordered and chaotic. Because of this internal complexity, random disturbances can produce unpredictable events that reverberate throughout a system, creating novel patterns of change. The amazing thing, however, is that despite all the unpredictability, coherent order always emerges out of the randomness and surface chaos.
>
> (Morgan 1997: 262)

Such processes of spontaneous self-organisation, therefore, can be detected over time, particularly if the system has a sufficient degree of internal complexity and diversity. In this way, diversity and instability become resources for change, with the role of management involved in shaping and creating contexts in which appropriate forms of self-organisation can occur (Cummings 1989, Morgan 1997, Stacey 1996, Weick 1977). The future of the organisation cannot, therefore, be predicted by knowing its present state. Stacey (*op. cit.*) indicates that this has important consequences for creativity and control in organisations, with spontaneous self-organisation emerging out of political interaction and group learning.

On the basis that chaos theory can be applied to everything around us, with everyday experiences legitimate targets for inquiry and consideration, the concept of the learning organisation may be appropriate within this context. This implies that the focus of attention needs to be directed to traditional organisational approaches and the barriers to learning and change that they continue to create. In this way, organisations need to be seen as complex, dynamic systems in which cultures, structures, processes and people allow new patterns of behaviour to emerge. Thus, by rejecting the traditional rationalist mentality prevalent within many organisations in order to think at a higher level of intellectual complexity about activities and interactions, organisations may be better equipped to survive and grow in an increasingly complex arena.

But generating and transferring learning throughout the organisation is acknowledged to be problematic, giving rise to differing schools of thought on the feasibility of the process. Grundy (1994: 20) classifies these as the prescriptive, the impossibility and the pragmatic schools of thought. The prescriptive school (Burgoyne 1992, Garratt 1987, Pascale 1990, Peters 1992, Senge 1990) believes that organisations must learn in order to survive; their ultimate goal is to become learning organisations. The impossibility school (Argyris 1991) contends that attempts to generate and spread learning within organisations must cope with resistance, politics and barriers of uncertainty. Finally, the pragmatic school (Grundy *op. cit.*) suggests that despite such barriers, islands of learning can be created within organisations, which, over time, may develop into a critical mass of learning throughout the company. Grundy (*op. cit.*: 24) argues that while the learning organisation may be a distant vision there are opportunities to create and develop a network of 'islands of strategic learning.'

Conclusion

The chapter has shown that innovative approaches that enable organisations to successfully deal with the rate and pace of change in the environment continue to pre-occupy managers and theorists. Over time, it can be seen that these have developed in their urgency and sophistication, with contemporary theory now recognising that organisations can make choices and can be proactive in creating their own environments, together with the basis on which change occurs. This represents a significant departure from the traditional view that implied that organisations were passive, and often unwilling, recipients of imposed external forces over which they could exert little influence.

Developing organisational learning in order to maximise the potential of the company's resources, whether by declaring enthusiasm to become a 'learning organisation' or just by placing a greater investment in the development of people, has increasingly captured the attention of managers. This would appear to indicate that more radical and deep-rooted approaches are being sought to deal with the complexity of environmental change. Accordingly, Morgan (1993) suggests that society is leaving the age of 'organised organisations' and is moving into an era where the ability to understand and encourage processes of self-organisation will become a key competence. Clearly, this will require continuous learning throughout all company levels to enable widespread responsiveness to a dynamic environment and a commitment to any changes that may emerge. But whilst the concept of organisational learning may present an attractive alternative to traditional organisational approaches and design, for many managers knowing which way to adapt to a complex environment and to develop a learning orientation continues to be problematic in practice. It would appear that cultures and structures within organisations need to be adapted and redefined simultaneously, in order to encourage new approaches to work, behaviour and the employment relationship itself to emerge. The task therefore represents a dynamic process of continuous learning and change.

It may also be that society's understanding of learning (and indeed not learning) is also changing. Hawkins (1994: 9) observes that we are beginning to learn more about how we learn and that our understanding of how we learn has 'begun to catch up with what happens in practice.' It is suggested that it is successfully managing this connection, between abstract conceptualisation and practical experimentation and implementation, that determines the organisational outcome in terms of whether change, learning and transformation can successfully occur. Theoretical and practical perspectives on developing learning in organisations will therefore be explored in the following chapter in order to identify traditional approaches that may impede the process, together with contemporary developments that are intended to encourage its occurrence.

3 Learning in organisations

Theory and practice

Summary

Following the discussion of the historical and conceptual foundations that under-pin organisational learning, this chapter considers the theoretical and practical perspectives associated with developing some form of receptivity to the approach. It discusses contemporary organising principles that are founded on under-standing and managing the complex nature of environmental change in order to ensure competitive advantage and future survival, exploring how learning can promote or inhibit the process. An analysis of learning as individual, group and organisational activities is then undertaken, identifying potential levels of learning and their implications for the development of people and their subsequent contribution to the organisation. The discussion then considers the barriers to learning that confront people within traditional organisational arrangements, preventing them from challenging existing norms and promoting learning and change. The chapter concludes with an exploration of practical approaches that involve fundamental changes to work organisation that are likely to offer contexts in which people may be receptive to engaging in the processes of double-loop learning and change.

Organisational learning as the way forward?

Burgoyne (1995a) suggests that contemporary, dominant organising principles of change programmes, which he considers include total quality initiatives, business process re-engineering, becoming 'lean', the mission-vision-commitment-empowerment formula, have their limitations for generating and sustaining organisational effectiveness. As more organisations develop the same approaches, there is difficulty in establishing any uniqueness and/or variety. As Salaman and Butler (1994: 34) assert 'if every organisation changes in the same direction, where is competitive advantage?'

It is for this reason that a more developmental form of organisation, such as that proposed by the concept of organisational learning, now seems to be a more attractive goal for managers. Burgoyne (*op. cit.*) locates this development within an emerging, sequential context that has moved from agriculture, manufacture, mentofacture to spiroculture. He describes the agriculture–manufacture transition as the industrial revolution, with organisational contexts and meanings derived from the church, state and military. The manufacture–mentofacture transition is the information and knowledge revolution in which technology has the simultaneous capacity to control, monitor and liberate. Spiroculture, the continuous, life-giving nature of relationships, is seen as the contemporary emergent phase in which Burgoyne considers that people look to organisations to provide meaning and identity. The organisation is all-inclusive, offering emotional involvement to workers and customers alike, ostensibly replacing their belief in the church, the state and science.

Burgoyne (*op. cit.*: 23) argues that these changes are assisted by what he terms 'transitional myths' or 'ideas that make sense both in the outgoing and incoming worlds, and hence, help people step between them.' While the Protestant work ethic was the transitional myth of the industrial revolution, belief in the entrepreneur and the autonomous self was the transitional myth of the information revolution. It would appear that the concept of the learning organisation, together with contemporary emphases on continuous improvement, quality and excellence, are the transitional myths that bridge the gap from mentofacture to spiroculture. Burgoyne suggests that they 'make sense' in the mentofacture–spiroculture transition because they relate not only to the adaptive performance required for manufacturing and knowledge work, but also pose ethical and spiritual questions such as what kind of excellence do we want? What are the reasons for quality? Why should we involve ourselves in learning for change?

Within an environment of increased competition, continuous improvement and rapid technological development, we are told that the primary source of competitive advantage in the future is likely to focus on learning and creating new knowledge in order to cope with change (Hirschorn and Gilmore 1992, Nonaka 1991, Zuboff 1988). Moreover, Burgoyne (*op. cit.*) and Drucker (1989) contend that as organisations have become increasingly concerned with mentofacture (knowledge and information creation using the mind) ownership of the critical means of production has shifted to employees. Ideally, if and when this potential is disseminated widely throughout the company, it should, in turn, lead to continuous innovation and receptivity to change. On this basis, it would appear that organisational learning to promote continuous innovation and change should thus be a priority objective for organisations that aim for competitive advantage and future survival.

But Nonaka (*op. cit.*) suggests that, traditionally, Western management consider the organisation as a machine for information processing with the only useful knowledge being formal and systematic. Such perspectives limit the creation of new knowledge, making organisations unlikely to be responsive to profound and continuous change required for survival. Nonaka indicates that creating new knowledge is not simply concerned with processing objective information. Rather, new knowledge always begins with the individual. It depends on eliciting the insights and intuitions of individual employees and making them available to the company as a whole. He suggests that the key to this process is personal commitment and the employees' sense of identity with the enterprise and its mission. Indeed Burgoyne (*op. cit.*) suggests that employee commitment and involvement have become the key issues in contemporary corporate management.

On this assumption, it would appear that there is a strong requirement that organisational learning to cope with environmental change should be continuous within society. Under changing circumstances, it is therefore important that elements of organisations are able to question the appropriateness of what they are doing and modify their actions to take account of new situations in order to improve performance. Essentially, as Morgan (1986) implies, a new philosophy of management is required to root the process of organising into open-ended inquiry, to remain open to changes in the environment and to challenge operating assumptions in a fundamental way.

Theoretical perspectives on organisational learning

Garratt (1995) suggests that theoretical perspectives on organisational learning have been influenced by a convergence between a number of disciplines that include psychology, sociology, cybernetics, economics and ecology. He considers that combining these with industrial disciplines such as finance and production resulted in an embryonic management education system that developed nearly forty years later as the learning organisation. He cites that the necessary conditions to create both the intellectual and practical basis of a learning organisation were in place by 1947. Influential figures at this time were Revans (action learning), Schumacher (the 'small is beautiful' school of economics) and Bronowski (the inter-relationship between arts and science). In parallel, Garratt recognises the ecological contribution of Ashby's (1960) work on requisite variety and the notion that, to ensure survival, the rate of learning needs to be equal to, or greater than, the rate of environmental change. He also suggests that Wiener's (1961) work in cybernetics, together with the contribution of the emerging work on socio-technical systems at the Tavistock Institute, played a significant role in the theoretical underpinning of the emergence of the learning organisation.

Contemporary views would also appear to be founded in the work of systems perspectives (Bateson 1972) and behaviourist views (Burns and Stalker 1961). These are embedded in the concept that innovative organisations should be designed as participatory learning systems which place an emphasis on information exchange and being open to inquiry and self-criticism. The emphasis is placed upon a vision of purposeful self-direction in development rather than individual and organisational futures determined by outside forces. Indeed, Argyris and Schon (1978) suggest that the need for organisational learning has never been more acute. Their work has emphasised the links between the laboratory training and T-group values established by Kurt Lewin in the 1940s, in which was stressed the need for the integration of theory, practice, and experiential learning. His most famous quotation 'there is nothing so practical as a good theory' symbolises his commitment to the integration of scientific enquiry and social problem-solving (Lewin 1952). This was illustrated during a training event in which it was suggested that learning is best facilitated in an environment in which there is dialectic tension and conflict between immediate concrete experience and analytic detachment.

The work of Argyris and Schon (1978) and indeed that of the behaviourist movement *per se*, has stimulated the core values of participative management philosophies to which much of the ethos of the learning organisation can be traced. They maintain that learning from experience is essential for individual and organisational effectiveness; and that learning can occur only in situations where personal values and organisational norms support action based on valid information, free and informed choice, and internal commitment. This is linked to Thompson's (1967) view of systemic organisational intelligence which focuses on information and the understanding of cybernetic systems that encourage the philosophy of learning to learn and questioning. Bateson's (*op. cit.*) work in cybernetics focuses on systemic notions of difference and meaning in which structure and processes are integrated. He has criticised the view that people traditionally are trained to see separate objects rather than patterns and relationships between them.

Cybernetics (the study of the organisation of systems in terms of communicational pathways and self-corrective patterns of circular process) addresses this by promoting the ability to remain open to changes in the environment and challenging operating assumptions in a fundamental way. The importance of feedback is significant in so far as information about the system returns to it, thereby influencing it. Positive feedback changes the system's stability; negative feedback stabilises the system's changing. It is also important to consider the inter-related sub-systems within the organisation (individuals, groups, departments, divisions, etc.) which are themselves complex open systems on their own account, also characterised by a continuous cycle of input, internal transformation, output and feedback. In this context, it is important to establish congruencies between different systems and to identify and eliminate potential dysfunction. By their elimination through differentiation (recognising difference in terms of change and opportunity) and integration (integrating the difference within the organisation) the ultimate goal is synergy – working together as a whole to achieve far more than the individuals, working separately, might have done (Carter *et al.* 1984).

Stacey (1996), however, argues that all organisations operate in a chaotic arena of non-linear feedback, often varying from a positive to a negative state to create complex patterns of behaviour. Those organisations that are successful operate in states of bounded instability, facing predictable short-term futures but totally unknowable long-term ones. As Prigogine and Stengers (1984: 12) observe, 'time and reality are closely related. For humans reality is embedded in the flow of time . . . the irreversibility of time is itself closely connected with entropy'.

If companies are to transform themselves through learning and self-organisation, then they will inevitably heighten their state of chaos. To effectively manage this may require a redefinition of traditional interpretations of decision-making and control, and how both are practised within organisations, so that strategic direction and change emerges from learning. Burgoyne (*op. cit.*) suggests that the notion of the learning company represents a view of what might be possible in terms of the management of the organisation's own learning processes to its advantage. Nevertheless, he warns that the learning organisation may represent a management excuse to de-layer or to downsize the business, demanding that people either leave or work harder for the same, or less, reward. He considers that the associated ideas of the concept may therefore become discredited before they have a chance to take hold.

Thus, organisational learning has captured the attention of academics and practitioners alike and there are indications that companies, keen to maintain their competitive advantage in an environment that many see as characterised by change and uncertainty, are embarking upon interventions that encourage its development. This is considered to be informed by the nature of change and development within society itself, together with the consequent relationship that would appear to be emerging between individuals and organisations, based upon a deeper level of involvement and commitment. This climate seemingly requires the generation of new ideas and knowledge within a framework that encourages autonomy, self-organisation and toleration of uncertainty. For traditional organisations, clearly, the significant changes to management structures, work practices and cultures that are required may prove to be so profound, lengthy and difficult that the concept may be diluted and/or misrepresented, creating further uncertainty and dysfunction. Moreover, the usefulness of the term 'learning organisation' is questioned on the basis that it may be seen as one of a succession of contemporary management tools employed to exploit the employment relationship. Notwithstanding this caveat, it will be useful at this point to examine how organisational learning, as opposed to the learning organisation, may assist or inhibit the change process in order to identify its practical potential.

The organisational learning process

In order to explore the impact of organisational learning it is important to examine the levels upon which the process of learning can occur as this will have considerable effect upon whether change is a feasible proposition. Hence, by identifying the characteristics of single-loop, double-loop and treble-loop learning (Bateson *op. cit.*) and their potential for challenging the status quo, thereby creating changed behaviours and approaches within organisations, the implications for the development of people may be more apparent.

Argyris and Schon (1978) argue that how organisations function and how decisions are made and problems solved succeeds in complicating issues, thereby reducing learning opportunities and performance. Their view is that organisational learning can occur only when its members are allowed to act as learning agents for the organisation, responding to changes in the internal and external environments by detecting and correcting errors in the organisational theory-in-use. They discuss single-loop learning (from Bateson *op. cit.*) by which individuals respond to changes in the external and internal environments by detecting errors and modifying strategies within the existing norms of the organisation. They consider that these are learning episodes that function to preserve a certain kind of constancy that does not present any significant challenge to the organisation. Bateson indicates, however, that the organisation's ability to remain stable in a changing context also denotes a type of learning. Burgoyne (*op. cit.*), nevertheless, describes this as the lowest level of learning in which habits are learned and as such, they are resistant to unlearning and hence are likely to prevent future learning.

Bateson goes on to identify deutero-learning, second-order or double-loop learning, which draws a distinction between the process of learning and the process of learning to learn. Simple cybernetic systems learn by detecting and correcting deviations from pre-determined norms. More complex systems, such as the human brain, have the capacity to learn to learn; they can reflect and inquire into previous contexts for learning or failure to learn, and can question the appropriateness of their actions. In this way, self-questioning and experience enables people to assess the wider context and perspective by re-framing the problem statements in order to restructure and change the theory-in-use (Garratt 1987).

It is suggested that the notion of agency is the key to this activity. Individuals and groups in the organisation act as learning agents on behalf of the organisation. They detect a match or mismatch of outcome to expectation and by means of collaborative inquiry and experience, people discover the sources of error and attribute them to the operating norms or theories-in-use within the organisation. They must then invent new strategies to reach organisational effectiveness, based on new assumptions to correct error, after which they must evaluate the results of the action. In this way, error correction embodies a complex learning cycle (Kolb 1984).

Burgoyne (*op. cit.*), relating these findings to the company context, describes this as the adaptive organisation and identifies this as the level at which most contemporary theory and practice of corporate strategy and the management of change is located. He suggests that it involves learning how to 'read' the environment, to understand the competition and to position the company and its people to manage change effectively. Such a company is therefore dynamic and adaptive, context and customer-driven, and it reflects the contemporary popular image of the 'learning company.'

Bateson also identifies treble-loop or third-order learning which poses teleological questions about purpose. Hawkins (1994: 18) suggests that this represents transformative learning, which focuses on aligning the operational (single-loop), strategic (double-loop) and service levels. He indicates that in this dimension

> on the individual level it is necessary to move into exploring the fundamental perspectives through which we view the world and the paradigms which shape our understanding. . . . At the organisational level it involves change in the collective mindsets of the organisation's culture and the emotional ground in which these are rooted.

Burgoyne (*op. cit.*) and Morgan (1997) suggest that at this level the organisation creates its environment at least as much as it adapts to it. They also consider that this is reflected in the ability of the organisation to stabilise the context in which it operates and/or its relationship with it. Clearly, it is only at this level of learning that the concept of the learning organisation can fully emerge, in so far as it profoundly challenges interpretations of existing experience and reality, together with traditional interpretations and understanding of the management of people and organisational cultures.

If the learning company is to become the primary focus of corporate change strategies in the future, this should have direct implications for human resource management. In particular, this will impact upon attitudes towards, and provision for, individual and collective development initiatives and interventions. On this assumption, one of the most powerful observations was that made by Knowles (cited in Mumford 1994) in his statement that adult learning crucially depends on individual interest in resolving relevant problems. Another was that made by Kolb (1984) who identified that not everyone learns or experiences events in the same way. In terms of the process of experiential learning, Kolb has illuminated an approach that clearly places individual learning and development as a self-directed responsibility.

Kolb sees learning as a continuous process or flow that is determined by concrete experience, reflective observation, abstract conceptualisation and active experimentation. When viewed from Kolb's perspective, learning is seen as a continuous cyclical process whereby planning, actions and concepts are modified by reflecting on experiences rather than from outcomes or results, hence by engaging the process of double-loop learning and change. He identifies adaptive learning activities that are commonly known as creativity, problem solving and decision-making. Holman *et al.* (1997), however, in their evaluation of Kolb's theory, consider that it is practical argumentation with oneself and in collaboration with others that forms the basis for learning and that to place too much emphasis on individual reflection alone, is counter-productive.

In connection with the ways in which people learn, Honey and Mumford (1992) describe a learning cycle, which is used to identify people's preferred learning styles. They contend that if learning styles can be identified on the basis of whether the individual is an activist, reflector, pragmatist or theorist, there is a greater likelihood that individual development can occur if opportunities are offered in the style most preferred by the recipient. Reynolds (1997: 128), however, critiques this analysis on the basis that it has 'reinforced a perspective that is both individualised and decontextualised'. This would confirm the importance of understanding learning as a process of socialisation (Hendry 1996). These findings would appear to have clear implications for those organisations that want their employees to engage in the process of learning. Unless the organisation can develop an understanding of how learning occurs and can offer environments in which it is encouraged, it is unlikely that any commitment to developing a learning approach will be fulfilled.

It is clear that the process of learning is a complex social, cultural and cognitive phenomenon and is dependent on variables that influence how far extant patterns and norms can be challenged and revised by individuals. Hence, the levels at which learning occurs will determine the extent and depth of change that an organisation may experience. Single-loop learning results in no significant changes to existing systems, whereas double-loop learning provokes change by learning to learn. Treble-loop learning creates transformational change in which developments may emerge from the system itself and it is at this level that the organisation may have more influence over its own environment. Clearly, if it is accepted that individuals contribute as learning agents for the organisation, then the conditions under which they learn most effectively must be present if they are to maximise both their own potential and that of the organisation. In contemporary organisations, it is now recognised that developing the individual is an important source of competitive advantage but for many this means over-coming established systems and processes that do not encourage learning and questioning. On this basis, it appears appropriate to examine how far traditional approaches to work organisation inhibit double-loop learning and change.

Learning in organisations: problems and barriers

Established systems within traditional organisations influence receptivity to learning and dictate how far the individual may challenge existing operating norms so that change can occur. Accordingly, any barriers to the encouragement of a learning environment must be dismantled before the individual can engage in the learning process themselves and on behalf of the organisation. Whilst there are many aspects of the nature of work and organisational life that might be identified, the section considers organisational culture, individual receptivity to learning and the approach of management as highly integrated and potentially influential in preventing the development of a learning approach. It suggests that there is need to explore alternative approaches that transcend reliance on the individual in favour of learning being seen as an activity that is the responsibility of the whole organisation.

Individual and organisational learning are often characterised by barriers that prevent their fulfilment. Honey (1991), for example, states that the problem within many organisations is that people learn whether management want them to or not but most organisations are designed to encourage the acquisition of practices and behaviours they wish they had less of. His view suggests that the learning organisation attempts to create an environment where the behaviours and practices that promote continuous improvement are actively encouraged.

It is here that there is a divergence in the views of theorists in terms of how organisations, as opposed to individuals, learn. Honey (*op. cit.*), for example, considers that the notion of organisations learning as opposed to the individuals in organisations learning together, introduces an unnecessary level of abstraction to the debate. Morgan (1993) endorses this view when he states that a learning organisation cannot be created, but that people's capacities to learn can be enhanced and aligned in creative ways. Indeed, while some organisations, through individuals learning, have successfully developed systems that have the capacity to challenge norms and procedures in relation to changes in the environment, many fail to do so. This would appear to be evident from those companies that, over time, cease to exist (Senge 1991). Moreover, sometimes their systems and structures manage to obstruct the learning process altogether. Morgan (1986) confirms that traditionally, bureaucratic organisations do not encourage employees to think for themselves, information tends to be closely guarded by those in control and attempts to challenge the status quo are discouraged.

Indeed, Argyris (1992: 26) indicates that many individuals in traditional organisations appear to be programmed with what he terms 'model 1 theories-in-use'. These dictate that they (a) strive to be in unilateral control; (b) minimise losing and maximise winning; (c) minimise the expression of negative feelings; (d) be rational. On this basis, it is considered unlikely that they will engage in double-loop learning and therefore, attempts to create learning environments within organisations will be inhibited. In an earlier work, Argyris (1990: xii) identifies 'designed error' or second-order error which he considers to be at the heart of ineffectiveness. He considers that the problem within many organisations is that producing such error is often covered up, and the cover-up is covered up. It becomes accepted that this helps organisations to survive and such actions are then seen as necessary and even caring. On this assumption, Argyris suggests that the individual's action can be explained in two ways. First, as 'skilled incompetence'; by stating that they were not aware of producing error while doing so, or they know they are producing an error but have found ways of making the error look as if it was not an error. Moreover, Argyris (1992: 40) goes on to discuss a second strategy, that of the use of 'defensive routines' which he states can be a policy or action that prevents someone (or some system) from experiencing embarrassment or threat. He suggests that this prevents anyone from correcting the causes of the embarrassment or threat and that they inhibit learning.

He further suggests that such organisational defensive routines are learnt through socialisation; they are taught as strategies to deal effectively with threat and/or embarrassment; they are supported by the culture of the organisation; and they exist over time, despite differing individuals moving in and out of the organisation. Earlier Argyris (1987) argued that the manner in which the organisation functions and in which problems are solved only succeeds in complicating issues and reducing rather than improving performance. Indeed, while some organisations have successfully developed systems that have the capacity to challenge norms and procedures in relation to changes in the environment, many fail to do so. Often their operating procedures manage to obstruct the learning process altogether.

Argyris (*op. cit.*) therefore suggests that the evolution of a learning organisation, and the development of the individual, are directly influenced by the type of situation in which that individual works. This, in turn, will influence their ability in terms of positive or negative contributions to the organisation. Following from the analysis of clinical psychologist Maslow (1943), Argyris sees each individual as having a potential for self-actualisation that should be addressed by the organisation. If this can be fulfilled, there are considerable benefits in terms of development and receptivity to change, not only for the individual but also for the work group and the organisation itself. Often, however, organisations operate in ways that prevent such development, which means that the generation of a learning climate can be problematic.

Argyris suggests there are three factors that influence the individual's ability to relate to organisational life and which have a direct bearing on organisational performance and learning. He identifies these as:

(1)   The nature and culture of the organisation;
(2)   The development of the individual towards psychological maturity;
(3)   The ability of management, work supervisors and other group members in terms of interpersonal skills and competence.

Organisational culture

Schein (1993) claims that culture plays a strong role in determining an organis-ation's ability to learn and change direction. Culture often embodies an accumulation of prior learning based on prior success that usually limits and biases people's capacity to perceive and understand a new vision and the need for change. On this assumption, Schein suggests that the cognitive capacity of the organisation is sometimes insufficient to grasp the complexity of changing situations, limiting the ability of leaders to develop realistic visions, and in turn the ability of the workforce to understand them. This promotes a situation in which members become anxious and develop fears of failure, particularly if the organisation has operated by means of a 'carrot and stick' philosophy in the past. 'Unlearning' such cultural norms is difficult because they are embedded, stable and predictable even when they become dysfunctional. Schein argues that con-structive motivation for change will only occur if it is based on valid disconfirming information. New responses and attitudes will only be learned if a climate of psychological safety is created that incorporates the opportunity to make errors, to practice and to innovate in a safe environment, as confirmed by Schon (1983).

Individual learning and maturity

Argyris (1957) describes a progression of seven stages from infant passivity, dependency and submission to control by others, to maturity whereby individuals develop the ability to see themselves from another's point of view, are able to foresee consequences and are prepared to accept responsibility for others. He considers such development as encompassing the potential for individuals to enjoy constructive release of psychological energy. Each individual has a set of needs and if offered the opportunity of satisfaction combined with challenge, they are likely to put all such energies into meeting that challenge. He suggests, however, that systems and procedures within many contemporary organisations prevent individuals from reaching maturity or releasing their full psychological energy. As a result, people are often myopic in outlook, unable to see future consequences and their attitudes to work are generally apathetic.

Responsibility rests not with the individual but with the organisation itself. This is particularly prevalent in bureaucratic organisations that prevent individuals from progressing from infancy to maturity. As a result, both the individual and the manager become frustrated at the lack of independence and innovation within the work group. Bureaucratic accountability implies that success is rewarded and failure is punished, creating a climate in which self-preservation becomes the ultimate goal. Management tends to respond by not sharing information and by applying greater control mechanisms. Workers, in turn, are inclined to put minimal commitment and effort into their work. Thompson (1983) describes this as 'masks for tasks' whereby people will keep up appearances in terms of performance and ability and tell people 'what they want to hear' (theory-in-use and espoused theory, Argyris 1991). They perceive this as maintaining their credibility with managers and it prevents them exposing their lack of knowledge, thereby avoiding blame as a result of failure.

Management

In terms of management capability, Argyris (1991) claims this presents one of the most difficult barriers to organisational learning. Often it is managers who have the most difficulty in learning because they misunderstand what learning is and how to bring it about. While he accepts that managers are skilled at single-loop learning, at performing well within their spheres of competence, this in itself contributes to their fundamental inability in double-loop learning. The fact that they seldom experience failure, and therefore have never learned from it, creates defensive mechanisms to compensate if and when failure does occur. Managers then tend to avoid criticism, blame others or ignore problems precisely when the ability to learn is most vital. Such 'defensive reasoning', Argyris argues, reveals a further incorrect assumption that organisations make about learning. Managers consider that if people are motivated and committed to the company, learning will follow automatically. In order to encourage this, managers embark upon structural realignments, performance reviews, cultural change and HRM strategies designed to improve employee involvement and motivation.

Despite the widespread appeal of such ideas, research in both the United States and the United Kingdom (Marchington *et al.* 1992) has shown that there are some doubts about whether there is any simple association between involvement, commitment and motivation which will create receptivity to learning. Guest (1989) for example, suggests that proponents of HRM assume that employee involvement will lead to greater organisational commitment, which in turn will lead to enhanced motivation and performance. However, the link is tenuous, partly due to the difficulties in measuring what is meant by commitment and whether this commitment is to the job, to work or to the organisation.

Similarly, Garratt's (1987) view of the dilemma within organisations that prevents the development of a learning orientation focuses on the attitudes and behaviour of managers. He suggests that managers must remove their traditional blockages to learning, which include the idealisation of past experiences, the charismatic influence of other managers upon their own behaviour, the belittlement of subordinates, and the impulsion to instant activity rather than taking time to reflect. It is also important that they abandon the notion of personal power, which inhibits companies from changing their traditional methods of organisation so that they move more towards co-ordinating rather than managing and controlling (see Table 3.1).

Garratt (1990) goes on to examine the crucial role of directors in encouraging a learning organisation. He indicates that there is a typical under-performance within organisations which is generated as a result of directors receiving inadequate training and development for their more strategic and generalist roles. As a result, they fall back on the 'comfort' of past positions and this has a profound effect on performance throughout all levels of the organisation. He considers that this produces an environment where there is minimal inclination to learn from others, together with a significant reluctance from managers to build effective teams within their organisations.

This results in a number of bottlenecks throughout the organisation, in which creativity is minimised and there is a tendency to operate with a blinkered and short-term perspective. Hence, when people and organisations maintain such defensive attitudes, this prevents them from developing more intelligent and creative approaches to the critical examination of their existence and actions. They may not be 'right' but opportunities for learning are diminished because they see merely what their established belief system expects them to see.

Nevertheless, for those managers who are attempting approaches to encourage learning their commitment would appear to have considerable resource implications for organisations. There must undoubtedly be seen to be tangible benefits in terms of return on investment if organisations are to be convinced of the value of the process. Controlling, monitoring and evaluating learning interventions against the business 'bottom line' is likely therefore to be difficult. In agreement, Garratt (1995) comments that learning in organisations may be the 'biggest payoff of all' and that its credibility may be achieved by reflecting it in some way on the balance sheet.

Clegg *et al.* (1996: 207) however, in their discussion of the role of managers in promoting organisational knowledge and learning, suggest that:

> Top management has an important role to play in the acquisition of the learning skills that institutionalise innovation. This . . . includes linking the organisation to key outside contacts that serve as 'learning agents' ; cultivation of technical skills; encouraging an innovative mindset among personnel; locating, defining and linking skills . . .; matching skills with the strategic plan.

Table 3.1 Management approaches: disabling and enabling (adapted from Pearn *et al.*
1995)

Approach	Disabling	Enabling
Change management	Manager plans and communicates to team	Manager initiates process but works closely with the team to develop
Leadership style	Close direction and supervision	Manager creates a vision but control and monitoring is with the team
Decision-making	Manager decides	Manager provides a framework; individuals have responsibility
Training and development	Manager determines and organises all training	Manager helps the person determine own learning programmes
Communication	Passes information needed to complete tasks	Consistently open and honest
External relationships	Focus is own aspect of the organisation	Develops close working relationship with other areas

Beyond individual learning

Clearly, this develops the debate in so far as it would appear that learning itself has to be seen as more than a practical, individual concern but rather as a multi-dimensional facet of organisational life. Hawkins (*op. cit.*) suggests that it is important that organisational learning is seen as a reflexive process, how the world is understood and what the implications may be for individuals in organisations and for how the whole organisation learns. The notion that learning resides not just within the individual but within systemic patterns, 'circuits of mind' or 'psychic fields' (from Bateson *op. cit.*) created by people within organisations, is postulated by Hawkins (*op. cit.*). This has clear implications for learning and change, in so far as they become the responsibility of wider society. To entrust learning purely to individuals acting as agents for the organisation, as suggested by Honey (1991) and Morgan (1993), without acknowledgement of the cultural and emotional interconnections, would therefore appear to jeopardise the process.

In order to evolve beyond their present level of meaning and understanding, so that they increase their capacity to learn and change, it seems that organisations need to remove the structural and cultural barriers that the nature of work and organisational life have traditionally created and that prevent their achievement. As Argyris (1987: 88) suggests, 'the organisation of the future will vary the strategy it uses and thus its structure according to the kinds of decisions it faces'. It is significant, nevertheless, that in times of crisis, transition and transformation, learning and development appear to become most intense both on individual and organisational levels yet budgets are often reduced or withdrawn. The focus for contemporary organisations is therefore to acknowledge the reciprocal nature of learning and change and to harness the energy of the relationship to achieve continuous improvement.

It has been argued that problems and barriers preventing learning that are embedded in culture, individuals themselves and management approaches exist within traditional work organisation environments. Only by recognising their negative implications can they be eradicated so that the conditions under which learning is more likely to occur can be created. Furthermore, there would also appear to be a requirement that the organisation looks beyond the immediate internal environment and its traditional interpretations of reality. In this way, learning may be seen as a phenomenon located within the development of the emotional interconnection of the people within the organisation and beyond, and as such, is the responsibility of all to ensure it is promoted and sustained. The chapter therefore continues with an examination of some of the practical approaches that are being considered in order to assist in the creation and development of a learning environment.

A learning approach involves challenging the status quo and hence, the encouragement of double-loop learning to reconstruct the theory-in-use; otherwise continuous improvement and change will not occur. This will require significant changes to established practices, processes and procedures within traditional organisations. It is therefore likely to take considerable time to accomplish successfully. Argyris's (1991) research supports the view that effective double-loop learning involves more than changes to structures and processes. It involves how people think, how they use reasoning to design and implement their actions. He indicates that defensive reasoning can block learning even when the individual is highly committed to it. Nevertheless, he acknowledges that there are problems to do with human behaviour if individuals are required to reason in every new situation. He suggests that they may display resentment, cognitive dissonance and work-related stress. Often there is discrepancy between what is 'said' and what is actually 'done'. This, Argyris suggests, represents 'espoused theory' and 'theory-in-use.' People are reluctant to reveal shortcomings, to expose their inability because they are afraid of appearing vulnerable. This in itself limits their learning experiences and opportunities. When such attitudes prevail, the opportunities for learning about group dynamics and solving problems in the workplace are limited. If attention is directed to removing such blockages by learning how to learn (double-loop learning), Argyris considers, there is considerably more potential for continuous organisational learning to evolve.

Potential for organisational learning is embodied in the original insights of Revans (1982) who stimulated interest in action learning in the 1970s. Essentially, action learning is a process of learning from and with others, which clearly embodies a systemic approach, together with promoting the development of learning to learn. Revans, echoing Ashby's view (from Garratt 1995) considers that the degree of learning within the organisation must be equal to, or greater than, the rate of change in the environment. The conditions under which people will be keen to learn must be present and the climate within the organisation must tolerate sufficient difference within work groups – too much similarity reduces the ability to adapt and learn. This is confirmed by Pascale (1990) who, drawing upon Ashby's (1960) work on requisite variety, comments that too little internal variety reduces tolerance of external variety. In this way, the development of a learning culture is encouraged which is positive and enabling.

Additionally, action learning attacks the inherent need of the teacher (or manager) to be the centre of attention as the 'expert' and places ownership for development and learning with the person concerned (Mumford 1991). Clearly, action learning complements self-development, as the individual has control and choice over what to learn, how to learn it and how to share that learning. This view is confirmed by Pedler *et al.* (1989) who suggest that confronting real problems, rather than being taught, is the major source of significant learning or development. Similarly, there is also commonality with the ethos of the learning organisation, as Mumford (*op. cit.*) suggests; working on real projects with a specific learning objective is a significant part of the process of an organisation constantly changing itself.

Senge (1990) elaborates Mumford's perspective in his conceptualisation of five interrelated disciplines that need to be fostered among individuals and groups for organisational learning and success:

(1) Personal mastery, which he describes as personal growth and learning;
(2) Mental models or deeply ingrained assumptions that affect the way we think about people, situations and organisations, often creating contradictions between what we say and what we do (from Argyris – espoused theory and theory-in-use);
(3) Shared vision, which Senge considers should not be imposed as it may discourage people in the organisation from learning;
(4) Team learning is seen as essential but Senge discusses how this can be impeded by various defensive routines;
(5) Senge cites the fifth discipline, systems thinking, as being integrative and most important of all. He describes how organisations tend to focus on one or two parts of problems rather than on the entire 'system'. As a result, they are drawn to simple explanations and solutions. As he puts it (1990: 73):

The art of systems thinking lies in being able to recognise increasingly (dynamically) complex and subtle structures . . . amid the wealth of details, pressures and cross-currents that attend all real management settings. In fact, the essence of mastering systems thinking as a management discipline lies in seeing patterns where others see only events and forces to react to.

The importance of systems thinking is seen as enabling people to understand the whole and to perceive the interrelationships or structures which underlie complex change situations. It also detects patterns of change over time, so that people can come to see that cause and effect are seldom close in timescales. As Stacey (1996: 312) confirms, non-linear systems can operate in a state of far-from-equilibrium whereby the links between cause and effect are lost in the complexity of interactions within and between systems [and] patterns of behaviour [that] emerge are essentially irregular . . . not simply because of environmental change, but because of the very structure of the system itself.

Strategic management

Traditional patterns of strategic management in organisations appear to inhibit the learning process and prevent recognition of the unpredictability of dynamic systems. Only if the long term for an organisation is a repetition of its past can it control using strategic plans and milestones. Nevertheless, the traditional approach is to produce a defined plan in which long-term goals, objectives and targets are articulated and imposed, with a tendency to adhere to them despite change events in the task and contextual environments. This results in a framework for single-loop learning but tends to inhibit double-loop learning. The process of learning to learn hinges on an ability to remain open to changes occurring in the environment, and on an ability to challenge operating assumptions in a fundamental way. Unless planning is determined by inquiry-driven action, some theorists (Ohmae 1986, Pascale 1990, Stacey *op. cit.*) consider that it is likely that companies will suffer due to failing to keep abreast of the requirements of changing environments.

Hampden-Turner (1990) considers that strategic planning might be approached from a creative, learning dimension. The process is summarised in seven steps that start with identifying the opposing values that form the core of the problem. Then the opposing values are located as two axes, helping managers to identify where they see themselves or their organisations. This is followed by re-framing the problem statement into processes that imply movement that loosens the impression of opposition, thus preventing one value from becoming superior to the other. This offers the opportunity for creative strategies for improvement in opposing contexts to emerge by moving away from static thinking. The strategic path towards improving both values will involve cycles in which both values will 'worsen' for a time. At a more fundamental level, however, learning is occurring, which will enable the next cycle to reach a higher plane for both values. Finally, the ultimate goal is to achieve synergy (working together) where significant improvement is occurring along all axes of all relevant dilemmas

In terms of approaches to strategic management within organisations, Morgan (1997) reinforces the importance of learning to learn, together with the effective contribution of individuals and the integration of sub-systems. He suggests that cybernetic principles create greater degrees of freedom so that the organisation can evolve by formulating a mission in terms of what is to be avoided rather than what is achieved. This enables a choice of limits rather than a choice of ends, creating greater organisational flexibility in terms of strategic management, vital to accommodate change in the environment.

It would appear that strategic management therefore could be designed to aid learning to learn. Whilst traditional models emphasise setting goals and targets to respond to threats and opportunities in the environment, this may inhibit the inquiry that challenges the basic operating norms of organisations. On this basis, the process of learning to learn requires organisations to be responsive to challenges and if necessary even the re-formulation of mission. By avoiding the imposition of goals and objectives, direction may emerge from participative learning approaches from all levels of the organisation rather than passivity and reaction.

If learning is to occur within organisations they need to encourage and value an openness and reflectivity that accepts error and uncertainty as part of the learning process. That problem-solving should explore different viewpoints with constructive conflict and debate can be seen as part of the process. Pedler *et al.* (1989) confirm the importance of a learning approach to strategy in which there is capacity for business plans to be developed, formulated and revised as the company goes along. In this way, managerial acts are seen as continuous experiments rather than set solutions. They consider that participative policy making is an essential factor if a learning organisation is to evolve. There are deliberate efforts made to involve all members of the organisation in planning, to reconcile conflicts and tensions and to reach decisions that all members are likely to support. 'Members' are widely defined and diverse and include employees, customers, suppliers, owners, neighbours, the community and the environment as stakeholders in the organisation. Attitudes to such diversity require that the organisation assumes that all groups have the right to take part in policy making, that it is valuable in so far as it will lead to creativity, better ideas and solutions.

The shadow system

In connection with this point, Stacey (*op. cit.*: 378) sees management recognition of the 'shadow system', the informal, self-organising organisation as pivotal in coping with ambiguity and uncertainty and so that emergent strategy might be generated. He suggests that if organisations are to cope with change, they must be capable of 'novelty and surprise'. He adds, however, that 'one form of novelty is creativity and innovation and another, of course, is crisis and disaster.' It is the management of the paradox that has to be developed. Stacey suggests that the creative process is evident within the organisation's shadow system, which exists alongside the legitimate system, essentially because often the formal system (such as the bureaucracy) does not work. Characteristics of the failure of such a system include alienation and powerlessness, immaturity, passivity and dependence as identified by Argyris (1957), feelings that work is meaningless, and the notion that work gradually becomes de-skilled. The shadow system, however, provides an alternative platform for organisational expression and development. Stacey (1996: 382), drawing upon the work of Barnard (1938), discusses the importance of communications and the social network and indicates:

> their function [the social group] was the communication of intangible facts, opinions, suggestions and suspicions that could not pass through the formal

channels without giving rise to public conflict. [They] made it possible for individuals to exercise influence far greater than the position they held in the hierarchy might indicate.

In support of this, Stacey suggests that the notion of 'learning communities of practice' (Brown and Duguid 1991, see also 'communities of inquiry' in Fisher and Torbert 1995) are an alternative conceptualisation of the shadow system. A community of practice is a group of people that carries out similar tasks but their significance is that they engage in dialogue; they discuss what they do and how they do it. In other words, they share experience, skills, knowledge and learning but in an informal, social setting. It is this aspect of individual and group learning that would appear to be vital for the transference and development of organisational learning. Stacey (*op. cit.*) remarks that organisations can deal with predictable situations using established procedures and regulations and can prepare people by means of training and development interventions. When confronted by unique situations, however, they often have to learn by being members of a community of practice. If organisations are to harness the potential of this phenomenon, however, there has to be recognition of its existence, its contribution and its value. The implications for leaders are fundamental, as this will inevitably require a different approach to that traditionally employed in order to gain the commitment and consent of employees.

Leadership and control

Deming (cited in Pedlar 1991) considers that it is an attitude of 'performance for someone else's approval' that has created an emphasis on mediocrity and the lack of ability to learn within Western organisations. Schein (1993) considers that to survive and grow organisations are now required to learn and adapt faster and faster but major problems arise because leaders and academics cannot readily admit that the current situation is turbulent and that they do not have a clear way forward. He considers that in an environment in which there is too much information, organisations now appear to have limited cognitive abilities to think in systemic terms. Additionally, managers are unwilling to contravene cultural norms that say leaders are in control and have solutions to problems. If they admit confusion, followers will express concern and be disillusioned. They know they must learn how to learn but are afraid to admit it. Schein suggests that it is important to cope with this anxiety in order to facilitate learning within organisations.

Responsibility lies with leaders to move away from the traditional view so that they develop an understanding of how organisations learn, how to accelerate that learning and how to integrate it at all levels. Senge (1990) for example, considers that the role of leader moves away from that of the charismatic hero making key decisions, to one of designer and steward. Inevitably, new skills are required in the form of the ability to build shared vision, to challenge basic assumptions and to encourage more systemic patterns of thinking. Change can be difficult, especially when it seems to attack the very values and processes to which managers owe their present positions. In order to overcome this barrier, it is considered important to assist managers in their ability to learn, to change and to develop. If an essentially empowering culture is to emerge from such development, then this will inevitably enable people to affect the way in which they are managed (Clegg *et al.* 1996). Central to this process is for managers to recognise their role as one of team leadership, legitimised by employee consent rather than positional power.

Team learning

Further to the previous discussion of learning communities of practice, Garratt (1987) also argues that an organisation will only operate effectively if it is seen as a series of teams working across the horizontal and vertical groupings within the organisation. He identifies the need for balance between the individualism of the West and Eastern approaches that are driven by clearly defined work teams. Senge (1990), however, considers that while organisations are being encouraged to develop a team approach, in reality teams can operate at a level of intelligence substantially lower than that of each individual in the group. He suggests that they organise and operate in ways that are efficient at keeping themselves from learning, often managing to reduce to sixty three the collective IQ of a team of managers with individual IQs above one hundred and twenty. Essentially, team learning is a team skill that really needs to be practised if it is to result in organisational effectiveness and learning.

Schon (1983) describes freedom to experiment in a 'virtual world', a constructed representation of the real world, as a valuable approach to team learning. Experimentation can be in the form of scenario planning, discussion, computer simulation, case study, drawing, modelling, planning, etc. Its value lies in the fact that it can slow down the pace of the real world; it can remove some of the complexities within the environment or can alter the structure of the variables. In organisations, although team learning requires this type of practice, there are few opportunities to become part of a 'virtual world'. It is usual for decisions to be discussed but implemented immediately, without the opportunity to assess outcomes or to reflect on how the team might have approached the task differently.

In support of this theory, solutions are offered in the form of the workplace seen as a 'learning laboratory' (Kenney and Florida 1993, Leonard-Barton 1992) in which an experimental approach is developed. Similarly, de Geus (1988) (former Head of Planning for the Royal Dutch/Shell Group) developed a technique of scenario planning in which institutional learning is encouraged. This is described as a process whereby management teams change their shared mental models of their company, their markets and their competitors. de Geus claims that experience has demonstrated that institutional learning is more difficult than individual learning, confirming theorists views that teams can block learning. He suggests that it is pain which makes people and all living systems adapt, but crisis management is a dangerous way to manage for change. The challenge for organisations is to recognise and react to environmental change before the pain of a crisis. In this way, change will grow out of an organisation's knowledge of itself (its self-identity) and its environment. He thinks this form of experiential learning is more effective than traditional teaching methods, proven to be among the least efficient ways to convey knowledge. Indeed Holt's (1983) research endorses this view and indicates that only 25 per cent to 40 per cent of what is taught in a traditional sense is received by learners.

Management development interventions within Shell have revealed to de Geus that institutional learning is essentially a process of language development. He considers that as the implicit knowledge of each learner becomes explicit within the organisation, this contributes to the overall institutional mental model. Clearly how significantly this develops will depend on the structure and culture of the organisation. Consequently, managers are required to revise their views of the world. They become team members within flexible structures, recognising that the most effective learning occurs in teams which develop a systemic under-standing that the whole is larger (and different) than the sum of the parts.

Notwithstanding these points, although experiential learning in the form of creative tension and difference can be used as a productive tool to improve team performance, there is a tendency to avoid this within many organisations. As de Geus suggests, members may embark upon defensive routines that limit their ability to learn within the team setting, leading to inertia, under-performance and disillusionment. The more effective the defensive routines are, the better they mask the problems and the more the team will come to rely upon them. The paradox, Argyris (1987) considers is that when such defensive routines disguise immediate problems, they also prevent people from learning how to reduce what causes the problem in the first place.

Additionally, this also prevents teams and individuals from knowing that they are indulging in defensive routines, from verbalising problems or even acknowl-edging them to themselves. As in Shell, it seems that teams do have the capacity to reverse this situation by learning and by creating a vision of what they want in terms of the business; how they want to work together; and by developing a commitment to telling the truth about the current 'reality.' By analysing situations for example, in terms of Holman *et al.*'s (1997) argumentation process of thinking, reflecting, experiencing and action, teams have the capacity to learn and break out of the defensive routine mode. By so doing, they may be able to realise that they have the capacity to change the current reality and to move forward.

Dixon's (1994) organisational learning cycle supports and reinforces the importance of widespread involvement and participation in the learning process. She identifies four stages that first involve generation of information by a variety of internal and external information gatherers or 'boundary scanners'. This is followed by integration of information into the organisational context by means of recording and sharing through information technology and 'boundary spanning' people in order to facilitate shared understanding. As a third step, she stresses the importance of collective interpretation of information and authority to take responsible action on the interpreted meaning. This would include not only managers but also all those affected by the information, operating within a participative culture of decision making. Finally, there is the authority to act on the interpretation and Dixon suggests that the requisite skills of contemporary leadership are to distinguish appropriate lines of decision-making authority in a participative and empowering context.

Conclusion

From the perspectives examined, organisational learning occurs in a complex arena. If profitable learning is to emerge, it requires recognition that organisations are unpredictable, chaotic systems that display both stability and instability; embedded within this notion are the requirements to maintain the system and to change it. By making use of these diametrically opposing perspectives and achieving a balance between them, it is possible to maximise the creative potential that self-organising systems can generate so that they can learn and move forward.

At the individual level, this requires the ability to gain insight and understanding from experience. It involves observation, experimentation, analysis, willingness to tolerate heightened risk, the unique and the unknowable. In many ways, this involves moving away from established paradigms and 'unlearning' (Nystrom and Starbuck 1984) previous mindsets, acknowledged to be difficult tasks in themselves. If organisations are to seek not simply change but transformation, however, it would appear that they must encourage attitudes and patterns of behaviour that proactively support learning at all levels so that the way forward becomes self-generated. Nevertheless, the vision of such transformation may be elusive and difficult for companies to legitimise if seen from the perspective of developing the 'learning organisation' *per se*. Indeed, this may result in Burgoyne's (1995a) suggestion of the abuse of the term in order to introduce change. Hence, managers may be more inclined to avoid taking risks, to continue established systems and procedures that have enabled their organisations to survive to the present day, despite the pressures for change which surround them.

If, as some theorists suggest, learning is to be a critical success factor for the future, survival will be dependent upon a more proactive and creative interaction with, and interpretation of, the environment in which organisations exist. In this context, learning is seen as a multi-level concept that involves processes of skill learning, self-awareness and an understanding of transformational change (Hawkins *op. cit.*). It may be that by weaving a more direct linkage between learning and the preoccupation of contemporary organisations to 'manage change', there will be greater potential for the effective pursuit of both. Accordingly, the theoretical relationship between learning and change, together with practical suggestions for frameworks that encourage both processes that have been advanced in the literature, will be explored in Chapter four. This will provide a theoretical foundation and context for interpreting and analysing the contemporary approaches undertaken in the case study organisations examined later in this book.

4 The relationship between learning and change

Summary

The challenge of managing change preoccupies management in many if not most contemporary organisations. Its significance is reflected in the burgeoning number of publications that discuss and examine both the theoretical and practical nature of its importance for commercial and industrial society. The apparent absence of explicit and coherent learning theory, however, in much of the literature on change would appear to indicate that understanding, managing and sustaining the change process may produce incomplete and limited results. To explore the connectivity between learning and change, it seems appropriate to examine traditional and contemporary perspectives on the management of change, together with those learning theories currently in use within this arena, in order to trace some parallel themes. Following this, practical approaches to learning and change are explored, taking internal and external factors into consideration, with particular reference to the implications of resistance, power and control.

The nature of change

Stewart (1996) indicates the internal and external contextual changes facing organisations in the 1990s are multifarious and include increasing commercialisation and competition, technological advancement, customer sovereignty and political influences. Indeed, changes in global politics and technology create economic and social consequences that impact upon all levels of society. Additionally, the pace of change is now considered to be so rapid that many businesses face constant market realignments and managers must respond quickly if their organisations are to survive. Nevertheless, it is not sufficient that organisations merely recognise and respond to the changing contexts in which they exist. There must also be recognition of the need to change (Carnall 1990, Clarke 1994), together with appropriate internal realignments surrounding the management of the employment relationship in this changing context. For example, the emergence of HRM literature in the past decade identifies the role of the organisation as a source of meanings and super-ordinate goals, together with its strategic focus on the integration of people's contribution to business performance (Blyton and Turnbull 1992).

The need for change is perhaps difficult for many organisations to legitimise unless (and/or until) provoked by a crisis or 'trigger' for change (Boddy and Buchanan 1992). This might include loss of market share, increased competition, reduced profits and/or increasingly, year-on-year pressure to cut costs from industry partners. Legge (1995: 76) states:

> Several buzz words signify these changes: intensification of international competition, globalization, the Japanese Janus (threat/icon), cultures of excellence, information technology, knowledge-working, high value added, the enterprise culture. The phrase that encapsulates them all is 'the search for competitive advantage'. The effect of these factors lies in their reinforcing interrelationships as much as in their separate existence.

Thus, academics and practitioners alike acknowledge that the organisational environment is turbulent and unpredictable for the majority of companies. This is not disputed, although the extent of these conditions being novel and unique to contemporary times continues to attract debate. Thompson and Davidson (1995) for example cite the works of Drucker (1959, 1968), Nohria and Eccles (1992), Naisbitt (1994) and Toffler (1971, 1981) to illustrate that the urgency of coping with change has been preoccupying organisations throughout the second part of the century. Essentially they see this as the result of the emergence of a mass global market for management texts, particularly from the 1980s onwards.

Thompson and Davidson (*op. cit.*) assert that the necessity for change being driven by turbulent times has been a longstanding feature of management discourse and is therefore not new. In criticism of 'pop-management gurus' advocating radical organisational change driven by environmental uncertainty, Thompson and Davidson suggest that the 'unpopularity of bureaucracy' has generated the need for a panacea in the form of an ideological illusion of organisational transformation, impacting upon structures, cultures, work practices and human resource management. They argue that evidence to support this trend lacks research and academic credibility.

Notwithstanding these concerns, there does seem to be increasing evidence to support the view that organisational members should be skilled in understanding, learning and coping with change. Indeed, managing change has become a crucial element of competitive edge and Thompson and Davidson (*op. cit.*: 22) identify the difficulties that some individuals experience with change interventions that establish new work practices and production systems. They suggest that employers are often finding that lack of education and social skills are barriers to the development of team working and quality systems.

Stewart (*op. cit.*: 14) summarises the key points that surround the analysis of change and its impact upon individuals and organisations. He states that change is a natural phenomenon that is continuous and ongoing. The main purpose of change is to aid survival and growth but survival is dependent upon adaptation to a changing environment and the development of experiential learning. Importantly, (and linking back to the systemic principals identified and discussed in Chapter two), the environment can be shaped by the organisation and within it, individuals and organisations change in both unique and common ways. Clearly, this analysis of change includes some parallel themes also common to the process of organisational learning. The nature of both learning and change is identified as an ongoing process; they are both characterised as essential for survival; and experiential, double-loop learning promotes adaptation and change.

Approaches to change

Contemporary perspectives on the management of strategic change can be positioned along a continuum. This ranges from 'recipes' and checklists in diagnosing, managing and implementing discrete change projects (Carnall *op. cit.*, Boddy and Buchanan 1992), to analytical and theoretical approaches aimed at understanding the process of change *per se* (Dawson 1994, Mabey and Mayon-White 1993, Wilson 1992). However, the integration of theories of change with practical management methods is increasingly being addressed in order to provide both academic and practical value. Whilst contemporary management texts have relied upon Lewin's (1952) three-stage model of planned change (unfreezing, changing and refreezing), its appropriateness in a dynamic environment is increasingly questioned (Dawson *op. cit.*, Wilson *op. cit.*). A planned process for freezing changed behaviours would appear to discount the complex and ongoing nature of environmental and change processes, failing to address crucial issues surrounding the continuous need for employee flexibility and structural adaptation. Wilson (*op. cit.*) indicates that the nature of planned change is stated in advance and is heavily reliant on the managerial role, whereas emergent change is a process of the interplay of multiple variables (context, political processes and consultation) within the organisation. This process-based approach, which is less prescriptive and more analytical, therefore enables a broader understanding of the problems and practice of managing change within a complex environment.

Accordingly, Dawson (*op. cit.*) contends that strategic change should not be solidified or seen as a series of linear events within a given period of time. The processual and analytical framework described is one of conception of the need to change; a period of organisational transitions characterised by disruption, confusion and unforeseen events rather than a sequential series of steps; and the operation of new work practices, often over long timeframes. These are further refined and developed during ongoing processes of change. A processual analysis of change therefore reveals that there can be no simple prescription for managing organisational transitions successfully due to temporal and contextual factors. Neither can change be characterised 'as a rational series of decision-making activities and events . . . nor as a single reaction to adverse contingent circum-stance' (Dawson *op. cit.*: 181). Nevertheless, as Burnes (1996) suggests, the planned and emergent approaches to change have their own limitations in so far as they were both developed with particular situations and types of organisations in mind.

Their universal applicability must therefore be questioned in order to allow 'approaches to change to be matched to environmental conditions and organisational constraints' (Burnes *op. cit.*: 198), so that these develop along a continuum of best and unique practice.

Within this context, Clarke (1994) suggests that mastering the challenge of change is increasingly part of every manager's role within contemporary organisations. Those who are effective at creating sustainable change have an extensive and systemic understanding of the business environment, can identify the external drivers for change and can diagnose internal, cross-functional organisational capability to respond in a systemic way (McCalman and Paton 1992). Therefore, unless change is linked with the complexity of changing market realities, the transitional nature of work organisation, systems of management control and redefined organisational boundaries and relationships (Dawson *op. cit.*), any one-dimensional change interventions are likely to generate only short-term results and to increase instability rather than reduce it.

The external environment

The main impetus for change would therefore appear to be scanning the business environment to understand and assess systems linkages and the potential holistic impact on the organisation (McCalman and Paton *op. cit.*). This will include exploration of markets/customers, shareholders, the economy, suppliers, technology and social trends. These, however, cannot be seen as discrete elements, as boundaries and relationships between the organisation and its environment can be blurred and are also subject to change. For example, customers may become competitors, suppliers may become partners and employees can become marketplace, suppliers or competitors.

Pettigrew and Whipp (1993) suggest that managing strategic and operational change therefore comprises five interrelated aspects, including environmental assessment, leading change, coherence, linking strategic and operational change, and human resources viewed as both assets and liabilities. In this way, organisations become open-learning systems with strategy creation emerging from the way the company as a whole acquires, interprets and processes information about its environment. In this context, Clarke (*op. cit.*) argues that continuous stability in contemporary environments is an unrealistic expectation. Organisations cannot assume that future survival can be based on extrapolations of historic behaviour. Identifying environmental and market change quickly and opportunistically is seen as the key to survival and growth. Leading from this, it would seem that there is need for management to assist people in understanding why change is necessary. Drawing upon the work of Greiner (1972), Clarke suggests that all organisations experience stages of evolution and revolution, and need to change at each stage in order to survive. In terms of the world economy, Clarke (*op. cit.*: 10) cites Kondratiev's view, that all capitalist systems are subject to long-wave cycles that provoke profound change, and considers that technology is now the emergent catalyst for environmental change.

Wilson (*op. cit.*: 84) suggests that the external legitimisation of change, or the extent to which changes conform to established change patterns in the operating environment, will determine how it is hindered or facilitated in the organisation. As Benjamin and Mabey (1993) indicate, the main stimulus for change may be forces in the external environment; so how change is accomplished rests with the people within the organisation. But change is often difficult for people to comprehend and accomplish due to its nature: change being frequently a future state and hence 'far from certainty' (Stacey 1996). As a result, Stacey considers that people tend to demonstrate higher levels of anxiety and conflict the further from certainty the context in which they must make decisions and take control becomes. It is, he suggests, by achieving an understanding of the external environment, through the development of a supportive internal environment comprising systems and processes, that the process of change may most effectively be assisted.

The internal environment

The dynamics of change therefore demand an appropriate response within the organisation, one that is not hindered by attempted extrapolations of past success in current, changed contexts. It is a response that should promote widespread and deep understanding of strategy, structure, systems, people, style and culture and how they can be seen as sources of inertia that can block change, or alternatively, levers to encourage an effective change process. As Wilson (*op. cit.*: 81) indicates, 'the key to understanding change is individual cognition and interpretation of the external environment'.

In terms of strategic direction, various writers inform us that the pace of change dictates that this is too complex for a small number of organisational members (senior managers) to predict. The responsibility for strategic change appears therefore to be becoming more diffused through the organisation, increasingly 'bottom-up' as well as 'top-down'. Pettigrew and Whipp (*op. cit.*) suggest that receptivity to change is dependent upon four key conditioning features. These involve the extent to which key players in the organisation are prepared to champion environmental assessment techniques that increase openness, structural and cultural characteristics; how far an assessment occurs; and how effectively it is integrated with central business operations. The main conclusion is that there are no universal rules with regard to leading change; rather it involves 'linking action by people at all levels of the business' (Pettigrew and Whipp *op. cit.*: 6).

Organisational structure

Concomitant to developing an understanding of the internal environment is the use of organisational structure as a lever for change, only used effectively if there is recognition of the informal as well as the formal (Brown and Duguid 1991, Hendry 1996, Stacey *op. cit.*). Power, politics, history and culture, social groupings, and the impact of physical structure define how people relate to each other, how effectively they interact and influence how the momentum of change can be created (Clarke *op. cit.*, Dawson *op. cit.*). The 1990s are, therefore, witnessing flatter organisational structures, in which levels of management are reduced in an attempt to cut costs and improve communication flows up, down and across the company. Another trend is to create a customer-centred organisation with structures that reflect and are responsive to different markets rather than different functions. Customer responsiveness places significant emphasis on effective horizontal processes – everyone becomes someone else's customer. The network organisation that is said by some theorists (Handy 1989, Moss Kanter 1989, Peters 1987) to be emerging as a result attempts to respond rapidly to change by breaking down internal barriers, quickly disseminating information and knowledge and building synergy across and between organisations.

Snow *et al.* (1993) suggest that these market-guided entities or dynamic, network organisations that are emerging have resulted in the displacement of centrally managed hierarchies, and that this creates a new agenda for managers in responding to change. They cite the driving forces of globalisation, competition and technological change that have created a new competitive reality, whereby specialisation and flexibility in all employees are required. Nevertheless, Thompson and Davidson (*op. cit.*) contend that the restructuring debate from which the post-bureaucratic organisation emerges is based upon unrepresentative examples from selected industries. Moreover, they claim the 'new' organisational structures and practices are even more dependent upon central planning and control systems to make them work. For example, the heightened emphasis on customer-orientation demands that targets are set and standards are identified, within a time-bounded quality framework for delivery. This, they suggest, creates a more rigid control framework for the management of people than that evident in the past.

Management and leadership

Within this dynamic context, and notwithstanding the previous assertions, the manager's role increasingly appears to be developing towards one of broker operating across rather than within hierarchies and handling resources often controlled by outside parties (Snow *et al. op. cit.*). Clarke (*op. cit.*) claims that the challenge that faces organisations is to adapt to a changing context of management in which key areas of expertise will focus on strategy formulation, human resource management, marketing/sales and negotiation/conflict resolution. Management style to implement these functions effectively is a key issue; changing management style (or indeed changing management?) may be, according to Clarke (*op. cit.*) an effective way to develop a definitive and coherent agenda for organisational change.

To engage the commitment of others to change, managers therefore may need to begin by challenging their own assumptions, attitudes and mindsets so that they develop an understanding of the emotional and intellectual processes involved in the transition (Clarke *op. cit.*, Buchanan and Boddy 1992). This links with theoretical perspectives on organisational learning that suggest it is only by challenging the status quo that double-loop learning and change will occur

(Argyris 1990, Bateson 1972). On this view, the essence of change is the move from the known to the unknown (Clarke *op. cit.*); hence the toleration of risk, transition and ambiguity are essential. This clearly can only be achieved through open and active communication between those participating in the change process, particularly if the organisation operates in a dynamic environment (Pugh 1993).

As Clarke (*op. cit.*: 172) says, 'while top-down, unilaterally imposed change does not work, bottom-up, early involvement and genuine consultation' are essential to effect the process. This can only be achieved through open communication that permeates the organisation via groups and individuals by means of both formal and informal channels. Wilson (*op. cit.*) therefore argues that the relevance and efficacy of change programmes will be coloured by the contexts in which they are applied. Indeed, application of the formal, programmed top-down approaches (such as TQM, management training, reengineering, competence frameworks, etc.) to effect change

> often fail to yield benefits proportional to the financial and human investment made in them. Seventy per cent of all corporations report that TQM has not lived up to their expectations.
>
> (Beer and Eisenstat 1996: 597)

Instead there is a suggestion that managers should consciously and proactively move forward incrementally and by adopting participative approaches. In this way, the quality of information utilised in strategic decisions may (or may not) be improved. Managers may be encouraged to acquire and develop a range of interpersonal skills that enable them to deal with resistance and political pressures more effectively (Buchanan and Boddy 1992). They may also be encouraged to build awareness and commitment for implementation. The promotion of interactive learning between the organisation and its environment may be encouraged; and the quality of strategic action may be improved through involvement and participation of those closest to the decisions (Quinn 1993).

Without understanding and mobilising the commitment of teams and individuals, current perspectives therefore suggest that the change process will not be sustainable. To this end, organisational development interventions (transactional analysis, teamwork, group problem solving, role-playing, etc.) may be employed to create a climate for change (Coughlan 1993, McCalman and Paton *op. cit.*). The role of the internal facilitator or change agent is therefore seen as pivotal in a group engaged in change management (Mayon-White 1993, Buchanan and Boddy *op. cit.*). Ideally, it is the role of the facilitator to encourage shared learning and experience through adult/adult relationships, whereby team members themselves are the main source of, and achieve recognition for, ideas in any change exercise. Carnall (*op. cit.*) confirms that this provides the framework and support appropriate for the emergence of creative solutions to novel problems. It also encourages a sense of commitment, involvement and ownership of the change process.

But whilst people can be a source of leverage for change, they can also be a source of inertia (Beer and Eisenstat *op. cit.*, Denison 1990, Hendry 1996). It is therefore important in the change process to assess levels of skills-mix and whether management attitudes and styles are appropriate for the future the organisation is attempting to create. Most significantly, achieving and sustaining any change intervention requires recognition of the intrinsic connection between operational and cultural factors.

Organisational culture

The essence of sustainable change would appear to involve an understanding of the culture of the organisation that is to be changed. If proposed changes contradict cultural biases and traditions, it is inevitable that they will be difficult to introduce into the organisation. Galpin (1996) suggests that the purpose of managing culture during change is to ensure that change is made important to people and so they understand the need for change. Creating cultures seen to be appropriate to dynamic and changing environments, foreshadowed by the emergence of the culture–excellence debate (Deal and Kennedy 1988, Pascale and Athos 1982, Peters and Waterman 1982), continues to be discussed in contemporary literature. Indeed, the notion that culture is not static but subject to change is without doubt. Burnes (1991 and 1996: 115) comments that although culture is influenced by external and internal factors that provoke culture change,

> given that it [culture] is locked into the beliefs, values and norms of each individual in the organisation, and because these are difficult constructs to alter, this type of organic cultural change will be slow, unless perhaps there is some major shock to the organisation.

He goes on to stress that it is when culture becomes 'out of step' with changes in the environment, structures and practices of the organisation, that dysfunction occurs and it becomes inappropriate or detrimental to effectiveness.

Johnson (1993: 64) suggests that strategic management of change is 'essentially a cultural and cognitive phenomenon' rather than an analytical, rational exercise. In attempting to realign internal behaviours with external demands Dawson (*op. cit.*: 45) suggests that change strategies need to be 'culturally sensitive'. Organisations must be aware that the process is lengthy, potentially dangerous and demands considerable reinforcement if culture change is to be sustained against the inevitable tendency to regress to old behaviours.

Galpin (*op. cit.*) indicates a range of components that establish an operational description of organisational culture which include rules and policies, goals, customs and norms, rewards and recognition, organisational structure, management behaviour, physical environment and communications. These provide tangible elements of culture that he considers can be managed, ideally simultaneously, in order to implement and sustain change. Watson (1994: 66) develops this perspective in his suggestion that the 'existence of a strong and clearly articulated culture' enables the activities of people within organisations to generate effective performance. Wilson (*op. cit.*: 91), however, considers:

> to effect change in an organisation simply by attempting to change its culture assumes . . . a linear connection between culture and performance [but] it is not always clear how culture and performance are related, if at all.

Denison (*op. cit.*) considers this perspective in his analysis of the relationship between culture and effectiveness. Drawing links between organisational adaptability, consistency, mission and involvement, he considers that responsive cultures are those that demonstrate high degrees of flexibility in interpreting historical and future timeframes. The existence of sub-cultures, with their own characteristics distinct from those of the dominant culture, provide an added complexity, particularly if conflict arises within and between them.

Nevertheless, the legitimacy of culture change continues to attract debate (Schein 1985, Uttal 1983 from Burnes 1996) in terms of it being a means to manipulate labour and the employment relationship. An observation surrounding contemporary organisational culture metaphors proposed by social scientists is that they have transformed 'compliance into co-operation, consent into commitment, discipline into self-discipline, the goals of the organisation into the goals of the employee' (Hollway 1991: 94 quoted in Starkey 1996: 365). Indeed, the central focus of HRM is the development of the organisation as a 'source for meanings and superordinate goals for its employees' (Sewell and Wilkinson 1992a: 100).

Pollitt (1990), however, offers an alternative perspective and warns that management does not 'own' the organisational culture and is usually in no position to manipulate it for its own objectives. Similarly, Lynn-Meek (1988: 470) confirms that 'culture is not an independent variable, nor can it be created, discovered or destroyed by the whims of management'. Nevertheless, Beer, Eisenstat and Spector (1993) suggest that the most effective way to promote change is not to attempt to change organisational behaviour. Rather, it is to place people in a new organisational context that imposes new roles, relationships and responsibilities upon them. This then forces new attitudes and behaviours upon people.

It is clear that promoting change cannot be accomplished quickly, especially where there are strong reinforcement mechanisms such as how people are recruited, rewarded and promoted. Similarly, if these aspects are complemented by well-defined reactions of leaders to problems and failures that promote fear of risk, it is unlikely that people will be convinced that change will take them somewhere better. Clarke (*op. cit.*) comments that creating a culture for change means that change has to be the norm, rather than as an added extra. In order to achieve a culture for change, it must be legitimised and 'sold' internally. This means that opinions are tested, perceptions are analysed and potential sources of resistance identified. Nadler (1993) suggests that a commitment to change can only be mobilised through heightened employee awareness, leading to joint diagnosis of business problems. Inevitably, this will have implications for the level of skills and knowledge present within the organisation and how people are mobilised to participate and contribute.

Approaches to change can be positioned along a continuum that ranges from the planned and prescriptive to the processual, evolutionary nature of the phenomenon. Creating an environment in which people understand the need for change means that they must become so familiar with the forces of change by learning about the external environment, that they are then able to translate these forces into effective action. This requires the alignment of internal structures, systems and processes involving culture, management and leadership so that fear and resistance do not prevent the successful instigation of change interventions. This will only occur if people are enabled to challenge the status quo and then to devise new operating norms and assumptions. This clearly takes the discussion into an examination and analysis of the impact and influence of learning and how this might usefully be viewed as an integrative process, fundamental to initiating and sustaining change in organisations.

Organisational learning and change

Dale (1994) indicates that the organisational environment is now iterative and unpredictable with change becoming part of normal reality. But the notion that change is inspired by, and is a direct result of, society's own progression, learning and development tends to be overlooked. If organisations are considered as organisms (Bateson *op. cit.*, Morgan 1997, Revans 1982), then their survival is dependent upon the rate of learning being equal to, or greater than, the rate of change in their environment. In addition, many of the decisions faced by contemporary organisations are characterised by change that takes the form of one-time events, discontinuities or changes that are unique and have never occurred before (Mintzberg 1994). This accentuates the need for any change processes, whether internally or externally induced or driven, to capture and maximise the organisation's capacity for double-loop or transformational learning (Bateson *op. cit.*).

The fragile nature of organisational longevity and/or success would appear to confirm that society's learning has not kept pace with the changes it is intentionally, or unintentionally, instigating. As a result of what some suggest as the unprecedented rate of global change, it is apparent that organisations must be prepared and equipped to increase their rate of learning in order to sustain survival. This, however, assumes a passive and reactive stance towards change on the part of the organisation and its members. A further dimension to be considered is the organisation's ability to alter its own environment and to provoke self-generated instability (Morgan 1997, Stacey *op. cit.*). Indeed, much of the uncertainty that is typical of contemporary business environments has emerged as a result of the changing nature of industrial and commercial society and its desire to exert greater controls over its destiny through choice. As Burnes (1996: 322) says, 'though organisations do try to align and realign themselves with their environment, they also try to influence and restructure the environment and other constraints in their favour.'

It is possible, therefore, to change the organisational environment. It can also be re-framed through learning. As Dixon (1994: 2) suggests 'knowledge that we create through learning allows us to change our environment, whether by re-framing it, physically altering it or both. The two factors, learning and change, reinforce each other'. Cunningham (1994) describes this form of learning as pattern change or reshaping what people already have and know so that it becomes part of second-order learning – people learn about how to learn for themselves (Bateson *op. cit.*). In essence, this confirms the view that organisational culture is a learned group phenomenon (Hendry 1996). The most obvious and profound example is that of technological advancement and society's entry into an informated age (Zuboff 1988). Martin (1988 quoted in Scarborough and Corbett 1992) indicates that the major resource redistribution by technological change is knowledge and that groups with knowledge of the old system may lose control of knowledge under the new system. This suggests that user participation in, and/or exclusion from, the technology process will impact upon its development.

Increasingly, the view of the organisation as a machine for information-processing, with the only useful knowledge being formal, objective and systematic, is being displaced in favour of a process that encourages creativity and innovation that, in turn, leads to change. Nonaka (1991) describes this as using the insights and intuitions of individual employees and making them available to the company as a whole. Against this background, it would appear that society is reaching a moral and ethical watershed in terms of how the reciprocal processes of learning and change are managed and understood by members of organisations. Srivastava *et al.* (1995) observe that social theorists agree that we are in the midst of a global revolution or paradigm shift (Kuhn 1962) in the way we understand the world. In agreement with Hawkins (1994), they consider that a boundaryless world is emerging, influenced by changes in the way that people gather knowledge and information. Using the metaphor of the 'global meeting', they consider that the task of learning from (and with) others who have differing ways of 'being, knowing and doing' is paramount for generating dialogue and collective learning and action.

Collective learning

Burgoyne (1995) also proposes that the manner in which the individual learns is undergoing profound change. Individual learning from concrete experience (Kolb 1984) is based upon the transitional myth of initiative, enterprise and self-development (the transition from manufacture to mentofacture). This now seems to be augmented by collective learning in social contexts (the organisation) based upon the transitional myth of pursuit of quality and excellence (the transition from mentofacture to spiroculture), embedded within the concept of the learning organisation. Burgoyne (*op. cit.*) states that the critical moment in learning is not so much an individual event but more closely aligned to group interaction and the creation of joint meaning. Cook and Yanow (1996) confirm this when they suggest that organisational learning involves shared meanings associated with and carried out through cultural artefacts, therefore becoming an activity of the organisation as opposed to the individual. Similarly, Holman *et al.* (1997) in their analysis of experiential learning stress the importance of social constructionism and activity theory, rather than purely cognitivism, as offering a different way of thinking about learning.

Hendry (1996) argues there are two types of group learning mechanism with different motivational bases and different consequences that are often intertwined. The first depends on positive reinforcement through successful problem solving, leading to shared understanding and group self-image. The second focuses on anxiety-avoidance, which leads to random management of trauma and threat – if successfully handled then similar strategies are adopted, regardless of their future relevance – what Argyris (1991) calls 'defensive routines.' Testing these assumptions reveals the limitations of the course of action and leads to consequent learning on an organisational level.

Scarborough and Corbett (1992: 69) support this to some extent when they suggest that the introduction of 'new work rules' embedded within a framework of 'technology' makes it appear legitimate and inevitable to the group. They consider, therefore, that the 'meanings attached to technology can exert considerable behaviour change in particular groups.' Potentially it can create a collective need and enthusiasm to change and learn, rather than be left behind. In terms of human resource development, this reflects the evolving nature of concern for facilitating self-development, towards creating learning organisations by means of the integration of individual and collective learning through participation.

Burgoyne (1995) postulates that it is dialogue (the creation of the flow of joint meaning) rather than debate (attempts at mutual persuasion or win/lose outcomes from individualised points of view) that is of value to the pursuit of organisational learning. This is confirmed by Srivastava *et al.* (*op. cit.*), who indicate that newer insights into management and organisational learning are needed in order to develop the potential of systems to succeed through co-operative rather than competitive strategies. Burgoyne (*op. cit.*) further suggests that 'meta-dialogue' or dialogue about the basis for believing that things might be credible, valuable or useful, may be a crucial process and tool in learning from experience in its new, more collectivist context. Drawing upon the ideas of Mitroff and Bennis (1993), Burgoyne cites the appropriateness of the term 'guarantor' whose function is to guarantee that the system will produce what it purports to deliver. In terms of developing joint meaning through dialogue, this will be easier if agreement can be reached amongst those concerned about the legitimacy of the guarantors.

In the context of developing organisational learning, Burgoyne (*op. cit.*) proposes that collective learning from experience must be concerned not only with what is being discussed (dialogue), but also with the basis on which joint meaning can be believed in (meta-dialogue). This would appear to confirm the views of researchers (Carnall *op. cit.*, Clarke *op. cit.*, Dawson *op. cit.*) who indicate that people must be convinced of, and believe in, the need for change before they will accept it as a means for improving their current situation.

The essential issue, therefore, is to draw a parallel between the processes of learning and change and, as Cunningham (*op. cit.*) suggests, think differently about the nature of change in order to determine what we need to learn. He cites the work of Bateson (*op. cit.*) to distinguish between first-order change – change which occurs within set boundaries and usually involves doing more (or better) than, in the past, and second-order change which takes place beyond existing frameworks and fundamentally alters the organisation's systems and processes.

Indeed, if links are established between learning and change, then the nature of change as a learning process is most evident in the initial stages. This may be characterised as unlearning (Nystrom and Starbuck 1984), unfreezing (Lewin 1952), crisis (Wilson 1992), cognitive dissonance (Festinger 1957) or the challenging of dominant values and beliefs (Hedberg 1981). How learning contributes to organisational change, however, is subject to traditional limitations to understanding, and practical evidence to support the phenomenon. A typical reaction is that willingness for both learning and change often only emanates from the feeling that there is no other option, as identified as a crisis or trigger for change (Burnes *op. cit.*, Greiner 1972, Wilson *op. cit.*). It is important, therefore, to assist people to become so familiar with the marketplace, customers and competitors through learning that they are able to diagnose any need for change themselves.

On this basis, Revans' work on action learning (*op. cit.*) concludes that the key to accomplishing successful change is to create a coalition of power involving those who know about the issue, those who care about it, and those who can do something about it. This concurs with Brown and Duguid's (*op. cit.*) discussion of learning communities of practice and Burgoyne's (*op. cit.*) assertion that meta-dialogue between individuals and those accepted as 'guarantors' is likely to co-create the meaning of their shared experiences and arrive at shared diagnosis of business problems (Beer *et al.* 1993).

Wilson (*op. cit.*) states that learning and change are precipitated by making impending crises real to everyone in the organisation (or perhaps even engineering crises?) by 'unfreezing' or encouraging group and individual dissatisfaction with current systems and procedures. This reinforces the findings of Knowles (1984) who, in attempting to create a unified theory of adult learning, contends that adults tend to prefer self-direction and become aware of specific learning needs when these are generated by real-life events. Also adults' experiences are a rich source of learning and they learn more through experiential techniques such as discussion and solving problems than passive listening. Finally, adults are competency-based learners: they will learn a skill or acquire knowledge that they can apply pragmatically to their immediate circumstances.

Approaches to learning and change in organisations

Despite such research findings, there still exists the dichotomy between traditional classroom-based training interventions and creating a learning environment that focuses on solving performance problems and encourages continuous improvement within organisations. Whilst evidence would support the shift towards learning as opposed to training in many high-profile organisations, there still exists a widespread reluctance to abandon traditional approaches altogether, despite counter indications of its usefulness to adult learners (Gill 1995). Indeed, in the change phase, the development of specific skills, knowledge and abilities to enable people to perform differently in terms of their roles and relationships is often neglected (Beer *et al. op. cit.*).

Clarke (*op. cit.*) and Nadler (*op. cit.*) confirm that enabling people to learn through effective top-down communication, promoting self-development and confidence may encourage commitment and shared ownership of business vision, actions and decisions that the future external environment demands. To generate the need and climate for change, therefore, it seems apparent that people within the organisation need to be involved in joint diagnosis of business problems and solutions for improvement (Pugh *op. cit.*). Inevitably, this involves encouragement and dialogue and it is only by challenging established norms and shifting perspectives that innovation and opportunities for change can occur. Pettigrew and Whipp (*op. cit.*) confirm that profound conditioning features based more upon collective learning need to be embedded in organisational systems, for sustainable change to occur. This would appear to confirm the view that it is culture and collective memory that are instrumental in recognising and legitimising the need for organisational learning and change.

Pettigrew and Whipp comment that the use of such learning ensures that the full implications of the organisation's view of its environment can then inform subsequent actions over the long term and, in turn, the way in which future shifts in the environment are approached. As Carnall (*op. cit.*) indicates, it is learning from the experience of change that determines how far organisational effectiveness can be sustained. Accordingly, Benjamin and Mabey (1993) consider that as employees' learning becomes more valued and visible within the organisation, questions about corporate action and purpose become more necessary and urgent to address, particularly if there is a high-profile commitment to aspire to become a 'learning organisation'. However, Burgoyne (*op. cit.*) cites Bateson's (*op. cit.*) famous metaphor 'the menu is not the meal, one should not eat the menu, but nor should one throw it away, it should aid choice'. To over-emphasise 'the learning organisation' *per se* as a panacea for organisational change and survival, detracts from the development of knowledge and understanding of organisational learning in itself. As Thompson and Davidson (*op. cit.*) warn, management theory and behaviour have always favoured one best way or ways. The danger may be that by attaching a 'label' to describe what would appear to be a significant and valuable progression in human resource management may sharply define the parameters by which it is understood and implemented within organisations. It may be that legitimising the learning organisation by embedding it within a theoretical framework of change management will be the safest way to ensure that it remains a positive platform for organisational and individual development.

It seems, then, that the nature of the relationship between learning and change demonstrates a complex, continuous process with no beginning or end. The dilemma for organisations is to acknowledge and understand the complementarity between learning and change, and to manage both simultaneously in order to avoid resistance and failure. This clearly involves recognition that traditional approaches to managing and developing people may need to be revised in order to accommodate the more collectivist basis on which individuals learn and interact within organisations. Inevitably, this will present its own challenges. At this point it seems appropriate to consider issues relating to resistance, power and control in organisations, together with their implications for the revised basis on which organisational learning and change may occur.

Resistance, power and control

Issues surrounding the tensions between control, learning and change need to be explored because people within organisations may demonstrate fear and resistance if they feel that their established power base, and/or position, is threatened. If this occurs, then it is unlikely that any proposed changes would succeed, thereby preventing the organisation from maintaining or improving its position. In order to connect with the context of the empirical research cited in later chapters, therefore, perspectives surrounding resistance to change in the automotive sector will now be examined. The section concludes with a critical analysis of organisational approaches to human resource management that aim to counter resistance by encouraging understanding of, and involvement in, the learning and change processes.

Given the encouragement that contemporary management is receiving with regard to the development of organisational learning to ensure the ability to change, clearly there is a need to recognise the tension between control and learning. Argyris and Schon (1978: 4) contend that 'to focus on learning without taking into account the legitimate need for control is to embark on a romantic and usually fruitless exercise'. Yet initiating, managing and sustaining the change process creates its own unique problems within organisations that centre upon issues of resistance and control. Productive learning and change cannot occur unless such issues are recognised and managed.

Clarke (*op. cit.*) states that there is no significant difference between personal change and organisational change. Both always involve losses – loss of the past, loss of routine and loss of relationships – that all provoke dissonance. In order to manage change, it therefore seems reasonable to start with the central assumption that change 'hurts' (Schein 1993). This will identify the need for appropriate support mechanisms to be in place to help the organisation move through what are, essentially, the predictable phases of change (i.e. Where have we been? Where are we now? Where are we going?). Dealing with the 'pain' of change therefore provides the key to management action and creates the need to anticipate and translate negative reactions into positive perceptions of change. Indeed Hendry (1996) indicates that as organisations develop their values over time, it is unrealistic to expect them to change quickly.

Clarke (*op. cit.*) cites loss of control, lack of understanding, uncertainty, ambiguity, elements of surprise and increased workloads as the main generators of resistance to change. Carnall (*op. cit.*) links these to perceptual, emotional, cultural, environmental and cognitive barriers that prevent change and creative problem solving within organisations. Hendry (1996) and Beer and Eisenstat (*op. cit.*) confirm that it is behaviour that has to change before a new or modified value system can become a reality.

Nadler (1993) observes that, despite the unique characteristics of each situation, any change will encounter three general problems: resistance, control and power. The overall implication is the need to motivate change, manage the transition and shape the political dynamics of change. Moss Kanter (1989) considers that in new forms of organisation, political action increases in conjunction with external turbulence and that political skills are at a premium if organisations are to cope. To effectively accomplish this change, managers need diagnostic models to understand problems, as well as guidelines for implementing the change process. Hendry (*op. cit.*) however, considers that an over-emphasis on the political 'recipe' for successful change perhaps neglects the value and contribution of learning.

In order to build a culture that is receptive to change, Clarke (*op. cit.*: 108) agrees that resistance is the primary factor that needs to be addressed. She indicates that new patterns surrounding the message of change must be embedded so that resistance does not re-emerge to draw people back into former ways. In effect, what is involved is a change in the basic assumptions that result from past learning (Schein *op. cit.*). The usefulness of what would appear to be a 're-freezing' process is questioned, however, given the uniqueness of organisations, the context in which change occurs and the often continuously volatile nature of the environment that demands ongoing flexibility and realignment (Dawson *op. cit.*, Wilson *op. cit.*). Nevertheless, by anticipating, identifying and even welcoming resistance, there may be opportunities for organisations to convert objections into levers for change. Benjamin and Mabey (*op. cit.*) for example, indicate that attention needs to be given to the political dimension because change inevitably results in a redistribution of power within the organisation.

Hendry (*op. cit.*), however, warns that there is a fine line between defining change as a political issue or in terms of learning and unlearning. He goes on to state that resistance can be managed by political action – removing people, or by adopting an educational approach. Allowing people to voice fear and reluctance enables managers to reflect on their own motivators, the reactions of others and encourages those with doubts to realign their views towards generating ownership of the change process. One outcome is that a shared vision of the future can be created which enables change to occur and assists in overcoming the costs of failure. Scenario planning (de Geus 1986, Hampden-Turner 1990) and envisioning new direction through joint diagnosis and participation become the role of the visionary leader who can effectively communicate the journey, so that the organisation is able to change and move away from the past. As Hendry (*op. cit.*) suggests, political strategies may be necessary but more importantly, redirecting people's attention is an essential part of change.

Resistance in the automotive sector

Change leading to new work practices and organisation have resulted in industrial relations throughout the automotive sector during the 1980s and 1990s undergoing considerable transformation with a relatively low level of shop-floor resistance towards management. Darlington (1994), in his discussion of the shop stewards' organisation in Ford Halewood, states that the more conciliatory stance towards management, encouraged by the hostile political and economic climate at this time, helped to dilute resistance and sapped shopfloor confidence and morale.

Industrial sociologists and organisational theorists continue to debate the changing nature of the employment relationship and its implications for resistance, power and control. Thompson and Ackroyd (1995) suggest that changes in the labour market and the transformation of production have been instrumental in shifting perceptions of labour's role in the workplace. Concurrent is the alleged drift from collectivism and the belief that conflict in the employment relationship around the frontier of control has been replaced by the new metaphor of evolutionary journey and perpetual change (Dunn 1990 quoted in Thompson and Ackroyd *op. cit.*). Within a learning organisation, where power should become less prohibitive and more productive, 'mutual investment in the process of learning on the part of management and other employees should enable the former to move the frontier of control' (Coopey 1996: 354).

Evidence, however, appears to indicate that despite new forms of organisational structures and work practices (team work, flexibility, employee involvement techniques, etc.) and the decline of trade unions, no new system of representation or human relations management has completely replaced traditional industrial relations (*Workplace Industrial Relations Survey*, 1990). Writers, however, suggest that the employment relationship has taken on a less confrontational stance as a result of the emergence of concepts surrounding HRM with an associated emphasis on cultural control and its contribution towards the functional, strategic integration of work organisation. Legge (*op. cit.*: 91) suggests:

> the rhetoric of HRM becomes an agent of change, concerned with the management of beliefs, with the manufacture of acquiescence in corporate values, with the production of images.

Indeed, Burgoyne (1995a) comments that empowerment, autonomous group working and participation in decision making offer forms of inner control (the capture of hearts and minds) to replace traditional forms of outer control embodied within job descriptions, objectives and formal rules.

On the basis that trade union decline appears to be synonymous with a concurrent decline in workplace resistance, the form that this takes is likely to be more difficult to assess than in the past. Willmott (1993: 520) suggests that 'programmes of corporate culturism, HRM and TQM have sought to promote or strengthen a corporate ethos that demands loyalty from employees as it excludes, silences and punishes those who question'. For those academics and practitioners who are committed to the 'learning organisation' and all that it aspires to be, this is a substantial contradiction to the concept of learning from experience and mistakes.

Resistance, nevertheless, constitutes 'a form of power exercised by subordinates in the workplace' (Jermier *et al.* 1994: 49) which draws upon various forms of knowledge and, as this knowledge increases, it may be that scope for resistance may widen. The writers identify the forms that resistance in the workplace might take in terms of 'resistance by distance' and 'resistance by persistence'. It would seem that as workers' knowledge and management controls increase within changeable internal and external environments, 'the material and symbolic insecurity for those in subordinate positions is intensified' (Jermier *et al. op. cit.*: 57). Tendencies to resist may, therefore, be interpreted as a 'wrong' definition of reality and treated as deviant and unjustifiable by management.

Within this somewhat paradoxical and confusing arena, the widespread adoption of total quality principles requires responsibility to be pushed down the organisational hierarchy, with an accompanied flattening of structures. This decentralisation of tactical responsibility would appear to occur even though strategic control is centralised (Sewell and Wilkinson 1992b, Thompson and Davidson *op. cit.*). In effect, responsibility is passed down but only under rigid monitoring and compliance with instructions (Sewell and Wilkinson *op. cit.*). Sewell and Wilkinson discuss the utilisation of just-in-time (JIT) and TQM regimes in contemporary organisations to illustrate that instead of devolved responsibility and autonomy at shopfloor levels, what is occurring is 'the authoritarian use of groups' (Thompson and Wallace 1996: 104). Control and discipline are transferred to the scrutiny of the peer group in the team or cell. In addition, powerful and elaborate information systems at management's disposal enable the close surveillance of worker activity and performance. When combined, the two systems provide horizontal and vertical controlling mechanisms that are more refined and intense than in previous work regimes.

Theorists argue that because the 'lean' production systems are highly visible and easily understood, there is less chance that people can 'hide' any defect or poor quality work. Similarly, synchronised production with *kanban* control of the flow of materials prevents the opportunity to create 'idle' time. Within an environment where productivity performance is usually measured against daily (or more frequent) targets, critics have suggested that the result is 'management by stress' (Slaughter 1989 quoted in Sewell and Wilkinson 1992a: 279). It is stated that its increasing appearance in the automobile industry in the United States has been identified with the creation of team-based assembly regimes. Evidence from the German automobile industry, however, indicates that whilst workers and management agree that teamwork is a useful concept in that it 'creates a forum in which the effects of Fordism and Taylorism could be discussed' (Murakami 1995: 303), most agree that it is implemented primarily for management's benefit.

Involvement and empowerment in groups

Whether these observations surrounding resistance, power and control are endorsed or not, the key issue is that the process of learning is also a process of socialisation – the way people attach meaning and their strategies for action are inevitably associated with values developed in social or interpersonal situations. People in organisations learn within a group context and the increasing use of teams in organisations would appear to indicate that positive environments for learning and change are intentionally being created (Brown and Duguid *op. cit.*, Stacey *op. cit.*). Hendry (*op. cit.*) goes on to support the view that the practice-based management of change literature advocates the use of groups for spreading and stabilising change, but the group as a unit of analysis for learning and change has been neglected in favour of the individual (see Kramlinger 1993). It may well be that it is the group-based environment rather than the individual that becomes the most powerful arena for learning to occur in and from which to be transferred to the organisation as a whole.

Similarly, the increase in adoption of employee involvement techniques by employers in the 1980s and 1990s (Marchington *et al.* 1992, Storey 1994) were intended to increase employee commitment to their work and/or to their organisation in order to promote workforce flexibility. Empirical research into how far groups stimulate learning in order to facilitate change within organisations is comparatively limited. The extent to which groups help to modify employee beliefs or performance with any significant outcome is debatable (Cunningham *et al.* 1996). However, the use of the group as a unit of analysis instrumental in assisting learning and change is a rich source of research for the future.

It is, perhaps, the notion of empowerment that has done most to capture the attention of management, having become a popular approach to generate involvement practice within organisations during the 1990s. Its characteristics include the alteration of management and non-management roles. In effect, it amounts to the people closest to market outlets ostensibly becoming empowered to solve problems and make decisions. In the context of HRM, employees are seen as proactive, capable of development, and offered opportunities to collaborate and participate (Legge *op. cit.*).

If managers are to relinquish any aspect of control and reallocate authority, this means that there is an organisational requirement to train and develop non-management to plan, make decisions and to work as part of a team, with management developed to coach and facilitate the process. Clearly, empowerment requires toleration of a greater degree of risk-taking within organisations, together with the development of a 'no blame' culture. Evidence, however, would appear to suggest that in some organisations there is no clear definition of what the concept means or who is allotted more power or discretion in their job roles (Cunningham *et al. op. cit.*). In addition, within some organisations conventional forms of discipline and control remain intact, perhaps even leading to closer control over non-management employees if line managers and supervisors are given responsibilities in areas such as recruitment, discipline and absence control. As Cunningham *et al.* (*op. cit.*: 153) suggest:

> Organisations appear to be focusing at least part of their managerial training and development on these 'harder', more 'control' centred aspects of employee relations. . . . It is therefore arguable as to what extent empowerment represents anything new or radically different from routine involvement schemes which Marchington *et al.* (1992) found typically did not 'involve any *de jure* sharing of authority and power'.

Similarly, in terms of the distribution of power, Coopey (1996) suggests that the effect of the characteristics of the learning organisation on the distribution of power may tend to favour those formally appointed as managers. Typically, they will have access to increased information, or conversely, if they feel threatened by fragmented control systems, are likely to behave defensively (Argyris 1991), so reducing the potential for collective organisational learning. Indeed, Whittington (1993: 130) comments that managers may 'refuse to learn because they understand perfectly well the implications for their power and status. Resistance to change may not be "stupid" . . . but based on a very shrewd perception of the consequences.'

So, whilst the concept of organisational learning as a means to cope with change appears a positive way forward, with practical guidance in developing the approach offered in an increasing number of texts, consideration must be given to the dangers of its use and misuse (Burgoyne 1995a). Citing the work of Giddens (1979), Coopey (1996: 365) warns:

> those who propagate the principles of a learning organisation risk opening the latest phase of a long history of metaphors which have been used manipulatively by managers with a long pedigree of instrumental interest in social science as a means of solving industrial problems.

Developments in work organisation have resulted in transformational practices that have influenced the labour process. But it is possible that HRM, which is central to the concept of the learning organisation and the movement of control further down the organisational hierarchy, may be in danger of becoming

> a mechanism through which managerial control is improved under dramatically changed external circumstances. If this were so, employees could be expected to resist managerial pressures to conform, using their transformative capacity in defensive ways inimical to the aims of a learning organisation.
>
> (Coopey *op. cit.*: 356)

Darlington (1995), for example, in his analysis of employment relations in the automotive sector, warns that a new sense of workers' confidence in terms of bargaining leverage might be felt in the future, depending upon changes occurring within the internal and/or external environment. He considers that there is no reason to assume that the current climate that exists and appears to represent a new form of industrial relations will persist other than as a cyclical phenomenon.

Conclusion

Instigating and sustaining change therefore involves 'unlearning' past behaviours and learning new. It involves a realignment of systems, processes and structures on a continuous basis, so that learning to learn becomes embedded as a cultural norm. The responsibility of leaders is to ensure not only that the environment is monitored and understood by all, but also that the organisation can learn and act on such understanding over time. Commentators agree that it is a long process, for people need time to adjust to, and progress through, organisational change. While the environment may demand revolutionary change, the costs to the organisation may be dramatic if this is sought. Evolutionary change may therefore have a more enduring, and less devastating effect. Given the multiple stakeholders concerned with large-scale organisational change, the effectiveness of the process is difficult for organisations to define or measure. Carnall (*op. cit.*) proposes an assessment of change effectiveness based on people, marketing, finance, operations, and business development. However, even when change strategies have reached an organisationally defined conclusion, constructing a rational, linear and retrospective explanation of the experience and its effectiveness is likely to be problematic, given the complex nature of the variables influencing the process. As to whether change becomes embedded in organisational memory (Huber 1991), this will depend upon the depth and breadth of knowledge and learning acquired, and how effectively it is transmitted and transferred by agents acting on behalf of the organisation. Indeed Burgoyne (1995), Hendry (1996) and Senge (1990) confirm that knowledge, language and thought are inherently collective.

Nevertheless, if the change literature continues to emphasise purely management and/or externally driven approaches, then individuals and groups within organisations will inevitably appear passive and resistant. Conversely, if there is felt to be participation and involvement in the process of change, what writers (Brown and Duguid *op. cit.*, Hendry *op. cit.*, Stacey *op. cit.*) term the development of linked communities of practice, then these may form the basis of a learning culture. Perhaps, then, it is the cognitive, social, behavioural and emotional factors that members of the organisation encounter throughout the process of change that are influential in terms of individual, group and organisational learning. As Hendry (*op. cit.*) suggests, the difference is that the learning organisation is one that tries to build upon what it has learned from change itself.

In support of this, Quinn (1993) contends that the organisational mindset needed to accomplish change is one that emphasises process and incrementality over content. Change is seen as a holistic, emergent and continuous learning process rather than a series of programmes. In turn, continuous improvement would appear to be a translation of change and learning into organisational identity and reality. On the assumption that change is a continuous process, then problems and opportunities for learning within organisations will also be continuous. How far this potential is exploited will depend upon individual and group receptivity to and belief in double-loop learning that challenges the status quo. In turn, this will be dependent upon how far management encourages an environment that supports its development rather than one that promotes resistance and collusion.

Against this theoretical background, the next chapter outlines the research undertaken within the automotive sector. The case study organisations are the Rover Group, Volvo AB, Creative Engineering and XZZ Components and the analysis is concerned with identifying the key issues and themes that emerge from the data collection. From this we may understand how far the approaches of these organisations support or challenge commentators' claims about organisational learning and change and how people within the organisations perceive the significance and impact of the processes and experiences.

5 The case studies

The Rover Group and Volvo, Creative Engineering and XZZ Components

Summary

The automobile industry has been, and remains, one of the leading sectors for the adoption of new work practices and organisational forms. To compete with 'lean' production systems developed in Japan, many Western companies in the auto motive sector have been forced to undergo a transformation process, to re-invent themselves in order to remain in business. This has faced companies with two key challenges. First: to learn new skills and competencies associated with the new organisational forms that lean manufacture and continuous improvement demand; and second: to ensure managers and workers embrace and adopt them. It is therefore apparent that the critical factors for success in the sector are the ability to learn and change continuously. The key contemporary approach for achieving this is increasingly being seen as the creation of learning organisations.

This chapter outlines four case studies of international organisations in the automotive sector, two manufacturers and assemblers, and two component suppliers. They all acknowledge they are in the process of promoting organisational, group and individual learning. Their rationale for this approach is that continuous change becomes legitimised and accepted within a milieu of learning with industrial competitiveness maintained in a context driven by the notion of continuous improvement. The approach of each organisation has been inspired and dictated by different internal and external factors prevalent within their task and contextual environments. However, they all share the common goal of continuous improvement through learning and change in order to succeed in the highly competitive arena in which they operate.

Case study one, the Rover Group, stated by Bower (1993) to be a traditional brownfield-site organisation, experienced a period of falling market share, product decay and poor employee relations during the 1960s, 1970s and 1980s. During this period, which was characterised by crisis, reorganisation and national isation, it chose to address these issues by focusing simultaneously on changes to work practices and procedures, product regeneration through collaborative alliances with Honda, and on the contribution of the individual and the group (Burnes 1996, Pilkington 1996). Most significantly, to demonstrate the Rover Group's commitment, both internally and externally, to its people and their learning and development, it established a separate company, Rover Learning Business. From its creation, the purpose of Rover Learning Business was to assist the Rover Group in becoming a learning organisation, in order to manage change effectively. In 1996, after the company was taken over by German company BMW, senior management in the Rover Group decided to dissolve Rover Learning Business, considering that it had succeeded in its remit to establish learning as a fundamental process throughout the organisation.

The second manufacturer, Volvo AB of Sweden, is an international transport equipment organisation employing 70,000 people, with production in more than twenty countries. Since its formation in 1927 the company has experienced a series of changes that have threatened its future. By the end of the 1970s, industry analysts were saying that small companies like Volvo (which captures only one per cent of the global market of passenger vehicle sales) were doomed. Models were outdated, exports had shrunk and home market shares had collapsed. The problems were compounded by increased costs in Sweden in 1975 and 1976.

Nevertheless, Volvo has now become a niche player with an established repu-tation for vehicle safety, quality and consideration for the environmental impact of its products. In its work organisation and management practices, Volvo has established itself as a leader since the 1970s, when it began to move away from traditional methods of vehicle assembly and develop approaches that focused on work humanisation and job redesign. Periods of experimentation with the removal of the traditional assembly line, the development of team work and the instigation of reflective production techniques at the Kalmar, Uddevalla and Born plants are well documented (Berggren 1992, Burnes *op. cit.*, Karlsson 1996, Sandberg 1995). Despite the varying degrees of internal and external pressures for change over a twenty-year period, Volvo has maintained a continual commitment to improving the quality of working life through investment in a plurality of production concepts that promote individual learning and teamwork.

Recent developments following the collapse of a proposed merger with Renault saw Volvo embarking upon a joint venture with Mitsubishi in 1996 to produce co-operatively designed cars in Born, Belgium, in order to expand sales in Europe and America. Volvo has maintained an established reputation for vehicle safety and reliability and has moved on to produce a range that is stylish and techno-logically robust. The company's potential was identified by Ford, who bought Volvo in 1999 in a move to expand its (Ford's) product portfolio and to fill the gap between the most expensive Mercedes and the lower end of the Jaguar range. It is anticipated that Ford's intention is to maximise Volvo's 'established image capital of vast amounts of unexploited value' by using Ford's own superior advertising strategies to penetrate and establish products in niche markets (Bayley 1999).

The third case study, Creative Engineering Limited, is now a well-established supplier of components to the motor industry, with a reputation for quality that is approaching world class. Its development has been characterised by distinct periods of decline and recovery, with its most recent success driven by a focused strategy of managing change through continuous learning and improvement. Again, there is acknowledgement within the company that the goal of becoming a learning organisation is a constant, but often elusive, target that is well worth trying to achieve. In March 1997 it was announced that Creative and a United States company would build a world-class component plant, demonstrating the company's commitment to the support of the globalisation of the component industry and the needs of customers.

Case study four, XZZ Components, is an organisation that would appear to have begun a transformation process over the past ten years, through what managers believe to be a process of evolution rather than revolution. Similar to the Rover Group, XZZ Components was a traditional organisation with many problems of resistance to change throughout the 1970s and 1980s. Its previous success had promoted an internal complacency that was difficult to erode and it was not until the failure of piecemeal changes (the introduction of new technology, robotics, etc.) that it became clear that more significant interventions were needed if it were to remain competitive.

The company was restructured and close links were forged with customers such as Nissan in order to improve quality and learn best practices from them. Internally, there were concerted efforts to develop a culture of learning and participation by increasing communication and promoting training and development for all employees. Commentators now consider XZZ Components to be a good example of how traditional companies can orchestrate their own recovery through effectively developing the processes of learning and change. Notwithstanding this transformation, managers within the organisation believe that there is much more that can be achieved and this will only occur within a framework that supports the ability to learn and change continually. The key approach for achieving this is seen by many players in the automobile industry as the creation of a learning organisation. Whilst there is recognition of the validity of the concept within management at XZZ Components, there is a tendency to avoid the distraction of the label in the legitimisation of new practices and procedures.

The Rover Group

The Rover Group employs 33,000 people and is recognised as an organisation that has achieved recovery and growth in a highly competitive global industry that is characterised by increasing pressure for change and continuous improvement. Rover Group's achievement of a five per cent increase in sales in 1997 from the previous year and achievement of the Queen's Award for Technology, indicated that its troubled history of the 1970s and 1980s was over. It was beginning to establish itself as one of Europe's leading motor manufacturers. Assisted since 1979 by Honda's technology and knowledge that enabled the revival of the product range, Rover established a reputation for producing niche products that appeal to expanding markets.

Its potential was clearly apparent to BMW, the German manufacturer, with its

£800 million take-over of the company in February 1994. BMW's strategy was to gain entry into the expanding market for off-road vehicles and also to penetrate the market for small, front-wheel drive vehicles where future global market expansion is also forecast. Existing Rover products such as the Discovery, together with the Mini and Metro, clearly gave BMW a ready-made opportunity whilst at the same time reducing potential resource and development costs. The merged BMW and Rover businesses in 1997 accounted for nearly seven per cent of the European market, with a fuller product range than some of the bigger rivals in the automobile industry. In March 2000, BMW announced the sale of the Rover Group. Despite current uncertainty, there appears to be an intention by the British government and Phoenix (a consortium led by John Towers, former managing director of the Rover Group) to support the continuation of the company as a viable player in the global motor industry.

Thus, over the years, the Rover Group would appear to have achieved a high level of transformation. How this has been accomplished seems to be directly attributable to the fundamental changes that have occurred in the way that people within the organisation have been managed and developed. In terms of the contribution of the individual to the organisation, there has been a concerted attempt within Rover to see employees as their greatest asset rather than their greatest liability, embedded within a long-term and ongoing commitment towards becoming a learning organisation.

Background

The original Rover was founded in 1877 as a producer of pedal cycles. It was the philosophy of S. B. Wilks, appointed in the 1930s to rescue the organisation from severe financial difficulties, that shaped the Rover company into a manufacturer of quality vehicles that commanded premium prices and offered high standards of comfort and performance. The company's post-war success lay in craft-based production techniques and work organisation. But by 1966 Rover could no longer remain independently viable and it became a subsidiary of the Leyland Motor Corporation. Mass production techniques were employed at the Longbridge plant under the influence of Herbert Austin. The company then merged with the rival producer, Morris, to form the British Motor Corporation. In 1969, this was assimilated by Leyland to form the British Leyland Motor Corporation that encompassed most of the existing United Kingdom motor producers at that time (Pilkington 1996).

From 1973 onwards as British Leyland it had to contend with a number of financial, work organisation and human resource crises. Product lines had become dated and unprofitable; the company could not respond to Japanese and European competitors in terms of economies of scale. Similarly, it could not match the new model developments of Vauxhall and Ford in the United Kingdom. As a result, financial controls imposed by management caused industrial unrest and it became clear that recovery was likely to be difficult without assistance. Nationalisation followed in December 1974 and, as a result of the Ryder Plan (developed by Lord Ryder on behalf of the Labour Government), it was recommended that British Leyland should remain a manufacturer in all sectors, but that there should be a substantial programme of product rationalisation.

In 1978, when Michael Edwardes became Managing Director of British Leyland, the issues he had to address involved not only the serious financial problems already identified but also the hostile industrial climate that was widespread within the organisation. The company had experienced declining sales in the 1970s and constricted budgets for new model development. As a result, it was left with manufacturing facilities that were not competitive and unappealing products. By the early 1980s, British Leyland had received state aid of £2 billion and had still accumulated losses of £2.6 billion (Burnes *op. cit.*). Political pressure to dismantle and sell the company increased, and Unipart (the spares business) and Jaguar (now owned by Ford) were floated off as separate companies. The automobile business, however, remained intact and began to address the task of regeneration.

Attempts to regenerate the company

A process of decentralisation followed, involving restoring the individual cars' badges – Austin, Morris, Rover, Triumph – in an attempt to address the industrial militancy prevalent within the organisation and to re-establish management's right to manage. In 1979, because of a pressing need to develop manufacturing and design capability (Pilkington 1996), links were forged with Honda, many of which were at first project-based but which heralded a longer-term relationship, enabling Leyland to revive its product range and to launch new products onto the marketplace faster. A period of new product development was also commenced.

In 1982, Edwardes left the organisation and was replaced by Harold Musgrove. Industrial relations were more stable than in previous years and product regeneration began with the launch of the Maestro and Montego. By 1984, the company had launched 54 derivatives of new cars and vans since 1979. Constant changes in product designs, however, meant that new work processes and techniques were required. This demanded not only substantial resource allocations for training and developing the workforce but also changes to the structure and culture of the organisation. The 'them and us' culture that had sustained the industrial militancy of former years was clearly no longer appropriate for survival and competitiveness in the future.

This marked a shift in focus within an organisation that had, up to this point, concentrated essentially on recovery by means of increasing profit through improved products and work procedures. The emerging view, that people within the organisation might play a significant role in recapturing its effectiveness, was to take on a greater significance in years to come. The development of learning and the ability to respond proactively to change were considered to be essential factors for the regeneration and success of the company. Furthermore, there was a need to reduce the size of the workforce (from 60,000 in the 1980s to 32,000 in

1990) and to reduce the layer of middle management and essentially non-direct workers. It was intended to ensure that the ratio of direct to non-direct staff ultimately became balanced at 80 per cent to 20 per cent rather than the 70 per cent to 30 per cent of the past.

During the 1980s, it was clear that Rover comprised three disparate factions – employees, trade unions and management – all contributing to the decline of the organisation. By 1988, the company's falling sales, due in part to the increasingly competitive global car market, coupled with prolonged periods of industrial unrest, led the chief executive Graham Day (who had been appointed in 1986) to review the company's future. Day considered that Rover could only compete effectively and increase profit margins if it were to focus on providing its customers with extraordinary service, delivered by people who were empowered to believe in the significance of their own contribution to the success of the organisation. The P&A consultancy and the Electoral Reform Society surveyed a random sample of the workforce to gauge attitudes and impressions. Intended to be seen by the workforce as external and unbiased, it revealed that despite a number of negative findings, over 78 per cent of Rover employees were prepared to spend their own time developing themselves in outside activities. By harnessing these talents, it was judged that the organisation might maximise the potential of its employees and ensure profitable growth for the future.

Concomitant with this strategy was the need to focus on niche products, aiming at the top end of the market (competing with Audi, BMW, etc.), and to realign the business to become process rather than function-driven. Day clearly recognised the importance of people in generating profits and quality products by means of distinctive processes. He introduced a management-led total quality strategy that indicated that 'quality is about people'. With the assistance of managing director George Simpson, the contribution that training and developing employees could make to the organisation's performance began to achieve a higher status. Alongside the encouragement to develop a learning culture was the shift in approach from the traditional role of management towards developing people's ability to lead. A new vision was declared in which fourteen strategic projects were identified, each championed by a main board director. 'Success through People' was one such project and this later developed as the platform from which Rover Learning Business was launched. From this time, a number of internally driven, management-led policies and interventions were developed to encourage people to learn and to promote culture change.

In 1989/1990 for example, employee involvement was encouraged by means of suggestion schemes, with over 40 per cent of employees participating. Despite the significant changes that these initiatives achieved, their impetus had begun to plateau by 1989, leading a core of personnel staff (since called 'the November group') to conclude that the most important elements for continued survival were learning, development and training for people within the organisation. To address these issues through a clear demonstration of Rover's commitment to become a learning organisation, a separate business unit, Rover Learning Business, was launched.

Rover Learning Business

The profound change that Rover was attempting was accelerated in 1990 with the establishment of Rover Learning Business (RLB). The primary aim of RLB was to facilitate a top-quality learning and development service and to provide assistance to all employees wishing to develop themselves. Learning and self-development were to be considered the responsibility of the individual and the line manager rather than traditional training interventions administered and delivered solely through personnel departments. Managers in the organisation were aware that whilst training plays an important role, it is purely business-driven. In establishing RLB, Rover attempted to develop the wider processes of learning, development and education. To achieve this, it was considered that there was need to change the emphasis from 'training', a process which employees regarded as being done 'to' them, to 'learning' or achieving something for themselves and from which the organisation would ultimately benefit. This was seen as a means to develop a learning culture and receptivity to change within the organisation.

RLB's remit was to bring together the various disparate learning initiatives that the company was developing so that they became more focused and integrated. Formed as a separate business unit, RLB was given a budget of approximately £30 million so that it might direct, co-ordinate and develop the company's learning initiatives. RLB had its own chairman, managing director, executive committee and board of governors. The board comprised leading educationalists, members of the Rover Group Board and union representatives. A managing director was appointed some months after the business was established and had commenced providing learning packages and consultancy within the company.

It should be noted that employees played a significant part in the creation of RLB. As previously discussed, the company had conducted a number of attitude surveys in previous years. These had consistently revealed that (a) employees felt their skills and abilities were not being fully stretched and that they were prepared for faster and more radical changes than those experienced so far; and (b) employees wanted more information about opportunities for involvement, development and progression within the company.

Hence, and in tandem with the creation of RLB, Rover's commitment to profound culture change and the development of individuals was embodied in the launch of 'Rover Tomorrow – The New Deal'. This included no compulsory redundancies in return for a commitment from employees to continuous improvement and flexibility in work practices. The term 'associates' was to be used to describe all Rover employees, regardless of their job title. Harmonisation of terms and conditions between white collar and blue collar employees was to be achieved. White-collar employees should be prepared to work on assembly lines if necessary and all employees, even directors, should wear the same overalls. In establishing RLB, its early priorities were to forge links between learning and development and the business functions. Managers experienced in profit analysis, engineering, sales, marketing, styling, etc. were recruited to RLB to provide a business focus whilst at the same time the intention was also to retain a core of leading-edge people in learning design. Whether sufficient people were recruited who were skilled in the development of learning initiatives, however, has since attracted debate.

RLB's remit was to assist the Rover Group achieve the following objectives:

- To distinguish the Rover Group as the best in Europe for attracting, retaining and developing people;
- To emphasise the view that people are its greatest asset;
- To gain recognition by its own employees that the company's commitment to every individual had increased;
- To unlock and recognise employee talents and to make better use of these talents;
- To improve the competitive position of the company.

In 1992, George Simpson indicated the key role that RLB played in the changes undertaken by Rover:

> In an industry of dynamic competition, companies which learn quickest will be the winners. Rover Learning Business, as the driving force behind the basic foundation of success through people, will demonstrate that it is with our people that the winning difference lies.
>
> (RLB Annual Report 1992)

RLB's products and initiatives

RLB focused on the development of initiatives and 'core learning products' that promoted individual, team and corporate learning together with a wider remit to encourage an understanding of how the change process could be effectively managed.

(1) Rover Employee Assisted Learning (REAL)

This product was intended to assist in the development of skills not necessarily directly connected with people's work in the organisation. The only criterion was that it was a legitimate learning experience, receipted and delivered by a recognised body. The intention was to develop the confidence of those people who had, up to this time, only negative experiences of education and learning. It was also hoped that by encouraging interest in new skills, people would be more receptive to learning about skills associated with their work at Rover.

In 1992 the REAL programme was refocused due to widespread resource problems in the motor industry in Europe. Employees were encouraged to make more specific links between their learning interests and the potential benefits to their work within Rover. Work related activities continued to be broadly defined and any activities likely to promote leadership and team building skills, for example, were supported by the organisation. By 1992, however, employee involvement in the form of new suggestions was considered to have saved Rover over £10 million in the year. Nevertheless, the REAL product was not without its critics within the Rover Group; they pressed RLB to identify more explicit criteria surrounding structured guidelines and a business-related focus, but met with resistance from those within RLB who were reluctant to make any significant changes to the product.

(2) Personal Development Files (PDFs)

Confronted by traditional personnel systems and processes that were considered to be inappropriate for the new employment relationship that Rover was attempting to create, the alternative approach introduced was the Personal Development File (PDF). PDFs were designed both to look at past performance and also to measure individual learning objectives in relation to overall business objectives for the coming year. They were intended to engender a two-way commitment while at the same time emphasising personal responsibility for learning and development. The file was owned by the individual and was also intended to provide a logical progression for younger employees' records of achievement. In terms of the effectiveness of PDFs, RLB distributed 20,340 PDFs throughout the group from 1990 to 1994 but how many reached employees was unclear. In 1995, one manager estimated that over 70 per cent of employees had a PDF, with over 50 per cent regularly conversing with management on the topic.

Another manager, however, estimated in 1994 that 9,000 were being used, 'which is much less than 50 per cent'. This, he considered, was largely due to RLB creating no line management ownership of the product, resulting in the 'destruction of the marketplace'. Moreover, the issue of how 'live' a PDF was essentially centred on line manager commitment, so he doubted whether 50 per cent of employees were, in fact, regularly conversing with management on the topic. Also interest from managers, team leaders and supervisors appeared to be greater than that shown by shopfloor associates.

(3) Group Learning Exchange Network (GLEN)

An additional product developed by RLB was the Group Learning Exchange Network (GLEN). This comprised a database of information and case studies developed to assist Rover associates in benchmarking and copyplus (improvements to existing practice and systems) exercises. It was intended to be a single source of information regarding best practice within the organisation and people were encouraged to detail their improvements to work practices so that others could learn from their experiences.

(4) Managing change

To become world-best in a competitive global market, by 1994 RLB had become increasingly concerned with change management issues and how these contributed to the Rover Group's performance. This can be seen from the development of the aims and objectives of RLB since its launch.

PHASE ONE (1990–2)

The key initiatives for RLB were intended to complement the quality strategy in place within the Rover Group. These focused on individual learning through REAL and PDFs with the intention of energising and encouraging people within Rover to embark upon, or to continue with, self-development activities in order that they would be more responsive to change.

PHASE TWO (1992–4)

Moving from the individual level, the focus shifted to the development of team-work that encouraged group and corporate learning leading to the understanding and facilitation of change so that they would be accepted as priorities on the business agenda.

PHASE THREE (1994–6)

Working with personnel and training departments throughout the organisation, RLB began to monitor the wider external environment in an attempt to translate the forces of change into internal approaches to work organisation that enabled the company to meet these challenges. Phase Three therefore attempted to re-energise individual learning and to develop a focused strategy for corporate learning that would enable people to understand the changing environment in which they operated. Incorporated was a more international dimension, combined with the development of integrated business support systems. This was promoted through joint-venture activities with producers and suppliers, while at the same time focusing on continuous improvement and change management initiatives that involved and encouraged individual and team learning. RLB's aims and objectives would therefore appear to have evolved since its inception. The primary focus by 1995 had become the changing nature of the external business environment and how this might be effectively managed by the Rover Group through teamwork.

Towards a learning organisation?

In 1994, the profitable growth of the Rover Group in the future was to be achieved by accelerating the pace of change through global and team learning. Objectives of RLB were therefore embedded in offering learning opportunities to all Rover Group associates making a valuable and recognised contribution to the Rover Group and the extended enterprise. A further objective was learning from and sharing Rover Group and world-wide best practice, and using processes and delivering products/services which were considered to be world-class.

Nevertheless, the contribution of RLB to the performance of the Rover Group began to warrant increasing scrutiny from 1994 onwards. Some senior members of the Rover Group expressed concern that issues surrounding monitoring, assessment and evaluation of costs and activities needed to be more thoroughly addressed in order to justify its existence and to reveal its added value to the organisation. Dealer training, for example, was making an estimated loss of £0.5 million per year at this time. It was also suggested that there was limited assessment of what RLB delivered, how it was delivered and what the end result achieved.

Also, whilst RLB was familiar with the organisational culture, structure and processes, a possible disadvantage that was expressed by Rover Group employees was that it was too closely associated with the organisation and lacked the unbiased approach that an external consultancy might offer. Conversely, an alternative view was that RLB had the advantage of understanding the business, the political scenario, nuances, etc. whilst external consultants might be inclined to 'deliver what was wanted'.

In June 1994, a new general manager (who had formerly been employed at the Landrover plant at Solihull) was appointed to RLB, and the manufacturing director of small and medium cars at Longbridge was appointed as managing director (a titular head). Following the concerns expressed there was increased interest in justifying RLB's role and contribution. A manager in RLB considered that there was some evidence to measure the bottom-line contribution of RLB, such as improved performance in the dealer network, but that relationships between training and development managers within the Rover Group and RLB were tenuous. He suggested that qualitative evidence to support the success of learning and development initiatives may not just have reflected RLB's activity but also the greater efforts of the business units themselves. The new appointments to RLB therefore appeared both politically and practically driven and were based upon re-focusing and restoring RLB's image internally back to corporate and individual learning.

In 1996, after continuing to offer consultancy and learning products, it was decided to dissolve RLB. The general manager had opted to take early retirement and this was seen to be an appropriate time to re-assess the contribution of the company to the wider organisation. Former managers within RLB suggest that the closure was not connected with the take over of Rover by BMW, but that the company had served its purpose in energising the learning process throughout the Rover Group. One manager stated 'by 1996 what we were trying to establish from 1990 onwards had been institutionalised. People were comfortable with the approach and a learning culture was becoming evident throughout the organisation.'

Another former RLB manager suggested that by 1997 most managers automatically involved themselves in learning and developing both themselves and their teams and that there was no longer a need for the stimulus of RLB *per se*. As a result, it was reported that all members of RLB have been absorbed into the Rover Group and their approaches and activities support those of the existing training and development departments in the company. The organisation as a whole continues to participate in international learning activities established under the remit of RLB, such as the European Lifelong Learning Initiative (ELLI), and it remains a member of the European Consortium of Learning Organisations (ECLO). According to the BMW Annual Report (1997), Rover maintains a high level of employee involvement and a revised form of the suggestion scheme was re-launched in 1996. Further links have been established with educational providers, together with greater co-operation with suppliers.

Conclusion

The Rover Group's creation of RLB as a separate business unit would appear to have had profound implications. In creating such a milieu to promote individual and organisational learning, a range of positive and negative factors have emerged that have influenced its development and contribution to the Rover Group over time. Regarding potential change within RLB as a result of the appointment of new management in 1994, the general manager commented shortly after his arrival:

> People need to feel good, wanted and useful. We need to demonstrate this often in order to change their beliefs. There is still a core of long-standing employees who are sceptical about management's reasons for changing practices and we need to get over this if we want to succeed in the long term.

In terms of RLB's role in assisting the Rover Group to learn and to develop change management skills, it is clear that more questions than answers began to be generated about its contribution over time. When the company was taken over by BMW in 1994 it was anticipated that BMW's own approaches would gradually filter through the organisation. Despite the enthusiasm to maintain the focus on learning and development, it would appear that there has not been the same commitment to preserve RLB as a separate business unit, perhaps because it is considered that it has served its purpose of acting as a catalyst for change.

Nevertheless, BMW stresses the continuing need for employees to be flexible and to work effectively in teams; it has invested considerable resources in the development of such processes throughout the organisation. In so doing, it is continuing the previous attempts of the Rover Group to establish a culture that promotes teamwork and individual and group learning in order to maintain competitive advantage. However, the shift from established, traditional approaches to work organisation towards a more flexible and social organisation of production has profound implications for change. It would appear that, despite the advances that people believe have been achieved, it might take longer for contemporary practices to become embedded in organisational culture.

In comparison, the second case study, Volvo AB, would appear to have succeeded in creating a work environment that has promoted and established teamwork and flexibility as fundamental to the operation of the organisation. Unlike the Rover Group, which was forced to react to a series of crises from the 1960s to the 1980s that threatened its viability, Volvo began to experiment with small but highly innovative changes to work organisation during this period. The foundation for these approaches was the improvement of the quality of working life, focusing on teamwork, flexibility, job enlargement and job rotation. It would appear that these practices, together with acceptance of change as an ongoing process, have become more deeply established as part of organisational culture.

Volvo

Since the 1970s, new manufacturing techniques in Western organisations have focused essentially on lean production and have largely been associated with the impact and influence of Japanese producers in the automotive sector. In Sweden however, a distinct approach to automobile production developed during the 1970s and 1980s that resulted from repeated challenging of traditional approaches to work organisation involving the assembly line and established hierarchies (Berggren 1992).

In order to achieve more flexible work structures and to improve the quality of working life, Volvo sought a new model of production and experimented with a number of alternatives. These ranged from buffered flow systems to the complete dissolution of the assembly line by means of parallel dock assembly. This latter system allowed small teams of skilled workers to build complete cars or trucks, within a framework that attempted to reduce repetitive tasks operated within short, monotonous work cycles. Group work became a major feature of the approach with some workers afforded significant levels of autonomy and decision making.

Whilst group work features strongly in the Japanese lean system, the Swedish model differed in a number of ways. First, it recognised a real need to increase workers' autonomy and decision making. Second, it changed the role of first-line management from direct control to planning, co-ordinating and supporting. Third, it became clear that the Metal Workers' Union in Sweden in the 1970s was strongly in favour of a shift in the balance of power that represented a social compromise between the different interests of management and the trade union (Berggren *op. cit.*). Management wanted to delegate tasks and responsibility without yielding control, while the union hoped for a genuine shift in the balance of power in order to achieve a more egalitarian employment relationship.

It advocated the development of new organisational forms that strengthened team decision-making rights, as well as developing collective competence. In this environment, it would appear that over a twenty-five year period, Volvo has adopted an approach that instigated revolutionary changes, creating a series of new plant concepts (Karlsson 1996). Significantly, these changes are characterised by patterns of learning and unlearning in accordance with the prevailing environmental, social and economic conditions, and are highly influenced by the processes of experiential learning and learning by detecting and correcting error in current theory-in-use.

Background

Like the Rover Group, in the 1970s Volvo experienced poor industrial relations, manifested by high labour turnover, absenteeism, strikes, and recruitment problems. Whilst dissatisfaction with work conditions in the automotive sector in the West became increasingly vocal in the 1960s and 1970s, in America and Japan its importance faded due to energy crises and world recession. In Sweden however, pressure from the labour market to improve working conditions did not cease. Unemployment remained low and, through government policy, wage differentials between different sectors and companies were small. This meant that it was difficult for companies to compensate for poor working environments with high wages and other benefits.

The interest and influence of trade unions in work environments and organis-ation increased, and legislation in 1977 (the Swedish Co-determination Law – MBL) meant that companies were legally obliged to involve unions in any proposed changes. This legislation was passed in the same year that Sweden entered recession and the union agenda was diverted to dealing with plant closures and redundancies. But by the recovery of the 1980s, it was clear that there would be more scope for union involvement in the expansion and development of plants and new work practices.

In tandem with the global changes that were occurring in all industrial sectors were the increased demands for product variety and flexibility. Berggren (*op. cit.*) observes that the specific climate for change in Sweden focused on simultaneous pressure from product and labour markets. Increased demand for flexibility and quality required a stable and committed work force; it therefore became important that new production systems were adapted to human demands. The influence of the unions in aspects of planning and investment decisions also increased.

In this context, Volvo, under the leadership of Chief Executive Pehr G. Gyllenhammar, played a significant role in the search for alternative production systems that have continued to develop since the 1970s. The company chose to address the problems of labour turnover and absenteeism by attempting to make work more varied and attractive. At the same time, Volvo was conscious of its image as one of Sweden's largest employers and, aware of pressure to democratise the workplace, was keen to be seen to embark upon more radical forms of work organisation that have continued to gain momentum over time. Berggren (*op. cit.*) comments that the period from 1970 onward was clearly a period of learning, in which the experiments and experiences of the first reforms and innovations provided a platform for later stages of change.

The Volvo trajectory

Volvo's approach to reorganising work systems can be seen to have evolved through five distinct phases associated with innovative production and work organisation developments at the following sites – Kalmar, Torslanda, Uddevalla,

Gent and Born. The approaches have often been experimental, with some being abandoned or refined; some have been developed to become widespread in use and others continue to be tested within different plants to varying degrees. What is apparent is a transfer of learning within and between plants driven by internal and external change. Torslanda, for example, the main car assembly plant, continues to evolve by innovation and also by adopting refinements of best practices tested at other plants.

Phase one: Kalmar

Volvo opened its Kalmar plant on a greenfield site in 1974. Its significance was that it was the world's first auto-assembly plant for volume production without mechanically driven assembly lines. Its design, incorporating dock assembly, was facilitated by what was intended to be a number of small factories within the large factory. The purpose of this was to ameliorate high labour turnover and absenteeism by providing an environment that would promote teamwork and a sense of joint production, thereby reducing the work stress that accompanied traditional manufacturing approaches. The building was well lit, noise levels were low and equipment was arranged ergonomically to reduce unnecessary movement and effort for the individual.

Individually controlled 'auto carriers', on which parts were assembled and transported around the factory, could be tilted and/or rotated by 90 per cent to enable work on the under-body and allow adjustment to the best height for each individual worker. Workers could also stand on the moving carrier and perform tasks on parts that were, in effect, standing still relative to him or her. The layout at Kalmar also incorporated buffer stocks, which enabled employees to have some degree of control over work pace.

Innovations in building and work design promoted the development of a team culture and job rotation. The core ideal of the project was efficient production by motivated and capable co-workers. CEO Gyllenhammar is quoted as saying that:

> The objective at Kalmar will be to arrange auto-production in such a way that each employee will be able to find meaning and satisfaction in his work. This will be a factory which, without any sacrifice of efficiency or the company's financial objectives, will give employees opportunities to work in groups, to communicate freely among themselves, to switch from one job assignment to another, to vary their work pace, to identify with the product, to be conscious of a responsibility for quality, and to influence their own working environment.
>
> (Berggren *op. cit.*: 122)

The significance of the innovations at Kalmar were that they were management led and driven, with involvement from unions, health and safety advisors, and job design consultants.

Whilst improved work conditions and the move towards teamwork had been well received by workers, efficiency showed no significant improvement over other conventional plants so refinements to the control of the pace of work were made. Burnes (*op. cit.*) suggests that in the latter part of the 1970s there were indications that managerial control over the work process was tightened. Berggren (*op. cit.*) for example, notes that the ability of work teams to change the pace of work led to 'mischief'; 'for fun' one team would change the pace of another team.

Dock assembly had been abandoned by 1984 and replaced by an intermittent line. Compared with the traditional assembly line, however, job content was considered to be larger and less repetitive, but workers still believed there was a need to increase work cycle times. Although hailed as Volvo's 'best practice' plant in Sweden, Gyllenhammar declared that:

> Volvo Kalmar is no final solution. It is the first step on the road. But much remains to be done in the field of work organisation. I could imagine much greater freedom and independence at work.
>
> (Berggren *op. cit.*: 127)

In 1985 Volvo commenced planning the Uddevalla plant, which was to become the basis for a conceptually innovative approach to vehicle assembly and work organisation. In the meantime, alternatives to the traditional assembly line had been instigated at other plants, including Tuve, the main producer of trucks, and Torslanda, Volvo's main car assembly plant.

Phase two: Torslanda

Torslanda is the main car assembly plant in Gothenburg. From 1976 onwards, management has continued to experiment with alternative forms of production and work organisation at the plant. Similar to Kalmar, the use of dock assembly and autonomous work groups to assemble an entire vehicle was instigated initially. Within six months, however, the approach was abandoned due to poor productivity, resulting from what was believed to be inadequate skill levels among the workforce.

A period of training and development for all workers was instigated and by 1979/80 management embarked on an attempt to regenerate group-based assembly with the opening of the TUN facility. The workforce was selected from existing personnel and it was intended that the work groups would be responsible for their own quality, pace of work, job rotation, material supply management and some maintenance. After unions expressed concerns over the viability of the concept, what occurred was a somewhat diluted version of the proposals. Nevertheless, it was agreed by those involved to be an improvement over traditional approaches to vehicle assembly.

By 1986 management had instigated major changes at the plant, which continue to be revised. Unions were involved from the outset with the intention of radically transforming the process of vehicle assembly. The action plan drawn up placed considerable emphasis on continuous training to develop workers' skills in effective teamwork and problem solving. As a result, workers have increased control over the pace of work and the quality of working life within the plant is reported to have improved considerably.

Since 1986 the workforce has increased and ten years later Torslanda employed 5,500 people and comprised sixty nationalities, 23 per cent of whom were women. The factory produced 580 vehicles per day. The diversity of nationalities would appear to result from the company policy of employing 'guest workers' to compensate for shortages of indigenous labour. This appears to indicate that despite the more worker-friendly approaches instigated by Volvo individuals still remain reluctant to enter a car assembly environment. Management, nevertheless, considers that the recruitment and retention rate for employees is high, with absenteeism and staff turnover both at only 1 per cent. Whilst this may be attributed to prevailing labour market and economic conditions, it is considered by managers that improvements to work organisation play a major part in attracting recruits and encouraging people to remain at the plant.

THE APPROACH AT TORSLANDA

The selection process ensures that recruits to the organisation are well educated, possess a good college education and work well within a group environment. Further learning is encouraged, particularly if job-related. Upward and down-ward communication is considered to be extremely important and information is circulated freely within the plant by a variety of means, including daily meetings, notice boards and informal discussions. The factory is extremely clean and well lit with good ventilation and air quality; there are clearly identified work group areas, many displaying microwaves for the preparation of snack meals, with pot plants and hanging baskets for decoration provided by members of the team. Workers dress casually and wear no standard uniform; they have the opportunity to take part in a number of on-site recreational activities including gyms and a swimming pool, with restaurants and pizzerias that cater for the racial and cultural diversity of employees. Volvo also provides a creche for its workers, where care is offered for children for either entire or part shifts, particularly if both parents are employees of the company.

In work organisation, auto-carriers that can be adjusted to the height of the individual and enable vehicle parts to be rotated so that underbodies can be worked on without bending are fully employed. Robotics has replaced the more arduous and unpleasant aspects of the work tasks. Whilst there is still some resistance by the Metal Workers' Union seeking to protect traditional demarcations, this has significantly improved since 1991. There is now recognition by some workers that multi-skilling is occurring and jobs are rotated every hour in some parts of the plant. Workers feel that their jobs are as secure as they can be in such a competitive sector, and the plant has been recruiting for the production of the new model C70 that was launched in August 1997.

Phase three: Uddevalla

Planning for the Uddevalla plant began in the mid-1980s and was a radical attempt by Volvo to break away from the traditional Fordist production system. The company was experiencing problems of quality and the new approach enabled vehicles to be produced in forty eight parallel assembly teams, each comprising ten people. Each result-oriented team would produce a whole car with cycle times measured in six to eight hours rather than minutes, as in Fordist systems. Responsibility for pace of work, quality, internal job rotation, maintenance and administration rested with each group.

In terms of the social organisation of production, Volvo was clearly attempting to give employees a sense of ownership of the whole task, to develop a wider portfolio of skills in employees, and to provide a work environment that was relatively stress-free and reflective (Harrison 1994). Indeed, one person who had experienced the practices at the plant considered that it encouraged *medarbetarskap* or co-creativity. He stated that 'active and co-creative people were recruited who had the will and ability to gather, create and utilise knowledge – people were trusted to a level that was far beyond empowerment'. Karlsson (*op. cit.*) suggests that an extremely horizontal organisation resulted, with some vertical integration, responsibility for quality and collaboration with the sales function, sometimes to the extent of meeting customers who would buy the finished product.

Logistically, the process of building a vehicle had to be refined and made simpler to fit with the new approach. It was intended that the plant, when fully operational, would employ 1,000 people and have the capacity to produce 40,000 vehicles per year. As in the Kalmar plant, some of the anticipated innovations at Uddevalla had to be revised or abandoned due to internal pressures for change and union intervention. Notwithstanding these modifications, it was considered that the performance of the plant compared favourably to some of the best of the lean production plants of the time (Sandberg 1994).

In 1992, however, Volvo announced the closure of both the Kalmar and Uddevalla plants as a result of mounting losses. Some commentators were convinced that Volvo's innovative approaches to work organisation could not match lean systems and were therefore the cause of failure (Adler and Cole 1993, Wickens 1993, Womack *et al.* 1990). Conversely, Cressey (1996) suggests that the closure occurred for a combination of reasons, most of which gave a false impression of performance. He considers that Kalmar emerged as superior when compared to all the Swedish plants, as well as many lean factories. He also observes that Uddevalla displayed a curve of increasing performance unequalled in other plants.

Despite the closures, Volvo's innovations, particularly at Uddevalla, were significant not only for Volvo itself but also across the global automobile industry. That the company announced a joint venture with the British niche manufacturer TVR to produce convertible and coupe versions of the 850 model at the Uddevalla site in 1995 may mean that Volvo's unique production concept will have the opportunity for further development.

Phase four: Gent

Although the Gent plant began production in 1965, its significance in terms of innovation commenced in the late 1980s when a new production system was built. This focused on the development of the Volvo Europe Car (VEC – the 850 model) which was assembled within a lean production philosophy that incorporated VEC teams working along the line. VEC teams were characterised by members with no job classifications but who were supposedly multi-trained and multi-tasked, who worked in flexible groups, forming a team along the driven assembly line (Karlsson *op. cit.*). Significantly, the team also took responsibility for continuous improvement and within this framework, for building and developing a chain of internal customers. This supplier–customer relationship was developed and extended to other Volvo plants following the success of Gent, which was the only vehicle assembly plant outside Japan to gain the Total Productive Maintenance (TPM) award. Management at Gent also introduced the concept of separate workshops or small factories within the larger plant, as introduced at the Kalmar site, which may, in some senses, be indicative of a backward step. Also, the result-oriented team approach was implemented, but with a greater emphasis on the philosophy of continuous improvement through TPM and worker involvement.

Phase five: the Born plant

The Born plant in Belgium is the site of the collaborative venture between Volvo and Mitsubishi. Called Nedcar, the plant makes cars for both companies that share the same chassis and one third of parts. Created in 1996, the reciprocal benefits for the joint-venture production task are deemed Volvo's contribution to product technology and European access, and Mitsubishi's advanced process technology and production volume (Karlsson *op. cit.*).

   The underpinning goals that were identified for the success of the joint venture focused on the creation of a common industrial structure, product and brand integrity and world class efficiency. Karlsson (*op. cit.*) refers to this as 'uniqueness around conformity.' The uniqueness is that the common industrial structure enables a variety of body parts to be assembled for both manufacturers, but within a process layout that is common to all models. To ensure a smooth procedure, there are common suppliers for more than ninety per cent of the components. Similarly, whilst the system can incorporate different designs and product concepts, this was made simpler by both organisations being jointly involved at the design stage through the creation of the joint product development committee (JPDC). For the production system layout, the main objective is volume and there-fore a standardised mass production system is operated, indicating to some extent, a contraction of the integrated team concept evident at Uddevalla. Within the system, however, there exist opportunities for sub-assemblies or sub-activities to create flexibility, what Karlsson (*op. cit.*) terms a Christmas tree layout.

   Work organisation in the plant clearly combines practices developed by both partners. It is based on Mitsubishi's established systems of lean production, together with Volvo's practices developed at Gent, most notably the VEC team philosophy focusing on a programme of continuous improvement. According to *The Economist* (30 March 1996) 'Nedcar is already one of Europe's more efficient factories. It hopes to increase production to 200,000 cars per year, as many as Volvo makes in Sweden.'

Karlsson (*op. cit.*) suggests that Volvo's approach, particularly evident in Gent and Born, exemplifies new combinations of dimensions of production systems, placing emphases on different aspects, over time. To achieve volume, it would appear that there has been a return to more traditional approaches to manufacturing, but within a lean production philosophy, whilst at the same time attempting to maintain and develop the integrity of the team function that has been established in Volvo.

Conclusion

The development of work organisation within Volvo over a twenty-five year period clearly demonstrates a plurality of production concepts that have been introduced as a result of the political, social and economic contexts in which the company has operated over time. They signify periods of interpreting and interacting with the environment, learning and instigating change processes and learning from change *per se*. There have been periods when management has tightened controls over the workforce in order to establish new approaches to work organisation, new approaches that have in turn led to greater levels of autonomy being afforded to individuals and teams. Accordingly, after management's initial involvement, it would appear that the contribution of the individual and team has been encouraged in order to gain their involvement in interpreting changes in the environment, so that strategy may emerge from those closest to the point of production. What is significant throughout is that Volvo has been experimental and has not followed mainstream practices if they were not likely to be contextually appropriate. As a company, it has also been selective in exploiting practices with potential for further development and discarding those that failed or resulted in mistakes. It would also appear that management has displayed an interest in delegating and encouraging autonomy within the individual and team, but at the same time is reluctant to completely abandon hierarchical systems of work organisation and the control over performance that they facilitate. Nevertheless, that there is said to be no such thing as 'Volvoism' is perhaps indicative of the company's underlying reluctance to admit that it has perfected its approach to work organisation and that it will continue to remain an evolutionary, learning journey.

Having examined the approaches of the Rover Group and Volvo, two manufacturers operating in the automotive sector, the chapter will now explore the development of two component suppliers in the industry, XZZ Components and Creative Engineering Limited. The aim is to identify and compare their interventions to promote learning and change, and to consider their performance and activities in relation to those of the manufacturers, given that the buyer–supplier relationship dictates conformity and unity in approaches.

Creative Engineering Limited

Creative Engineering is a component supplier to the automobile industry. It is an example of an organisation that has succeeded in transforming itself over a fifteen-year period to cope effectively with continuous change in the industry. It is now recognised as a high-performing organisation providing quality products; an independent survey concluded in 1995 that it was one of the few UK companies that was approaching world-class status (Burnes and New 1996). In 1997, Creative won the regional Company of the Year Award and the Finance Director commented 'we see this as a team award and as far as we're concerned, it's the employees who have won it. What makes the difference is people and that we're continuing to learn.'

The significance of this transformation would appear to lie in the company's ongoing search for continuous improvement and learning. This is dictated by a vision that recognises that benchmarking processes and activities, both within and beyond the global automotive sector, promote the transference of learning and the ability to change.

Background

Creative Engineering Limited was formed in the late 1940s and began with the production of fancy goods. Soon after, the company also began to make small items, such as ashtrays, for the motor industry. In 1955 the Charles Colston Group bought the company, with the intention of producing a domestic dishwasher for the United Kingdom and European markets. Alongside the development of the dishwasher, Creative also embarked upon the manufacture of its 'own-label' paraffin heaters. Following the death of a family as a result of such a heater in 1961, albeit not a Creative product, the market rapidly diminished and the company focused on the manufacture of pressed parts for Colston dishwashers.

Unfortunately, the United Kingdom and European market for dishwashers did not develop as Colston had hoped. The company then began to supply components for twin-tub washing machines manufactured by John Bloom's Rolls Razor company. From initially producing one hundred twin-tubs per week, the market quickly grew and Creative was ultimately producing seven thousand units per week. This spectacular growth was abruptly halted in 1967 when Bloom's organisation collapsed. Creative was able to retain large stocks of appliances and equipment, and Colston Domestic Appliances was created to manufacture and market spin-dryers, automatic washing machines and new dishwasher models. The market for such goods, however, was volatile and Colston was unable to compete with the two market leaders, Hoover and Hotpoint. It was also unable to invest in new product development. As a result, in 1976 Creative was split into two separate units, one to service the existing range of Colston products, the other to develop a wider range of contract pressworks. By 1979 Colston had left the appliances market altogether, selling the business to Ariston.

The company's future appeared precarious at this time, as the whole of the manufacturing sector was suffering due to economic recession. New opportunities were difficult to identify but it was clear that unless they could be found, the company would cease to exist. At this time, the company managed to gain some business from Talbot's automotive plant in Linwood, Scotland, producing pressed metal fabrications. In 1980 a new managing director was appointed. He had joined the company as an apprentice and had worked his way up the organisation, experiencing a variety of roles. On his appointment, he was clear about the issues the company had to address if it was to survive in the future.

Creative in the 1980s: the strategy for survival

The managing director and the management team appointed by him had to contend with the deep recession in the United Kingdom economy at this time, with the north eastern region badly affected. This meant that business was difficult in many manufacturing industries and the prospects of export orders were poor. In addition, the work secured in the motor industry for Talbot appeared unlikely to last much longer, as rumours of the plant's closure were rife. Creative's turnover had halved by this year and it was clear that its position of over-dependency on Talbot (fifty per cent of current output was for Talbot) left it exposed and vulnerable.

The managing director saw that Creative needed to secure its future by attracting long-term business and finding a new strategic direction that differentiated it from the competition. He stated (in Laycock 1994: 4):

> We needed to 'break the mould' – look not only at products but also at processes – at how we were doing things and how we could do them better. The world was changing, old standards were no longer good enough. We needed to find a way to differentiate ourselves from other manufacturers serving our types of markets.

It was the managing director's vision, together with the support and commitment of the management team appointed by him, that determined Creative's approach and strategy for the future and was instrumental to the organisation's recovery and success.

His ideas for the success of the company focused on a proactive rather than a reactive approach to strategy making. He was committed to the achievement of quality and price advantages over the traditional products offered by competitors. The automotive sector was one of many sectors that were investigated by the managing director's team. Also included were consumer electronics, information technology and the growing DIY markets. Despite the turmoil the motor industry was experiencing in the 1980s (over-production throughout Europe, poor labour relations, low productivity, pressure for cost reductions, etc.), it was decided that this sector had the greatest long-term potential for Creative's future success.

This conclusion resulted from extensive research and benchmarking exercises undertaken by the managing director in Germany and Japan. There he witnessed better work procedures and processes, which helped create his vision for the future of Creative in the United Kingdom. In Japan for example, he was impressed by the use of robotics and innovative production processes that promoted teamwork and co-operation through the integration of functions. Most significantly, the managing director and his team sensed the beginnings of profound change within the industry, with a greater reliance on collaboration and co-dependency in order to achieve high standards of quality and continuous improvement. The managing director commented (from Laycock *op. cit.*: 6):

> I realised that if we were to have any part in the future motor industry we would need, ourselves, to take a different approach – to respond positively to the changes taking place. The old traditional methods of engineering production were being over-taken. Old comfort zones were rapidly being eroded. To have any chance, Creative would somehow need to become part of the 'new tomorrow'.

In order to accomplish the changes required, it was clear that the managing director had to establish how Creative should be organised. Using his experiences from Germany and Japan, most particularly Japan, he considered that to achieve the status of world-class supplier to the automotive industry, Creative would need to pursue, and achieve, Japanese standards of excellence.

Creative targeted Ford and the Rover Group, and managed to convince the companies of its intentions to become a world-class supplier to the automotive industry. It was successful in gaining orders for work on forthcoming models due for launch in 1983 but it was made clear to Creative that work would be shared with other suppliers. Future business would depend upon matching the quality, cost and delivery performance of those other suppliers. This challenge motivated Creative to set itself two clear objectives: to exceed the performance of other suppliers, and to become the sole supplier for the components produced.

Creative purchased new equipment at a cost of £1 million and began to deliver parts to Ford and Rover in 1983. Its success was marked by a five-fold increase in turnover from that of 1979/80. But by the late 1980s Creative had reached a plateau in its achievements. Whilst Ford and Rover work continued to be successful and further business was gained, the managing director recognised that performance could still be improved. He judged that the issues were senior managers being reactive rather than proactive; a lack of problem-solving capability within the organisation; and the need for cost reduction and improved levels of quality monitoring and evaluation so that long-term relationships with customers were established.

A learning approach to change

To address these issues and to demonstrate Creative's commitment to become 'world class', the management team established a number of key objectives. These included a move to just-in-time manufacturing (JIT) and the adoption of quality techniques such as statistical process control (SPC), pioneered by Deming and Juran. A fellow director suggested that the managing director at this time 'was steeped in the belief that technology and work practices were portable between one nation and another'.

Concomitant with these changes was the key initiative to promote employee participation through the introduction of cellular manufacturing, total productive maintenance (TPM) and team working at all levels. Core competencies and skills within the workforce were identified and began to be developed in line with business objectives. Teams were customer-focused and given responsibility for quality, work methods and costs and from their inception people were encouraged to make improvements to how the cells operated. By 1995 it appeared that Creative had successfully managed its own transformation. Turnover was £80 million and 850 people were employed. It had gained additional customers, including Nissan, and had established itself as a high-quality supplier in the automotive industry with a firm commitment to continuous improvement.

The change experienced within Creative clearly required a significant investment in training and development and marked a commitment to the pivotal role of learning in influencing the change process. Both management and employees within Creative are aware that success in the motor industry can be transient and that there is a real need to learn continuously and increase skills and knowledge in order to maintain the company's position. As one manager commented in 1996:

> We've only really been training for the last five years. Prior to that, everything went into engineering but if we were going to be world class we had to put money into people. We had to fire people up and then take advantage of their enthusiasm by giving them opportunities.

The approaches pursued would appear to have been successful at all levels of the company, and focus on both internal and external activities that ensure that Creative maintains its competitive position. In order to equip people for such change, Creative has developed the following initiatives and approaches that are intended to encourage people to continue with their own learning.

(1) The Employee Development Centre

In order to demonstrate Creative's commitment to offering opportunities to all members of the company, the Employee Development Centre was opened in 1996. This offers open-learning materials and skills training to all members of the organisation.

(2) The Employee Development Scheme

This has operated since 1995 and aims to align business objectives with individual objectives and operates within a framework of National Vocational Qualifications (NVQs) and degrees. All apprentices on the shopfloor follow the NVQ route and are given day release, where appropriate, although most training occurs on site. At management level, Creative offers full sponsorship to individuals who undertake development activities (internal or external) that are directly linked to business objectives. Selection is based upon an annual appraisal review and people can apply for hundred per cent sponsorship if appropriate. There appears to be a high success rate in achieving full or partial support. Feedback on performance is deemed an important aspect of the scheme at all levels, and people are encouraged to discuss their own development with their line managers on a regular basis. Learning contracts have been instituted, which are thought to give consistency in approach and provide an indication of the company's belief in the encouragement of self-directed learning and development. As one manager said 'technology helps the company to be world class but in reality, it's the people. Training gives people the feeling that they're worth investing in and it makes people feel secure . . . well . . . relatively secure.'

(3) The Joint Consultative Group

To increase and enhance the communication flows in Creative, and remove the traditional approach to wage bargaining, the Joint Consultative Group was established, with shopfloor members elected by their peers. The Group is informed of and can discuss any anticipated changes and business developments on a monthly basis. The result of this opportunity for regular dialogue between management and employees is considered by both managers and shopfloor members to be very positive.

(4) Total Productive Maintenance (TPM)

As part of a total quality management framework, the most influential system identified in terms of increasing productivity, reducing costs and assisting continuous improvement at Creative is that of total productive maintenance (TPM). The system is based upon benchmarking and identifying best practice within and beyond the automotive sector, and has been introduced by means of rolling training programmes throughout the production areas that seek to close the gap between Creative and its competitors. These training programmes have been devised after close analyses of both existing best practice outside the company and current performance within specific production areas in Creative (e.g. downtime, quality problems etc.). A TPM programme is then tailor-made for that production area based upon the initial analysis, although much of the programme may be generic to all areas. Individuals and teams are taken off the job for five days and spend time in the training centre, while TPM 'floaters' cover for them.

Management see TPM programmes as a means of promoting culture change – they help develop teamwork and informal structures in the organisation – and as a method of communicating change in the external environment to the shopfloor. TPM obviates the need for specialised maintenance staff (indirect workers) and transfers responsibility to operators (direct workers).

TPM has been introduced in those areas that supply to Rover and will be moving into the Nissan sections in its next phase. The approach encourages preventative, autonomous maintenance, with faults identified by operators. Operators are also focused to eliminate, rather than rectify, what are termed as the six big losses: breakdown, set-up and adjustment, idling and minor stoppages, reduced speed, reduced yield, and defects in process and rework. On the premise that TPM gives people time to consider preventative measures, to analyse down-time etc., one manager said that 'TPM is a powerful tool for forward planning and it gives people more fulfilment in their jobs. The company recognises that people are worth more if they can do minor repairs'. Another manager stressed the usefulness of TPM, saying 'it builds on the skills people already have . . . people have learned over the years by watching the maintenance people anyway'. Reflecting on what is agreed by managers and employees alike as the successful implementation of TPM, a director commented:

> If people within Creative resisted change, we would never have got TPM in. OK . . . there's a minority who say they don't trust management but this is only a minority. People feel they now have to use their brains more . . . they now say they want more information on TPM. I think this shows that Creative has a high adaptability to change.

The next anticipated stage in the process is to multi-skill those maintenance employees that remain and to create a team of 'individuals who are well rounded in all disciplines and can cover electrical, mechanical and computer aspects' (said a manager). It is then envisaged that a specialist core support team will operate to address specific problems in production areas.

Alongside TPM, Creative Engineering introduced team-orientated problem solving (TOPS) in 1997 which, in tandem with *kaizen* activities, aims to build team expertise in problem-solving techniques and activities. The company employs an Improvement Manager to operate *kaizen* but TOPS operates on a more formal basis by setting improvement targets. Teams are encouraged to make use of internal and external facilities to assist in improving their understanding of the causes of production-related problems and how they may be eradicated. In the early stages of the initiative, three teams from the Ford product group were engaged in TOPS activities, either after work or at weekends. The goal, according to a manager 'is to employ 850 industrial engineers and this will ensure that Creative will be a continually changing organisation and people will know why they need to change.'

The managing director recognises, however, the need for continuing inter-ventions to maintain the competitive advantage that the company has so far achieved. In 1997 he judged that globalisation and *kaizen* placed a growing need on the organisation to develop the workforce to become the best. Given the systems that had been established to promote learning he observed that 'we have the facilities and approaches here at Creative but we have not achieved a learning culture yet. It's up to us now to find out what the barriers are which prevent this happening.' He also stressed the urgency of removing such barriers given that he considered that 'suppliers such as Creative are subject to much more change than the majority of companies.'

Conclusion

Creative is an organisation that is still in the process of rapid expansion to further establish its position in the automotive sector. The implications of this strategy of growth are that it continually places heightened pressures on systems and people in terms of training and development, and requires management interventions to establish the parameters according to which this will occur. Those with ambition and an interest in learning think that they will be well placed to capture the opportunities open to the company and to the individual. Others feel threatened that they may be left behind if they do not keep up with the pace of change.

If Creative is to become a world-class company, management reckon there is still a long way to go in improving productivity levels, reducing costs, and increasing training and development interventions so that they accurately monitor and match contemporary business objectives. Essentially, management thinks that, over time, the culture of the company has become 'pro-change', with the structure of the company 'less hierarchical and firmly established around teamwork'. Nevertheless, in an industry that is characterised by mature markets and the continuing erosion of profit margins, it is aware that customers will try to make Creative share more of the risk, with increased activity in value/simultaneous engineering. This will create the need for continuing skills development and flexibility in the workforce, and a greater reliance on the contribution of the individual and team.

Faced with similar challenges is XZZ Components, a supplier that began the implementation of lean manufacturing approaches from the late 1980s onwards. While it would appear that significant advances have been made since then, there are indications that the company has not so far achieved the same depth of culture change that promotes learning to the level of that in Creative Engineering.

XZZ Components

XZZ Components is another organisation that would appear to have successfully embarked upon the process of re-inventing itself over the past ten years. It is a long-established organisation that was typical of many in the industry, in so far as when faced with increased competition it experienced serious problems of resistance to change throughout the 1970s and 1980s. Management found that 'significant interventions such as improving quality and developing the workforce to meet such standards were needed if it were to remain competitive' (Managing Director).

Following a change in management in 1989, the company was restructured and close external links were forged with customers in order to improve quality and to learn. Management encouraged a culture that promoted learning and participation by increasing communication and promoting training and development for all employees. XZZ Components won quality awards and turned a succession of annual losses in the 1980s to record profits in the 1990s. It is now considered by industry analysts to be a good example of how traditional companies can orchestrate their own recovery through effectively developing the processes of learning and change. Managers within the organisation, however, are far from complacent and believe that continued effectiveness may be maintained only within a framework that supports the ability to learn and change continuously.

Background

XZZ Components began to make constant-velocity joints which were its core business from the 1950s onwards. The launch of the Mini started the global trend for front-wheel drive vehicles and demand for the constant velocity joint increased to such an extent that by the 1960s, XZZ was unable to cope with demand. As a result, the patent was licensed to other manufacturers to produce the component in both the United Kingdom and Japan. This inevitably brought in substantial revenue for the company but it also camouflaged the real financial difficulties that XZZ was experiencing at this time.

The organisation, according to the current managing director, suffered during the 1980s due to its traditional approach to manufacturing. As an organisation it had grown complacent; management was autocratic and confrontational and did little to address the industrial relations issues that were prevalent in the automobile industry at the time. As a result, the company was losing money, XZZ was unhappy and the shareholders were demanding action. The customer base was rapidly changing with the entry of the Japanese as strong competitors in the global automobile industry. According to the managing director 'when the Japanese started transplanting operations in the 1980s, this heralded a massive pressure for change in the industry here'.

Although the company had convinced Nissan in Sunderland of its ability to supply parts, XZZ had difficulty in meeting Nissan's quality, cost and delivery standards, despite the somewhat piecemeal changes it attempted to instigate, such as the introduction of new technology incorporating a robot production line. To address the mounting losses, which by 1989 were £5.88 million for the year, XZZ replaced the existing management team and appointed a new managing director.

His first priority was to mobilise a process of management-driven change to stop the loss of £0.5 million per month that the company was experiencing. He and his 'strategy for success' team did this by creating a vision statement that indicated where they wanted the organisation to be in five years time: a leading manufacturer of drive-line assemblies. To achieve this, he judged that the company had to become 'masters of variety and complexity' and needed to concentrate on excelling in quality, value and delivery. It was recognised that not only was there a need for a revision of work practices and procedures, but also, as the managing director stated, 'we needed to start developing people and make full use of their potential'.

He reports that he was confronted with a traditional manufacturing plant that displayed little coherence among the different stages of the production processes. It also held high levels of stock and work-in-progress. It was clear that the system encouraged poor communication, slow decision-making and a divided workforce. He was also aware that a small core of full-time union officials controlled aspects of communication between management and the shopfloor. Within such an environment, it was unlikely that the company could compete to meet the standards required by its customers.

He and his team reorganised the factory by breaking it down into six smaller units, each responsible for a different stage in the manufacturing process (including 'the tulip factory', 'inners and cages' and 'the bell cells factory'). Each unit was given responsibility to identify and solve its own problems. Cellular manufacturing processes and team working were also introduced to some of the units (while some elements of batch production remain elsewhere), although the managing director suggests 'these were not well received at first'. To develop close co-operation with customers, inter-departmental business units were established, comprising representatives from production, quality, engineering and sales. Each of the main customers was assigned to a unit with a view to increasing collaboration in the development of new models. At the same time, some interventions to train and develop the workforce were commenced and, in an attempt to break down the traditional divisions between management and shopfloor staff, a harmonisation policy was introduced whereby everyone began to wear company uniforms and eat in the same restaurant.

The Nissan crisis

Despite these initiatives, the company faced problems again in 1992 when it supplied sub-standard parts for Nissan's new model, the Micra. It was stated that more than ten per cent of XZZ's product output for the model had to be scrapped or re-worked before leaving the factory. The crisis forced the company to re-examine its approaches in the light of more fundamental realignments to systems and procedures and it looked to Nissan to assist in the change process. As the managing director stated 'we needed radical change to our fundamental principles – the way we did things, developing and rewarding people. We needed massive improvement if we were going to survive.'

He galvanised union support for his proposals, many of which focused upon improving communication channels within the organisation, so that barriers between people and skills were removed. Weekly team briefings were introduced, together with an internal newsletter giving information about the plant's performance and activities. Notice boards were erected displaying targets for productivity and quality. The managing director thinks that by developing close contact with its Japanese customers, XZZ became 'steeped in Japanese manufacturing techniques to an extent that they contributed substantially to the company's turnaround'.

The pressure for change in the industry became clear and the union officials were forced to agree to what management suggested would ultimately be of benefit to the remaining workforce. Staffing was cut to 1,000 by removing a layer of managers and encouraging people in their late fifties to take early retirement. As the managing director suggests:

> We had to make people redundant and this was hard for the unions to accept. People would say 'why improve productivity if people are sacked?' But we had to do it if we were to survive – it cost us a lot.

The organisational structure is now flatter and involves shopfloor staff, group leaders, managers, operations director and managing director.

Partnership for Change

Notwithstanding the setback of recalled parts to Nissan, the company broke even in 1992 and it became clear that the new work practices and systems were succeeding. By 1994, the management team felt that they needed to embark upon the next step forward and 'Partnership for Change' was launched. The initiative included Targets for Operational Performance (TOPS), which outline annual targets that the workforce should strive to achieve.

Criticisms, however, focus on the momentum of change, with one manager commenting that this is slower than he had expected at the outset. Rather than confine lean manufacturing approaches to those areas in which cellular production has been introduced, his view is that it should be introduced throughout the organisation. He declared 'we are not here to negotiate with the shopfloor . . . we're here to explain the consequences of *not* doing what's needed. I want people to understand the need for quick changes . . . revolution, if you like, and I want to get this enthusiasm into the heads of all XZZ workers.'

Despite concerns that the change process is slow, there continue to be concerted attempts within XZZr to identify the development needs of individuals at all levels in the organisation so that people are more receptive to change. The training budget is used to finance internal and external programmes that seek to encourage people to take ownership of their own development. At senior level, these include director and management development initiatives. Other interventions span National Vocational Qualifications and higher degree programmes. Links with external educational providers have also been forged and the company has created its own workshop to train and develop apprentices, with one manager explaining that it was difficult for education to keep pace with the changes in industry.

Nevertheless, it was considered that individual enthusiasm for learning was often hard to achieve without the commitment of supportive line managers. It was acknowledged that there remain some line managers who retain traditional views of the employment relationship and that they frequently resist change. In support of this, a production manager declared that the essential ingredient for successful change is founded upon the way people are managed. To facilitate change, he suggested there should be a development programme for every individual together with a concerted attempt to enhance communications between shopfloor workers and line managers. More significantly, he suggested that 'putting people together and saying "you're a team" does not make a team. People need to be trained to understand how teams work . . . how to handle the politics of the workplace. But for some this is all too much and they'll always cling on to the old ways and views.' In support of this, a long-standing employee commented that 'the changes that the company has undergone make the work very different nowadays. You need more skills to work in teams and sometimes managers aren't sympathetic to those of us in our 50s who aren't so keen about change.'

Nevertheless, a shift manager observed that the company had made considerable efforts to involve shopfloor staff in the change process by allowing greater freedom to experiment. Mistakes, he stated, were tolerated and people were encouraged to identify them so that they can be rectified rather than hidden. He continued, 'You always get the odd person who won't come to the party – you can counsel them – but most people will change when they see there's no other option. Anyway, some people like an autocratic style of management . . . it makes them feel secure.'

Union perspectives on the change process in XZZ Components are generally positive. In the judgement of a union convenor of thirty-three years experience in the company, XZZ was one of the better companies in the area in terms of job security and conditions. He remarked upon the changed environment in which the company operates and how the employment relationship was affected:

> At one time your own employer was all you were bothered about. Now the problems are determined by the customer who imposes the work practices on us. There's often no discussions . . . just a veiled threat because they want more and more out of us for less and less.

Despite these comments, there are continued efforts to improve upward communication and to encourage people to contribute suggestions for improvements to work practices. Change, however, is recognised to be occurring only slowly and may be associated with the existence of a traditional dominant culture and impressions of the employment relationship, the implications of which mean that there are tendencies to regress to established behaviours. In this context, a member of the human resources development department suggested that the reality of achieving production targets in a manufacturing industry can often mean that the development of people is neglected. Notwithstanding these issues, internal and external development programmes are available, although the company tries to provide as much training in-house to meet the needs of the business.

For example, XZZ Components's apprentice scheme provides off-the-job, on-site training in a newly refurbished training workshop for thirteen candidates that matches the work environment as closely as possible. Two instructors have been recruited to operate the workshop on the basis that they can provide exactly what training the company requires to maximise the contribution of its employees. Nevertheless, whilst there is open access to development opportunities at any level in the organisation, there are clear requirements that are evaluated and justified against the business 'bottom line'.

Accordingly, approaches that ensure that the company's financial investment in training is used in the most cost-effective way are evident throughout the organisation. However, the emphasis is on solving performance problems that individuals are likely to encounter in the workplace. For example, the continuous drive to improve quality levels has seen the establishment of a 'concern management room' on the shopfloor. Workers are encouraged to enter the room whenever they have any concerns about their own work or that of their colleagues. Problems have to be tackled within twenty-four hours and a solution found within five days. Since its inception in 1994, customer complaints have reduced by fifty per cent and representatives from other organisations have observed the process. It is clear therefore that XZZ Components has done much to establish itself with its customers as an organisation that is committed to quality and continuous improvement. As a first-tier supplier, it continues to work closely with all its customers (Nissan, Toyota, Ford, Rover, Honda) in production and development initiatives and to exchange best practices.

The company also continues its attempt to generate greater involvement in the training process from line managers by encouraging them to initiate feedback from their teams on courses of study and training interventions. Whilst this is recognised to be a difficult change for many, the system is gradually becoming accepted by most line managers in the organisation. At management and director levels an appraisal system operates (not for shopfloor employees) and it is the main instrument for the identification of development needs. Opportunities for academic and professional courses of study are available for those staff members who are interested. The company also utilises a succession planning committee that involves directors and managers in the identification of employees with potential for promotion. Development plans are produced for their continued performance within the framework of a group management development programme.

The company has developed a 'fast-track' management/leadership programme that identifies managers with what is considered by senior management to be 'extraordinary potential' to be directors. Development interventions have also taken place with the Board of Directors on such topics as motivation, communication, problem solving and change management. Key areas for future consideration have been identified as coaching, mentoring and stress management, together with building greater awareness of team roles and functions.

Conclusion

XZZ Components would appear to have achieved a clear turnaround in terms of the performance and effectiveness of the organisation. The culture change that has commenced since the late 1980s, although recognised as slow and incomplete, can be attributed to the commitment of senior management and workers to re-invent and re-establish the company in a highly competitive environment. Whilst for some this has been a painful process, the company would appear to have tackled this by regaining management control and rationalising the workforce and encouraging those who did not support change to leave.

It is recognised that there are some members of staff who remain steeped in traditional values and are resistant, but for supporters of the change process, success has been marked by the recent winning of the Investors in People award. One human resource manager commented 'we didn't do anything extra to get it . . . the hard part will be sustaining the changes so that they continually reflect improved business performance'. The recognised danger is that the organisation may become complacent and stand still as far as identifying and evaluating future development interventions. Aware of this fear, it is likely that management in XZZ Components will continue to ensure that the lessons of the past are remembered, thereby enabling the organisation to continue to move forward by anticipating and dealing proactively with change through a learning approach.

Case studies: summary and conclusion

The research reported here has focused on four organisations that operate in the automotive sector and it has identified and compared their approaches and performance in dealing with the dynamic and competitive nature of the environment in which they operate. While the organisations have undertaken specific learning and development approaches to deal proactively with change as identified above, it is clear that they have achieved varying levels of success in the process. Volvo, for example, established itself since the 1970s as an organisation committed to innovative approaches that are founded upon the contribution of learning and teamwork, while the Rover Group commenced the transition from traditional practices and procedures in the 1980s. Some managers in Rover clearly are convinced that the new approaches are institutionalised while others question how deeply change has impacted on the organisation. Similarly, many members of Creative Engineering consider that teamwork has led to the development of a learning culture while some managers are aware that the nature of the environment dictates that the company is far from achieving this state. Like the Rover Group, XZZ Components would appear to have achieved a significant transformation, but there remain those who cling to traditional assumptions of the employment relationship, indicating that culture change so far may be superficial compared to that in Creative Engineering.

Nevertheless, as a generic approach, all of the companies have invested substantially in developing the workforce and in changing systems, structures and processes to maintain competitive advantage. This has involved the development of individuals in team-based structures that allow the expression of ideas for continuous improvement in order that learning and change can occur. But the shift to employee development and involvement was preceded in all the organisations by increased management intervention in order to re-establish management's right to manage. In Volvo AB for example, despite the more egalitarian basis upon which the employment relationship was historically founded compared to that in the United Kingdom, management would appear to have driven the changes and maintained some of the more established hierarchical control mechanisms that allow innovative approaches to be explored.

Similarly, it would appear that management in the Rover Group, Creative Engineering and XZZ Components were faced with industrial unrest, Japanese competition and hence, out-dated approaches to work organisation in the 1980s. They assessed the changes that were occurring in the environment and exerted tighter controls over their workforce in order to establish new work practices. It was from this control that greater autonomy and responsibility was gradually given to the workforce in return for an increased level of involvement and commitment. On the basis of the research surrounding the activities and performance of the organisations therefore, it would appear that the generic issues and key themes for consideration are as follows.

(1) Management identification of the nature of change in the external environ-ment and application of a top-down approach that establishes internal change in work organisation so that the company becomes proactive in dealing with change;
(2) Management recognition that to be proactive involves bottom-up approaches that lead to more emergent strategy making by the contribution of the wider organisation through continuous improvement;
(3) Cultures that support continuous improvement must be encouraged, through individual and team learning that challenges the status quo;
(4) Individuals must be developed so they can engage in double-loop (or second-order) learning, making it possible for change to occur.

Having explored the practical contexts and findings of the research, the next chapter will revisit the significant debates on learning and change in the literature in order to develop a more intricate picture of the issues and themes identified so far. This will demonstrate how the practical findings connect with academic perspectives, particularly those advanced by contemporary writers, thereby providing a framework that will underpin and inform the discussion and analysis in Chapters seven and eight.

6 Emerging themes for organisational effectiveness in the automotive sector

Summary

This chapter revisits the main themes examined in the literature in order to provide a theoretical foundation for Chapters seven and eight, which analyse issues that arise from the research presented in Chapter five. The chapter identifies the nature of change in the automotive sector that has led to new manufacturing approaches, and shows there is need to undertake concerted environmental scanning so that external change is accurately monitored and anticipated. Whilst this appears to be traditionally a senior-management activity, contemporary changes to work practices ostensibly seem to require wider involvement so that strategy emerges from the contribution of individuals and teams close to the production processes. In this way, the organisations may have more potential to develop a proactive relationship with the environment and may be more able to exert choice in their actions and decisions.

The chapter continues with an examination of the implications for organisational cultures and establishes that any realignment of the employment relationship would require that individuals engage in double-loop learning in order to promote organisational change and to facilitate emergent strategy. It concludes that for significant change to occur there must be recognition of the interrelationship between learning and change and that this may be a lengthy and difficult process involving varying degrees of culture change within organisations. Despite these caveats, it seems that if organisations are to continue with any degree of success they cannot avoid attempting to develop such approaches.

Background

The evolution of the automotive sector is characterised by change and uncertainty and has, historically, proved to be at the forefront in the development of innovative work practices. Henry Ford's mass production of the automobile in the early part of the twentieth century in the United States established a system that came to be known as 'Fordism', characterised by strict division of labour, bureaucratic control and accountability. Nevertheless, Thompson and McHugh (1996: 172) suggest 'the Fordist system of mass production is held to be incapable of permanent innovation' and this inflexibility manifested itself in terms of both products and the nature of the employment relationship. Over time, the Fordist approach has been questioned, particularly as people became more vocal and demonstrative in articulating their discontent with the ways in which they were treated/managed in the workplace.

What followed from the 1930s onwards were piecemeal attempts to redefine the employment relationship in the automobile sector. Encouraged by commentators like Mayo, McGregor and Barnard, managers began to pay more attention to what were seen to be the more 'positive' motivating factors such as communication, leadership and social interaction in the workplace. Nevertheless, Jones (1981) contends that whilst mass production was criticised, there was still the need to ensure that a tight framework for the control of workers was maintained, particularly during the 1940s and 1950s when competition in the industry intensified as European producers became serious contenders in the global market. Following continued periods of industrial unrest throughout the global industry in the 1960s, however, it became clear to some managers in the sector that they had to consider alternative approaches to work design if they were to re-establish control (Berggren 1992, Burnes 1996, Thompson and McHugh *op. cit.*). Work humanisation and quality of working life schemes were explored, most notably by Volvo in Sweden, in an attempt to address the higher-level needs of the individual, as identified by Maslow (1943). Also, to address the growing need for quality, industrial psychologists such as Herzberg (1968) and Argyris (1957) argued that if the individual was motivated and content in the workplace then this would enable higher quality vehicles to be produced.

Notwithstanding these developments, Jones (*op. cit.*) considers it was apparent that players in the global automotive sector continued to struggle for survival during the 1970s due to lack of product differentiation, the oil crises and depressed market conditions. Womack *et al.* (1990) suggest that the increasing penetration of established markets by Japanese producers, whose vehicles were characterised by their small size, competitive pricing and low fuel consumption, only appeared to exacerbate their problems. Japan's significance, however, was not only that it quickly established itself as a major vehicle producer, but also that it appeared to offer an approach to manufacturing that would challenge Fordist mass production. Womack *et al.* (*op. cit.*) suggest that the lean approach not only provided a viable alternative to Fordist production, but that it also required a revised approach to human resource management. They contend this offered a radical solution to the problem of dealing with the industrial unrest characteristic of traditional Western approaches. Storey (1994) argues that this was because it required the establishment of new work structures and employment relationships that focus on teamwork, flexibility, technology and continuous improvement.

As various commentators (Atkinson 1984, Bratton 1992, Piore and Sabel 1984, Storey *op. cit.*) suggest, although Japan's manufacturing practices acted as a major catalyst for change, it was clear that the global climate in a range of industrial and commercial sectors was changing from the 1970s onwards. For example, Piore and Sabel in 1984 identified the end of Fordist mass production and the beginning of an era of flexible specialisation. Bratton (*op. cit.*) argues that an increasing interest in human resource management from the 1980s onwards was beginning to recognise the significant role of individuals and teams in achieving organisational strategic objectives and quality, while Peters and Waterman (1982) ignited interest in the 'excellence' movement. This interest, together with the growing preoccupation with corporate culture as a milieu to promote loyalty and commitment (Deal and Kennedy 1988, Denison 1990), raised management's awareness of the 'softer' systems in organisations that could be used to encourage the change process. So, traditional manufacturing and production systems, together with the basis on which the employment relationship was established in these environments, came to be challenged. Moreover, addressing this challenge became all the more urgent in the automotive sector. As Womack *et al.* (*op. cit.*) suggest, Japan's producers threatened the survival of players in the Western industry due to their superior levels of quality, productivity, performance, and commitment of the workforce to achieving these goals.

Change in the automotive sector

Organisations in the automotive sector, hitherto operating within traditional management and work organisation frameworks, have seen the abandonment, to a greater or lesser degree, of Fordist approaches in response to radical change in the nature and degree of international competition in the contextual environment (Storey *op. cit.*). This appears to have been the result of a complex mix of developments in Western industrial approaches mentioned above and identified by commentators as follows:

(1) The influence of Japanese producers since the early 1980s and the dominance of 'lean' production techniques that include just-in-time (JIT), cellular manufacturing and total quality management (TQM). These approaches are recognised by some industry analysts to be the most efficient and cost-effective approach to manufacturing in the sector (Kenney and Florida 1993, Schonberger 1982, Womack *et al. op. cit.*). By others they signify 'management by stress' (Parker and Slaughter 1988), with heightened pressures upon the individual for continuous improvement (Berggren 1992, Briggs 1988, Kamata 1973).

(2) The end of mass production and the beginning of an era of flexible specialisation (Atkinson *op. cit.*, Piore and Sabel *op. cit.*).

(3) The increasing interest in and analysis of human resource management implications for new forms of manufacturing (Bratton *op. cit.*, Storey *op. cit.*).

Whilst there are a variety of labels attached to new methods of manufacturing, the implications for people employed within the organisations remain the same. Crises or 'triggers for change' experienced by the organisations generate uncertainty, in which it becomes clear that the organisation must change if it is to remain competitive. The 'pain' of such change (Clarke 1994, Schein 1993) requires that organisations be transformed. In such a context, people must embrace innovative forms of work organisation; they must adopt new roles and responsibilities and assume that change is a constant in an environment characterised by uncertainty and instability (Clarke *op. cit.*, Morgan *op. cit.*, Stacey *op. cit.*).

The implications are significant for both the individual and the organisation because how organisations respond and restructure work practices and systems are fundamental to their long-term survival and success. If people are not convinced that such change will lead to a better state, they are unlikely to co-operate without resistance. Hence, managers in the industry conclude that transformational interventions that offer improved organisational performance are required. These may be achieved in the automotive sector through a new 'social organisation of car manufacturing' (Hancke and Rubinstein 1995: 180) in which the emphasis is placed on continuous improvement in both individual and organisational activity.

Organisational learning and change

Storey (*op. cit.*: 4) in his analysis of 'new-wave manufacturing' points out that the keywords associated with the new approaches include 'flexibility', 'quality', 'teamworking', 'just-in-time delivery' (JIT), 'right-first-time' production, the elimination of waste and non-value-added activity, 'zero defects' and 'continual improvement'. He suggests:

> Arguably the separate elements are not so new. What is different is the way the new-wave manufacturing approach brings them all together into a new, mutually reinforcing whole. Hence JIT places a premium on right-first-time and total quality; continuous improvement requires involvement from everyone and some form of teamworking; in turn teamworking implies a need for flexibility, while flexibility means a better trained and more competent workforce.

Thus, since the 1980s increasing emphasis has been placed on the development of individuals in the workplace, in combination with the view that successful organisations are those that are committed to becoming 'learning organisations'. However, there are a number of key issues in the development of the learning organisation (see Table 2.2 in Chapter 2). It is clear that the approach involves learning at all levels of the organisation, the transference of knowledge within and between organisations and people, and a proactive attitude to change. Indeed, commentators such as Burgoyne *et al.* (1994), Garvin (1993) and Senge (1990) suggest that the key to competitive advantage in any sector is to promote individual and organisational learning on a continuous basis as a way of dealing effectively with environmental change and instability.

Garratt (1995) suggests that the emergence of the learning organisation as a dominant management approach has been influenced by the convergence of a number of disciplines, including psychology, sociology, cybernetics, economics, and ecology. Others (Ashby 1960, Revans 1982) contend that it is only by ensuring that the rate of learning is equal to or greater than the rate of change in the environment that organisations can ensure survival. Hence the importance of understanding the organisation and the environment as learning organisms is recognised, for there is much that management can do to influence and create their own environment on this basis (Morgan *op. cit.*). Similarly, if the organisation is recognised as a learning organism, then Stacey (*op. cit.*) suggests that organisations must be seen as complex, diverse and chaotic, but at the same time as having the potential for order and self-organisation. Such characteristics, he suggests, can become resources for change if management is proactive in creating appropriate contexts in which self-organisation can occur.

This clearly demonstrates the centrality of the importance of 'systems thinking' (Senge *op. cit.*) about the relationship between learning and change. For if change is to succeed, people must support and understand it through learning and development (Dawson 1994, Dixon 1994, Schein 1993). Moreover, for continuous improvement to occur, it is double, rather than single-loop learning (Argyris and Schon 1978) that must be encouraged in all aspects of organisational activity, otherwise the status quo will be reinforced and change will either not occur or not last. On this premise, various writers (Burgoyne 1994 *et al.*, Clarke *op. cit.*, Dixon *op. cit.*, Stewart *op. cit.*) suggest that approaches to learning and change must appreciate that organisations change in both unique and in common ways that reflect the organisation's environmental, cultural and developmental characteristics. These factors will now be examined in more depth in order to identify the key themes that are most influential in the development of a learning approach to change.

Environmental characteristics

Some commentators (Morgan *op. cit.*, McCalman and Paton 1992, Stewart *op. cit.*) regard monitoring and understanding the external environment as critical for the effective management of change. Boddy and Buchanan (1992) contend that the need for change is difficult to legitimise unless provoked by a crisis (such as Japan's entry into the global automotive sector). But Schein (*op. cit.*) suggests that this form of crisis management is not a recommended method of instigating or managing the change process. Essentially, it is a top-down approach and is limited to catching-up with competitors rather than determining the ground on which to compete as a self-generated activity. Moreover, theorists (Clarke *op. cit.*, McCalman and Paton *op. cit.*, Stacey *op. cit.*, Stewart 1996) argue that survival is dependent upon continued adaptation to a changing environment that cannot be predicted because it is complex and chaotic. But it must also be recognised that the environment can be shaped by the organisation. This supports analyses of organisations as open systems (Morgan 1986 and 1997, Stacey *op. cit.*) which stress the importance of developing a proactive relationship with the environment and anticipating change as a continuous, natural phenomenon in which choices can be made (Burnes *op. cit.*).

For example, if they were to remain competitive within an increasingly global environment, it seemed to managers in organisations operating in the automotive sector that the only way to do this was to adopt the same, or similar, production and manufacturing approaches to those used in Japanese organisations. Researchers who took up the technological/rational interpretation of 'Japanisation' (Schonberger 1982, Voss and Robinson 1987, Womack *et al. op. cit.*) promoted this view enthusiastically, arguing that these techniques were not specific to Japan alone, but were transferable throughout the world. Indeed, Japanese producers such as Nissan, Toyota and Honda proved this was the case by successfully establishing assembly plants and/or joint ventures in the United Kingdom and employing local workers.

Additionally, Storey (*op. cit.*) and Hancke and Rubinstein (*op. cit.*) suggest that lean production techniques required a revised approach that incorporated flexibility, teamwork and continuous improvement. They argue that these aspects were not new *per se*, but their arrangement in an industrial context meant a new social organisation of car production had to be established, replacing that of traditional Fordist manufacturing frameworks dictated solely by management control mechanisms.

Communicating the risks of the potential 'future state' (Stacey *op. cit.*) is therefore an important part of the process of encouraging organisational transformation and would appear to indicate recognition of complexity and chaos theory as relevant considerations when attempting long-term planning interventions. As Benjamin and Mabey (1993) suggest, this involves communicating the stimulus for change to the workforce and then creating a supportive internal environment comprising appropriate systems and processes to assist in the process of change.

Pettigrew and Whipp (1993) identify key conditioning features that indicate receptivity to change. These include key players championing external assessment techniques, information being openly circulated about changes in the environment, and new approaches being developed and effectively integrated into overall business planning. A central theme that emerges is management recognition of changes in the external environment so that they are communicated to, and understood by, the organisation. This would appear also to involve interpreting national characteristics relating to history, culture, politics and social groupings, then creating internal structures that are appropriate to how individuals relate to each other in this environment, thereby influencing how the momentum of change can be generated (Clarke *op. cit.*, Dawson *op. cit.*).

Cultural factors

Argyris (1957) suggests that bureaucratic arrangements in organisations limit the development of individuals and do not encourage them to think creatively or with a long-term perspective. In a later analysis Argyris (1991) argues that hierarchies place control in a management domain that establishes positional power and encourages preservation of the status quo. Communication is filtered and/or limited, so preventing people from fully understanding how they can meaningfully contribute to the organisation's performance. Benjamin and Mabey (*op. cit.*), however, suggest that creating a supportive internal environment comprising appropriate systems and processes is important in assisting in the process of change. The environment that organisations in the automotive sector are attempting to create, for example, requires more involvement from the shopfloor in ensuring that quality is the responsibility of everyone. To achieve this, people's abilities must be developed so they can operate the new technology and perform effectively in the changed contexts that the new systems demand. Similarly, people need to work successfully in teams in these contexts, so they must be flexible and able to perform a variety of tasks rather than just a limited number.

Moreover, the quest for continuous improvement in the industry means that the responsibility for strategy and change is beginning to be driven from the bottom-up as well as top-down. As Pettigrew and Whipp (*op. cit.*) indicate, strategy creation must emerge from the way the company as a whole acquires, interprets and processes information about its environment. People must contribute not only their physical abilities but also engage in dialogue so that ideas and creative solutions to business problems are encouraged. It is anticipated that emergent strategy and direction will flow from this, which will enable a more proactive relationship with a dynamic environment to be established.

Accordingly, managers need to employ various strategies (surveys, meetings, interviews with employees, etc.) to learn and gain an understanding of their company's cultures in order to effect the change process. Clarke (*op. cit.*) and Dawson (*op. cit.*) recognise the importance of management developing sensitive approaches to change that do not contradict cultural traditions and biases. Similarly, Galpin (1996) identifies a range of tangible elements of organisational culture that can be managed to implement and sustain change. These include payment, work conditions, communications and the physical environment.

A further tangible element of culture is management behaviour: the redefinition of the management role may contribute to learning and change. Garratt (1987) and Senge (1990) for example suggest this involves establishing a participative, co-ordinating approach to encourage the contribution and learning of the individual. Individuals in the lean manufacturing environment for example are given more information about the organisation and its production targets. They are required to reach a level of understanding about the information, and then offered the opportunity to question and challenge existing norms (double-loop learning) within defined parameters if they consider that improvements can be made that may result in more effective approaches leading to greater productivity.

Snow *et al.* (1993) suggest that managers in such an environment act as brokers and facilitators operating across, rather than within, hierarchies. For some, relinquishing positional power is a difficult process (see Figure 3.1 in Chapter 3). Argyris (1991) identifies defensive routines that individuals may adopt which generate tensions between what is said (espoused theory) and what is done (theory-in-use), leading to inertia that may sometimes obstruct the change process altogether.

Culture change of this nature is acknowledged to be a lengthy process by theorists and practitioners alike. Johnson (1993) suggests it is a cognitive phenom-enon, and it is clear that over time, organisations will display varying degrees of success in how far (and how deeply) the change process is accepted. Burgoyne

(1995) in his discussion of meta-dialogue (the basis on which joint meaning is understood and believed) suggests that managers must first establish the basis on which the current reality is understood and believed in by those in the organisation so that foundations for new approaches can then emerge. In this context, promoting the development of teamwork entails recognising the increasing importance of the informal organisation (Stacey *op. cit.*), and communities of practice (Brown and Duguid 1991) as focused approaches that will encourage both learning and change.

Nevertheless, Nadler (1993) and Benjamin and Mabey (*op. cit.*) argue that the political dynamics of change must be considered in addressing the tensions between control and learning. Indeed, Coopey (1996) suggests that mutual investment in learning should enable the frontier of control to be moved to a more participative, co-ordinating arrangement. However, tensions surrounding perceptions of management action are important considerations. Sewell and Wilkinson (1992b) for example observe, that in team-based, lean environments, tactical authority is passed down while centralised control remains intact or is enhanced. Furthermore, Thompson and Wallace (1996) suggest that teams create a milieu in which control is transferred to, and exerted by, peers rather than management. Similarly, the notion of empowerment and how far individuals are enabled to challenge existing procedures so that change can occur must be considered (Cunningham *et al.* 1996). Once people in organisations have more information about and understanding of the external environment, a second key theme comes into play, the potential for emergent strategy and teamwork to be used as agents of learning so that established norms can be challenged and change will occur.

In this connection, Clarke (*op. cit.*) argues that creating a culture for change requires that change becomes part of the accepted norm. Clearly, opportunity to challenge the status quo can occur only within a culture that is enabling, supportive and, as Argyris (1991) says, tolerant of experimentation and mistakes. However, the legitimacy of culture change may be an uncomfortable issue in some organisations, as noted by Lynn-Meek (1988), Pollitt (1990) and Schein (1985), who suggest that it may be interpreted as a means to manipulate the employment relationship. The third theme that emerges therefore involves the creation of cultures that enable strategy to emerge through the contribution of individuals and teams.

Developmental factors

Stewart (*op. cit.*) suggests that change interventions are accompanied by a significant investment in individual and organisational development. At the individual level, the introduction of new work practices in the automotive sector is often so radical that investment in developing skills needed for effective performance in the new environment is required. These may include communicating, problem-solving, teamwork and flexibility, together with skills-based training in the operation of new technology. In this way, as Wilson (1992) says, the relationship between change and learning is recognised by making the crisis associated with traditional manufacturing regimes 'real' to people in the organisations, thereby generating a learning need in them to adopt new manufacturing approaches. This supports the research of Knowles (1984) who argues that adults learn best by experience, self-direction and involvement, and that they are competency-based learners who will acquire skills they can apply pragmatically to their immediate circumstances. Moreover, structures that require effective teamwork mean that the basis on which the individual learns needs to be re-defined to allow more collective, social processes to emerge that may encourage deeper learning and change (Burgoyne 1995, Cook and Yanow 1996, Hendry 1996, Pettigrew and Whipp *op. cit.*).

To promote a deeper level of learning and change, more emphasis should be placed on the development of individuals so they are equipped to challenge existing norms. This is the fourth key theme identified. This requires training in a broader range of skills appropriate to people's roles; involvement in how work is organised and implemented; and revision of relationships so that individuals can question traditional management approaches. It also requires that more information is circulated about targets and performance, what is occurring in the external environment and how successfully their organisation is competing. Indeed, Morgan (1997) suggests that learning will occur by reducing the distance between the individual and the environment in which they operate and promoting the ability to challenge existing operating norms, thereby promoting double-loop learning and change.

Argyris and Schon's (1978) discussion of double-loop learning indicates that change will occur only if individuals are encouraged to challenge the status quo and that they can do this in a climate of relative safety. By this they mean there must be removal of barriers to learning, exemplified by defensive reasoning, inertia, positional power and failure to take responsibility for self and others. Grundy (1994) suggests that whilst double-loop learning may not be widespread, there may be identifiable areas in organisations from which the approach may gain momentum.

Thus, how far the development and encouragement of individual learning leads to an organisational response must be considered, because this will influence the continuation of learning approaches and the effectiveness of the change process (Dixon 1994). Hendry *et al.* (1995) offer an analysis of learning in terms of the individual, the organisation and the environment in which they draw upon March and Olsen's (1975) model (see Table 2.3 in Chapter 2). March and Olsen describe three distinct stages of individual learning ability – foundation, formation and continuation – by which the individual progresses from readiness to learn to becoming a self-motivated, independent learner. Hendry *et al.* (1995) draw a matching frame of reference at the level of the organisation. They suggest that organisations can display levels identified as dependency, transitional and independency. At the dependency level, the organisation offers formal job training and remedial approaches, whilst at the independency level there is broad commitment to work group autonomy and shared responsibility. Hence as the individual develops confidence as a self-directed learner, so the organisation will offer increased opportunities to maintain and support this state. It is clear, however, that this is a developmental process, and organisations may display varying stages of ability and response throughout their structures and lifecycle.

Conclusion

This chapter has identified the main issues in the literature that relate both to the generic nature of change in the organisational environment and specifically to change in the automotive sector. It suggested that lean manufacturing approaches emanating from Japan posed a threat to the viability of established organisations to such an extent that they were provoked to embark upon radical change strategies. Generically, it discussed how change impacts upon a number of organisational levels that include the environmental, cultural and developmental. From the discussion of these levels, four key themes were identified:

(1) the performance of the organisations in monitoring and communicating environmental change;
(2) the promotion of emergent strategy-making and teamwork;
(3) the development of cultures that support these approaches;
(4) the development and involvement of the individual to facilitate emergent strategy.

These key themes will provide a framework for Chapters seven and eight, in which the practical activities and approaches of the case-study organisations are analysed and evaluated. From this we can determine the range, extent and usefulness of their approaches to the promotion of individual and organisational learning, development and change.

7 Discussion and analysis
The Rover Group and Volvo

Summary

Chapter six revisited the main themes in the literature to identify the key challenges that influence organisations in the process of change, in order to provide a foundation for the analysis of the research findings in the following chapters. These challenges would appear to manifest themselves on a number of levels and they may be identified as follows.

(1) The organisation must perform well in monitoring and communicating change in the external environment.
(2) New work methods rely on teamwork and continuous improvement as fundamental to the production process. This provides the potential for emergent strategy formulation to flow from wider involvement in the process, but thereby requires the participation of individuals other than management.
(3) Emergent strategy can occur only in cultures that encourage individuals and teams to challenge established norms.
(4) If this is to occur, individual learning and involvement must be promoted within the organisation in order to facilitate emergent-strategy making.

This chapter will therefore explore how far the evidence gathered during research on the Rover Group and Volvo reflects and/or challenges the theoretical perspectives and key issues examined in earlier chapters. It will show that at the external level, both companies have made significant attempts to understand and communicate change in the environment to the wider organisation. At the individual level, it shows that both the Rover Group and Volvo are attempting to equip people with the skills and abilities to operate effectively in a changing environment. In Volvo it seems that such approaches are well established as part of organisational culture and people demonstrate a greater capacity for independent, double-loop learning. In the Rover Group, such characteristics whilst not yet fully established are beginning to emerge as individuals increasingly taking responsibility for addressing their own development needs.

(1) Environmental change in the automotive sector

Monitoring the external environment is a major preoccupation with organisations in the automobile industry seeking to remain competitive and to absorb and exchange contemporary best practice. The emergence of Japan as an industrial power from the 1970s onwards indicated that, formerly, insufficient attention had been granted to this activity. Hence, organisations in this sector were forced to embark upon radical change to transform their companies in order to regain market share. As a result, both the Rover Group and Volvo are sensitive to contemporary developments and are keen to maximise their potential for innovation and creativity through double-loop learning. The approach of each, however, is unique and is characterised by the nature of its development and the impending crises or 'triggers for change' induced by environmental events that it has had to face.

The Rover Group and the external environment

The Rover Group adopted a unique approach to manage the change needed to regain a competitive position in the automobile sector, in that in 1990 it established a separate business unit, Rover Learning Business (RLB), to assist in the process. This was intended as a positive signal not only to its employees but also to the wider environment that it was committed to transforming the company through learning and developing its people. In this way, it was committed to becoming a 'learning organisation'. The learning organisation concept involves developing and integrating double-loop learning by scanning the environment, challenging operating assumptions and developing strategic approaches that are participative and emergent (Hawkins 1994, Jones 1992, Morgan 1997). It is therefore appropriate to examine Rover's approach and performance in developing double-loop learning at the organisational level by scanning the external environment.

RLB assisted the Rover Group in commencing culture change (detailed later in the chapter), whilst simultaneously monitoring how the company might learn from its wider operating environment. Hence, the establishment of RLB and its board was intended to ensure not only that senior managers from the Rover Group were represented but also that people from other industries and educational establishments were also present. This action supports Garvin's (1993) point that learning from others in the wider environment is a vital contribution to inspiration and creativity that will encourage the transference of learning within and beyond the organisation.

Similarly, whilst Phase One of the Rover Group's planned change strategy focused on the development of individual learning interventions (discussed below), Phase Two from 1992 to 1994 looked towards the development of corporate learning, in tandem with individual learning, to embed learning and change processes in the Rover Group. This accords with Bateson's (1972) view of how learning can open up new opportunities. In this case Rover was not only becoming more aware of its position in the wider environment, but also recognised how it might influence it to its advantage, if appropriate internal learning and change responses were developed. This seems indicative of the company's belief that it was moving towards a different level of complexity in its approach, in so far as the whole organisation (as opposed to the individuals) had become the unit of analysis for learning, transferring knowledge and skills (Kramlinger 1992).

Moving into Phase Three of the change strategy from 1994 to 1996, RLB worked with personnel and training departments throughout the Rover Group, continuing to scan the wider environment by monitoring the evolving nature of the motor industry and attempting to use this information to the Group's advantage. Scanning the environment in this way offers a broad understanding of the wider context in which the organisation operates, making it more likely that change will be understood in terms of its impact on all stakeholders (McCalman and Paton 1992).

Suppliers and partnerships

Links between the Rover Group and suppliers such as Creative Engineering and XZZ Components have been strengthened by improved communication, joint activities for training and development, combined research projects, and the transference of best practices. This is a clear demonstration of awareness of the importance of continuously learning from the wider operating environment (Dixon 1994). Furthermore, RLB also assisted the Rover Group to learn from Honda during its partnership, particularly with regard to its activities in the United States. In February 1993 for example, the 'Learning from Honda' input focused on a series of workshops across the whole company, outlining new work practices and initiatives, and clearly demonstrating recognition of the value of benchmarking from others. By reducing the distance between the company and its customers and partners in this way, relationships based on openness and transparency are developed, thereby increasing the potential for double-loop learning and change to occur.

Members of RLB claim that reducing the distance between the organisation and the environment has been attempted in the widest sense. Looking beyond the automotive sector, links have been forged with academic bodies (including Warwick University, London Business School and Liverpool John Moores University) and Rover is represented on global networks that promote organisational learning such as the European Council for Learning Organisations (ECLO). These initiatives indicate that the Rover Group is exploring the context of its industry in relation to the wider environment.

Internally, the Group Learning Exchange Network (GLEN – a database of information and case studies developed to assist Rover associates in benchmarking and copyplus exercises) was developed to assist in the learning and change processes by making knowledge institutionally available rather than the property of select groups. This was to promote awareness of variations in processes so individuals might avoid becoming locked in single-loop learning that prevents significant or lasting change from occurring.

In February 1994 when Rover was sold to BMW it was thought that BMW would maintain the established commitment to learning and development for individuals and the organisation. Although employees confirmed in 1997 that this approach continues, RLB was dissolved in 1996, with former members claiming that the learning culture had been established and RLB had therefore achieved its purpose. Given that the company has undergone profound change since 1990 and that establishing new work practices takes considerable time and effort, it may be that the organisation has indeed advanced considerably but not so that learning is fully embedded in organisational culture.

Volvo and the external environment

The second automobile manufacturer, Volvo, has adopted a different approach to the Rover Group in managing and anticipating change in its operating environment. From the 1980s onwards, new manufacturing techniques adopted in Western organisations such as the Rover Group essentially followed the 'lean' route, with the standard approach in the automotive sector that of the 'Japanisation' of the industry (Ackroyd *et al.* 1988). This was not the case in Sweden, where a distinctive work organisation and assembly line developed during the 1970s and 1980s. This resulted from the repeated questioning of the traditional assembly line and established shopfloor hierarchies due to the distinctive nature of the economic, social and political environment in Sweden during this time (Berggren 1992).

Different social arrangements in countries lead to a range of solutions (Sandberg 1995). Learning from the changes occurring in its environment, Volvo opted to instigate a series of revolutionary changes by developing new approaches to production systems in order to achieve a level of stability for the company. Volvo was clearly demonstrating an awareness that future survival cannot be based on extrapolations of historic behaviour, but that, as Clarke (1994) claims, organisations must identify and respond to environmental change quickly and opportunistically if they are to survive.

This is not to suggest that the Rover Group did not do this. Rather, Volvo placed a greater emphasis on a series of revolutionary changes by experimentation, with innovative production systems utilised in a succession of plants that were directly influenced by previous performance, adjustment and learning from the experience of change. This would indicate considerable awareness and use of the experiential learning cycle (Kolb 1984) in creating and developing Volvo's approach to learning and change, confirming that 'approaches to change [should] be matched to environmental conditions and organisational constraints' (Burnes 1996: 196). Indeed, the unique conditions that prevailed in Sweden appear instrumental in shaping Volvo's approach to the nature of production and the terms upon which the employment relationship is based.

Environmental conditions specific to Sweden

Volvo, like most organisations in the global automotive sector in the 1970s, was characterised by poor industrial relations and employee dissatisfaction, with workers generally becoming increasingly vocal in articulating their discontent. In other parts of Europe, America and Japan such issues faded with the onset of the energy crises and world recession. This did not occur in Sweden, where pressure from the labour market to improve working conditions mounted. This was because unemployment remained low and wage differentials between different sectors and companies were small, making it difficult for Volvo to compensate for poor working environments with high wages and benefits. Moreover, the interest and influence of trade unions in work organisation was increased as a result. With high union membership, Volvo was keen to experiment with new ideas surrounding what were considered to be 'good work practices', rather than traditional Fordist approaches that were dependent upon moving assembly lines and hierarchical structures. Furthermore, in 1976, the Swedish Co-determination Law meant that companies were legally obliged to involve unions in proposed changes, significantly increasing their influence in work organisation.

Such conditions continued into the 1980s when the product strategy of Volvo was moving more towards upmarket product segments (Berggren *op. cit.*). An increase in product variation throughout the global automobile sector, together with a growing dependence on export sales, meant that Volvo had to respond to different consumer demands. These combined pressures from the labour market and the product market clearly required approaches to work organisation that were flexible and which in turn required a skilled and stable workforce. This encouraged Volvo to continue its rejection of Tayloristic approaches.

Volvo's approach

Volvo's scanning of the environment in this way enabled the company to detect the importance of shifting trends and patterns (Bateson *op. cit.*) in both the labour and product markets, thereby developing approaches that would appear to be creative and future-oriented. It can be seen from Volvo's Kalmar plant that initial attempts were made to deal with social change in the workplace by acknowledging that people were no longer prepared to tolerate work practices that did not offer the opportunity for personal growth and development. By abandoning the mechanically driven assembly line and offering employees the opportunity to work in small groups within an ergonomically planned production system, there was recognition, and an acceptance, that people in employment were concerned not only about financial reward but also about the quality of working life.

As a result, Volvo judged that a human-centred approach would be more appropriate for the nature of the social and economic environment in which it operated. The systems put in place at Kalmar were designed to allow teams and individuals a higher degree of autonomy and discretion than in traditional car plants. But when efficiency showed little significant improvement in the late 1970s, management refined the system, seeking to exert more control in order to deal with internal demonstrations of resistance to change. Acknowledging, as Schon (1983) suggests, that resistance must be managed and controlled if productive learning and change are to be achieved clearly demonstrates that double-loop learning was occurring.

Furthermore, what can be seen from the Torslanda plant is the development from 1976 onwards of experimental forms of work organisation designed to improve productivity and employee motivation, many of which have been taken from systems employed at other Volvo plants such as Kalmar, Uddevalla and Gent. For example, the abandonment of dock assembly shortly after its introduction in Torslanda in 1976 demonstrated that new approaches would succeed only if those responsible for their implementation were competent and well trained in their execution (Berggren *op. cit.*, Dixon *op. cit.*).

In recognition of this, by 1986 there was increased commitment from management to a programme of continuous training and development throughout Volvo plants. Organisational learning was promoted as a viable platform for change management. This was developed through job rotation, whereby workers spend time in different areas of the plant to learn new skills and to exchange best practice, together with the creation of increased communication channels so that people are informed of change. In some way this indicates recognition by management that, as Hendry (1996) suggests, one way to manage resistance to change is to adopt an educational approach.

This view was clearly apparent by the 1980s, when Volvo needed to expand its production capacity although the labour market was difficult (Sandberg *et al.* 1995). The radical solution was the design of the Uddevalla plant, in which attempts were made to provide systems that would integrate productivity and ideas of good work practices propounded by the Metal Workers' Union. By introducing a system that allowed groups of workers the autonomy to assemble entire vehicles, organisational learning is stimulated because work is varied, long cycle times are employed and people can communicate freely. The transference of learning can therefore occur with teams regularly communicating, sharing best practice and creating 'islands of strategic learning' that over time may develop into a critical mass of organisational learning (Grundy 1994).

Kalmar and Uddevalla – reasons for closure

The reasons for the closure of both the Kalmar and Uddevalla plants are complex and concern both internal and external environmental factors identified and analysed by theorists (Berggren *op. cit.*, Cressey 1996, Sandberg *et al. op. cit.*). The early 1990s saw a period of rapidly falling demand for vehicles throughout the world and in order to combat this, Volvo's strategy focused on:

(1) The closure of smaller plants lacking the ability to supply body shells.
(2) The preservation of the well-established and larger site at Torslanda, Gothenburg.
(3) The influence of traditionalist management and union factions who considered the new approaches too risky in the economic climate. In this connection Hancke and Rubinstein (1995: 193) claim that:

Uddevalla closed because it did not have a winning coalition that backed it. None of the social groups . . . could tie their fate in an almost existential way to Uddevalla's long term success: not the managers, not the unions and not the workers.

(4) Volvo's planned alliance with Renault (since dissolved), which determined that the company's future vision of car production was to be inspired and influenced by Renault's culture and philosophy.

What is evident is the development by Volvo of a clear and proactive approach to deal with environmental change in order to create stability and choice for the wider organisation. Faced with decreasing product demand, Volvo chose to consolidate its production facilities at the larger Torslanda site whilst at the same time transferring some of the more successful work practices developed elsewhere to that plant (Berggren *op. cit.*).

Partnerships

The closure of the plants, various industry analysts (Cressey *op. cit.*, Sandberg *et al. op. cit.*) claim, was largely the result of the influence of Volvo's proposed partnership with Renault, announced in 1993. The merger was seen to be 'the result of car wars making it increasingly difficult for companies to make profits in an industry whose excess capacity feeds saturated and cyclical markets' (Williams, Haslam and Johal 1995: 311). The influence of Renault was such that Volvo's economic difficulties at that time were attributed to new production concepts and low product volumes, which differed substantially in philosophy and layout from that of Renault. In addition, the economy in Sweden was undergoing profound change, with high levels of unemployment, high interest rates and no need to attract people by offering innovative work practices like those developed at Uddevalla and Kalmar. As a result of these crises or 'triggers for change', the plants were closed, indicating an acceptance of the need to accept the 'pain' of change by undertaking radical action where necessary. Moreover, there were managers in both Renault and Volvo who were concerned that the approaches were too innovative for the economic climate of the time and were not prepared to champion their continuation. This clearly recognises the role of effectively managing organisational politics in the change process (Hendry *op. cit.*, Revans 1982).

The joint venture between Volvo and Mitsubishi instigated in 1996 is based at Born in Belgium and provides a strong example of the two organisations developing a collaborative, creative approach to the production of vehicles and the development of mutually supporting work structures. Following the growing recognition of the limitations of the Japanese model of lean production (Altmann 1995, Parker and Slaughter 1993) and the momentum in Europe for more humane design of work, both organisations are seeing the context and activities of their industry in an imaginative way. As Garvin (*op. cit.*) suggests, it would appear that they have recognised the importance of creating new possibilities for the design and manufacture of their products that may lead to competitive advantage in the future. Incorporating both 'lean' and 'reflective' systems, the plant provides an example of the transference of learning within and between companies and cultures and demonstrates a clear commitment by Volvo to achieve the volume that lean production systems can offer without forgoing its established improvements to work design.

Conclusion

What can be seen in the Rover Group and Volvo AB are demonstrations of strategies that have developed from an internal to an external focus, with recognition that constant monitoring of both environments must be maintained. In RLB's approach, Phase Three clearly attempted to develop a focused strategy for corporate learning, but also incorporated was a more international dimension combined with the development of internal business support systems. These support systems were manifested through the development of joint-venture activities with producers and suppliers. They encourage transference of knowledge by focusing on learning, continuous improvement and change management through inward and outward benchmarking and what RLB call 'copyplus'. The dissolution of RLB in 1996 may indicate that there is no longer the need for a separate organisation to act as a catalyst for change, with many people believing that approaches have become embedded in practices and norms.

Conversely, it may be that BMW were not prepared to continue the investment, given that criticisms of the added value RLB contributed to the Rover Group had begun to emerge from 1994 onwards. Whilst it would appear that Rover has made considerable advances from 1990 and has achieved significant transformation, it is unlikely to have reached a similar position to that of Volvo, which enjoyed social, political and economic advantages that encouraged learning and change processes to become established much earlier.

Volvo is an example of a company that would appear, over time, to have learned and changed its habits to adapt to and take advantage of contextual changes. The company demonstrates considerable receptivity to environmental change in developing approaches that are dynamic, adaptive and consider the long-term macro-economic implications of its actions. By embarking upon collaborative strategies, particularly with other manufacturers such as Mitsubishi, Volvo has attempted to adopt a proactive approach that achieves the integration of some of the more effective aspects of two manufacturing philosophies. Indeed, Auer (1995: 455) argues:

> The automotive industry . . . should not push for a total cost reduction approach and the leanest of all worlds. Instead of a maximum in leanness, which might lead internally to fragile organisations and externally to a downward spiral in the economies, an optimum in leanness is required. Acceptance of some 'slack' in the production flow as well as the labour force might be functional for organisational and economic 'safety' alike.

Whilst it is important that organisations reduce the distance between themselves and their environments, so that change can be understood and approached proactively, internal systems and processes must be established that enhance, rather than prevent, the learning opportunities that such activity provides. Clearly, in the initial stages management in the organisations has taken a top-down approach in recognising that understanding the external environment is essential to sustaining competitive advantage. Whilst the organisations have displayed a variety of approaches, the link between learning and change has been recognised by senior managers at different stages of the transformation process, then developed by learning interventions specific to the company and reinforced over time (Vince, cited in French and Grey 1996). It would appear, therefore, that there has been recognition by managers in both the organisations that over time an investment in learning and development must be embedded in their approaches if change is to be successfully understood and accomplished.

However, there is increasing recognition that there is also need for bottom-up approaches that are emergent and flow from people within the organisations. The discussion will now focus on the second generic theme that emerged from the research. This focuses on the approaches of the Rover Group and Volvo and their encouragement of emergent strategic direction, with particular attention to the development of teamwork.

(2) Emergent strategy and teamwork

In order that organisations can develop their capacity to learn and change, new patterns of action must be allowed to emerge that consider the contribution of members of the wider organisation rather than those traditionally involved in management. In this way, learning evolves and is not constrained by planned approaches that encourage single-loop learning but prevent double-loop thinking and learning. This clearly requires wider involvement in the planning activity. In tandem there is need for an approach to management that avoids rigid controlling mechanisms that inhibit questioning and challenging established systems and processes.

New work systems incorporating just-in-time, total quality and continuous improvement that are evident in the Rover Group and Volvo, clearly indicate that people receive more information about the environment in which the organisation operates. From this, there is potential to engage in dialogue 'where both abstract ideas and personal feelings about them are shared in a spirit of provisionalism, mutuality and co-inquiry' (Kolb *et al.* 1994: 154). In this way, people may achieve a shared understanding of the 'current reality' and know what is required of them and the organisation in order to remain competitive (Senge 1990). A milieu for such activity occurs in the form of teamwork that encourages the translation of this reality into effective organisational performance. Indeed Morgan (*op. cit.*) argues that methods of generating continuous improvement such as *kaizen* and TQM are powerful tools to encourage double-loop learning in organisations because they promote the creation of values and mind-sets that make learning and change a priority. It is important, therefore, to examine how far the organisations promote learning and change through the emergence of strategic direction and teamwork.

RLB and the Rover Group

The Rover Group is unique in so far as a strategic initiative, Rover Learning Business (RLB), was created to promote learning and change within the wider organisation. This signifies a clear and deliberate intention at the outset to encourage individual and organisational learning rather than leaving it to chance. The creation of RLB provided a 'reference point' to guide future behaviour. In terms of strategic intent, therefore, it is important to evaluate Rover's performance by examining the outcomes and any consequent adjustments and changes to the strategy, in order to understand the usefulness of the approach.

An important issue is how far RLB acted as an effective reference point to provide a sense of the vision the Rover Group hoped to create in its commitment to becoming a learning organisation. This would appear to depend upon the clarity of the vision and how clearly articulated it was to the wider internal and external community. In turn, this would then be dependent upon the development of shared understanding and mental models describing the current reality for those directly involved in the process.

A further consideration is how far double-loop learning and change are understood by those involved in their promotion, and hence how effectively these concepts are communicated to the wider organisation to encourage organisational learning. A comment from an RLB manager suggested that it was to the detriment of RLB from its inception that the emphasis was placed on the business functions, with few people skilled in understanding and developing learning processes being recruited to RLB. This would indicate that from the outset the requirement to think creatively about the nature of change, in order to assess what the learning needs of the company were likely to be in the future, was not fully addressed (Cunningham 1994). As an RLB employee said, 'RLB has been effective in teaching Rover how to learn but not in enabling it to identify the specifics it needs to learn about'.

Whilst RLB's reason for creation was to assist the Rover Group in becoming a learning organisation, a manager in RLB observed that what had resulted was the development of a 'learning delivery' organisation. He felt that this was largely due to failure to establish at the outset the role and the identity of RLB and what it really was: 'people were confused between the business and the products, and also how RLB might be integrated within the Rover Group as a whole'.

For example, a manager within RLB reported that during the early 1990s it became difficult to establish criteria for the Rover Employees Assisted Learning (REAL) experiences because there were no guidelines, 'just philosophical statements'. This suggests that a common understanding of the vision had not been developed and communicated throughout the organisation. From 1991 to 1994 RLB was being pressed to identify criteria for structured guidelines and a business-related focus but this met resistance from those within RLB who were reluctant to make any significant changes to the product. This again appears to indicate a lack of vision, agreement and co-ordination, together with resistance to change on the part of managers within RLB once the organisation had established its role and culture.

An RLB manager reflected that in Rover Group's vision in 1986, the main focus on people provided only one of the strategic initiatives to re-vitalise the organisation. It was suggested that other issues (profit, product and processes) had to be addressed simultaneously in order to make the connection between people and structures. Indeed, Dawson (1994) and Beer and Eisenstat (1996) confirm the importance of a multi-faceted approach to change that simultaneously addresses issues surrounding work processes and structures as well as people. This appears to have led to confused signals within RLB and the Rover Group with regard to its contribution. This resulted in an inability to model behaviours in line with a clearly articulated vision, demonstrating a traditional, rather than a learning approach to strategy-making in RLB. A learning approach by contrast would enable plans to be revised and amended following the contributions of those closest to the action, individuals in the business units in the Rover Group itself.

This traditional approach appears to have resulted in failure to integrate sub-systems (i.e. personnel and training departments in the Rover Group) so that learning and development in the whole organisation is encouraged. In 1994, an RLB manager claimed that to individuals within the Rover Group, the value of personnel departments was greater than RLB in promoting change, stating 'RLB is not on people's lips as the fountain of knowledge'. A cell manager remarked that RLB was 'a bit remote from the action', perhaps indicating that RLB had not fully engaged in meaningful dialogue with groups and departments to achieve collaboration and 'joint meaning' (Burgoyne 1995). Neither does it appear to have been fully able to diagnose internal capability to respond to learning and change successfully. As a result, it may not have understood the development of the business units within Rover Group as a whole.

Monitoring and evaluation of RLB's performance

In terms of overall achievements, it is recognised that RLB placed organisational learning firmly on the business agenda and that it succeeded in assisting as acting as a catalyst to generate a climate for learning and change in the Rover Group. It has also succeeded in promoting a positive external image for the Rover Group as a learning organisation. Nevertheless, the central issue of the contribution of RLB to the performance of the Rover Group, and how its effectiveness might be measured, remained a challenge that the Rover Board itself expressed in 1994. RLB's internal work for the Rover Group was estimated to cost £1 million and there was a requirement that its added value to the organisation be examined through quantitative assessment. This would confirm Garratt's (1995) views that initiatives for developing organisational learning of this nature may finally be legitimised only through measurement against the business 'bottom line'.

This suggests that as the process of organisational evolution unfolded, RLB's own crisis or 'trigger for change' emerged. One member of RLB observed that the glossy image of RLB was successful externally but created resentment internally. This was directed at both associates on the shopfloor and the personnel departments in the business units, perhaps indicating that managing the politics of change had not been fully addressed (Moss Kanter 1985, Revans *op. cit.*). It might also be indicative of individuals in the Rover Group becoming ready to take more responsibility for the processes of learning and change without RLB's external assistance (March and Olsen 1975).

Reflecting on how far RLB was itself a learning organisation, one RLB employee stated in 1994 that 'we need to dismantle walls and the boxes people are in and unlock the managers so that they work together and learn from each other'. This would appear to reinforce Garvin's (*op. cit.*) observation that, while many organisations are skilled at acquiring and creating knowledge, few are skilled in applying it to their own activities and behaviour. Similarly, considering RLB's ability to manage change within the Rover Group, an RLB manager commented 'how can people in RLB influence change if they've never experienced it themselves?' In similar vein, a newly appointed RLB manager in 1995 considered 'RLB plateaued two days after it was launched and then it went downhill after that – the business needs to be shaken when it had previously just been stirred'.

Another RLB manager reported that to his knowledge, no members of RLB had ever made any suggestions for improvements to their own work practices or job roles, essentially, he considered, because people within RLB itself did not fully understand its role or purpose in the wider organisation. This relates to a further comment from a long-term manager: 'RLB does not model sufficiently the practices of a learning organisation to enable Rover itself to become a learning organisation'.

With regard to the future performance of the Rover Group, managers in RLB suggested in 1995 that there were a number of issues directly relevant to individual and organisational learning that needed to be addressed if the company was to remain competitive in a rapidly changing industry. In this sense, RLB was clearly engaging in double-loop learning and had detected that survival would be dependent upon its own learning and change. It was attempting to scan its external environment and anticipate future events. For example, the levels of complexity built into the process of building cars was a major factor to be considered by RLB, because it would have direct implications for production, assembly, labour supply, recruitment and selection, training and development, etc. for the Rover Group.

Some members of RLB declared that there was a need to become less reactive and offer more creative approaches than existing training departments within the organisation could provide. New management appointed in 1995 was, at that time, thought likely to herald a period of regeneration for RLB by re-focusing the company's image internally back to corporate and individual learning. In 1995 a manager commented that:

Over the last two or three years the individual business units have moved on and it seems that RLB has failed to service their requirements. The focus now is inward [on RLB] and we need new approaches to take RLB forward.

There was recognition that further development might be achieved by RLB through the transference of change skills by adding a new 'depth' to team learning. In addition, creativity among associates could be developed by engaging in real dialogue rather than just participation. As one member of RLB suggested, 'it's all very well talking about learning and training people – we all know the right language but maybe the systems aren't in place to allow the right actions to flourish?'

This indicates anawareness that by 1995, RLB needed to address the problem of how to create 'joint meaning' and shared understanding through the development of systems that would encourage the integration of individual and collective learning. RLB recognised that if the development of joint meaning and understanding was to occur, greater attention needed to be directed to managing and understanding the collective learning processes that emerge from teamwork and autonomy, so they could be harnessed to the advantage of the organisation.

Using the analysis of Hendry *et al.* (1995) (see Figure 2.3 in Chapter 2), this may also indicate that the organisation had travelled from the dependency phase to the transitional phase, in which the organisation attempts to respond to individuals by offering wider opportunities for teamwork and experiential learning. As Revans (*op. cit.*) suggests, this recognises the importance of the group in learning from and with others. The characteristics of an adaptive organisation (Burgoyne 1995a), one that is dynamic and can take advantage of contextual changes but has not progressed to third-order learning in which the organisation creates its own environment rather than adapts to it (Bateson *op. cit.*), also appear to be evident.

Despite the plans envisaged by management in 1995, it was decided to dissolve RLB in 1996. There are a number of competing explanations of this. Some say that after the BMW/Rover Group merger senior figures were not prepared to champion its continuation for political reasons. Others claim the company had achieved its original aims and had established learning and change processes, and/or that people within the wider organisation had assumed a greater role in training and development and could no longer see the relevance of RLB. Others again say that RLB had simply failed to have achieved its aims.

Conclusion

Whilst there were many positive appraisals of the contribution of RLB, some associates within the Rover Group and RLB itself became concerned about its contribution. These concerns may be listed as follows.

(1) RLB's collective leadership lacked power and direction over the period 1992 to 1994.
(2) Investment in learning process skills and competencies was also lacking.

(3) Line managers in the Rover Group assumed a leadership role for learning, resulting in less need for RLB's contribution.
(4) There was a failure to nurture strong partnerships with training and development departments within the organisation.
(5) The influence of lack of communication and internal politics within the Rover Group had the potential to affect the performance of RLB and its effect on the wider organisation.
(6) The business rather than learning background of managers within RLB meant that they were unfamiliar with learning processes.
(7) There was a failure to keep pace with the requirements of the individual business units, leading some senior Rover Group personnel to conclude that RLB added little to the organisation in terms of bottom-line contribution;
(8) There was a failure to develop stronger links with academic bodies that would ensure that RLB's involvement in learning and development was externally recognised.
(9) The lack of integration and little cross-functional teamwork within RLB led to lack of learning within RLB itself.
(10) Low investment did not facilitate RLB's emergence as a learning organisation in its own right.
(11) Limited experience of change in RLB itself made it difficult for the organisation to influence the process in the Rover Group as a whole.

Notwithstanding these concerns, it was clear that many people in RLB were aware that change was needed. It is also clear that the creation of a separate business to develop people and promote learning was, at the outset, a positive catalyst for change within the Rover Group. Externally, it helped to establish Rover's international reputation for a commitment to developing people; internally this helped RLB to promote the learning organisation approach in practical and analytical terms. Over time, however, the Rover Group's strategy may not have fully reflected the learning approach, due to a lack of vision, unclear strategic objectives and a failure to communicate with the organisation as a whole. Developments within the separate business units may have overtaken the development of RLB itself, creating friction and uncertainty regarding its role and purpose.

In support of this, Burgoyne (1995a) warns of the difficulties of the learning organisation label in so far as it may be seen as being used to 'sugar the pill' of what are considered to be exploitative work practices by those involved. For such reasons, it is important that learning and 'change [are] linked to the transitionary nature of work organisation . . . and redefined organisational boundaries and relationships' (Dawson *op. cit.*: 46). Otherwise they are likely to generate only short-term results and increase perceived instability rather than reduce it.

Emergent strategy and teamwork in Volvo

Whilst it is acknowledged that both the Rover Group and Volvo operate in the same task environment, their contexts and developmental stages in the learning process markedly differ. The Rover Group expressed commitment to the development of the individual through RLB and the concept of the learning organisation in order to accomplish change. Volvo, however, has focused on employing a learning, emergent approach to strategic direction, together with the associated modification of production systems that, over time, have become essentially team-oriented, rather than individually oriented. This recognises the value of the contribution of the work group in allowing strategic direction to emerge through learning, in so far as there is greater potential for systems to be challenged and revised through experimentation and innovation in a team environment.

The development of the Volvo approach to work organisation has been characterised by the use and development of the autonomous work group since the 1960s at a succession of plants (Berggren *op. cit.*, Sandberg *et al. op. cit.*, Thompson and McHugh 1995). It is clear that such innovative practices in production processes and work organisation have been the result of an approach to strategic direction that has been experimental and emergent within the company. This has encouraged double-loop learning and change to occur through the transference and adaptation of practices within and between plants (Berggren *op. cit.*), essentially due to an approach to team learning that has enabled groups to develop balanced skills through multi-dimensional alignment (Burdett 1994). Indeed, Anderson *et al.* (1994: 198) suggest that work groups or teams are 'the crucial medium through which new ideas are proposed, shaped and re-shaped through interpersonal negotiation and pursued towards implementation.' They identify the key determinants for effective team performance as:

- Vision – understood and shared by all members;
- Participative safety – involvement in the decision-making process and toleration of experimentation and error;
- Climate for excellence – constructive controversy is encouraged to improve standards and performance;
- Support for innovation – articulated, rewarded and financed.

Volvo's advances in this sphere show that the organisation has moved through the phases of 'dependency' and 'transition' identified by Hendry *et al.* (1995) and is approaching the 'independency' phase, in which there is a broad commitment to work group autonomy and shared responsibility for production goals.

The VEC team

This is evident from the production system developed in the 1980s at the Gent plant that focused on the Volvo Europe Car (VEC) team. The multi-trained and multi-tasked team took responsibility for continuous improvement and, within this framework, for developing a chain of internal customers that would evoke a future orientation and develop systems thinking in the organisation (Morgan 1997, Senge

1990). This supplier–customer relationship was developed and extended to other Volvo plants following the success of the Gent initiative. It would appear that the result-oriented team approach, with a greater emphasis on the philosophy of continuous improvement through total productive maintenance (TPM) and worker involvement, was implemented to integrate individual and collective learning through participation.

Using the Uddevalla plant as a further example, this was a radical attempt by Volvo to break away from the traditional Fordist production system by learning from the experiences at Kalmar, Torslanda and Gent. The company was experiencing problems of quality and the approach initiated at Uddevalla was intended to 'achieve quality by personal dedication' (Karlsson 1996: 12) by placing greater ownership and responsibility for the final product with those at point of production. The production system was planned with assistance from unions and industrial analysts with the intention that each result-oriented team would produce a whole car with cycle times measured in six to eight hours rather than minutes as in Fordist systems.

This is a clear demonstration of Volvo's efforts to gain wide involvement in developing the new approaches, so they would be accepted with minimal resistance. In tandem was recognition that the individual and group were instrumental in setting the pace of work, establishing internal job rotation and promoting quality, and hence double-loop learning and change. People 'are asked to dig beneath the surface of recurring problems . . . they are encouraged to examine existing modes of practice and find better ones' (Morgan 1997: 94). In designing systems that encourage these processes, Volvo was attempting to create an environment in which the organisation becomes a 'learning laboratory' for problem solving and experimentation (Kenney and Florida 1993, Leonard-Barton 1991, Roth *et al.* 1994).

In 1992, Volvo announced the closure of both the Kalmar and Uddevalla plants as a result of the mounting losses detailed earlier in the chapter. What is apparent is that Volvo rapidly acted on its reading of the environment and took strategic action to deal with the situation before it worsened; it did not attempt to maintain the status quo when it was clear that this would not succeed. In this way, the company did not accept the current reality as *the* reality but engaged in double-loop learning that assisted in implementing a radical change strategy.

Similarly, work organisation at the Born plant in Belgium combines practices developed by both Volvo and Mitsubishi that incorporate lean and reflective approaches, and advance the VEC team philosophy of continuous improvement. The development of a system that exhibits 'uniqueness around conformity' (Karlsson 1996) is indicative of the company looking beyond its own boundaries and undertaking an approach that recognises that the task of learning is changing. Transferring the analysis from group to organisational level, the collaborative venture recognises the value of generating dialogue (joint meaning) and meta-dialogue (the basis for believing that things are credible and useful) (Burgoyne 1995) with other organisations that have different ways of 'being, knowing and doing' (Srivastava *et al.* 1995).

Conclusion

It would appear that Volvo sought to create an environment that is supportive of learning and change by the development of systems and processes that focused initially on the participation of the individual and then of the group. This recognises that in developing a proactive approach to change, momentum to promote organisational learning must be maintained throughout. What is apparent is an organisation that is moving towards the 'independent' stage (Hendry *et al.* 1995) in terms of group and individual learning, with the emphasis on information exchange through partnership. This amounts to a clear attempt to influence and restructure its own environment in its favour (Burnes *op. cit.*).

The chapter will now consider the third theme identified as common to the case study organisations, that emergent strategy can occur only in cultures that encourage individuals and teams to challenge established norms.

(3) Creating cultures that challenge

Management interest in developing cultures that promote success has been evident since the 1980s, with the rise of Japan as an economic power and the associated literature surrounding the culture–excellence debate (Deal and Kennedy 1988, Pascale and Athos 1982, Peters and Waterman 1982). Whilst there are many perspectives on the influence of organisational culture on performance, Allaire and Firsirotou (1984) note that it is the product of a number of different influences that include society's values, the organisation's history and the context in which it operates. Watson (1994: 21) defines culture as

> the system of meanings which are shared by members of a human grouping and which define what is good and bad, right and wrong and what are the appropriate ways for that group to think and behave. A culture is, in part, a moral system. It not only defines values (ideas about what is good and bad, right and wrong) for those who subscribe to it, but contains assumptions about the nature of the world and of human beings.

On this basis, if organisations are to develop the capacity to engage in double-loop learning, cultures must enable traditions and ideas to be challenged and revised so that new values and assumptions can emerge. This activity must be seen and accepted as the norm, so that the principles of double-loop learning become apparent and lasting receptivity to change can be established. Hence people must first have a good understanding of the frameworks and operating norms that inform current organisational activity, and then be able to question, challenge and change them if and when necessary (Argyris 1977). In this way, internal systems can be matched to current and potential change in the external environment.

Concomitant with double-loop learning is Schon's (1983) account of 'framing' and 'reframing', which essentially suggests that organisational members must be reflective and skilled in understanding how the organisation operates, its mental models and reality, and then be able to adjust them or develop new ones when appropriate. In support of this, Senge (1990) considers that by sharing mental models and developing 'systems thinking' (understanding the connectivity between all aspects of the organisation's functions and actions), people will be better equipped to question and change operating norms. Thus it is clear that only by establishing a framework for its development in the organisation that double-loop learning can be encouraged. How far culture in the case study organisations stimulates double-loop learning and change will therefore be analysed now.

Culture plays a significant role in the performance of an organisation and its ability to learn and change (Denison 1990, Schein 1993). It is clear, however, that many organisations face difficulties in adapting established cultures to meet changed environments, because they often embody prior learning and experiences that people are reluctant to discard (Galpin 1996, Schein *op. cit.*). Burnes (*op. cit.*) suggests that it is when culture becomes 'out-of-step' with changes in the environment that it becomes dysfunctional and detrimental to effectiveness.

Both the Rover Group and Volvo have experienced periods throughout the 1970s and 1980s when their internal behaviours were at odds with external demands, and have had to embark upon radical change programmes to compensate. This has involved attempts to develop cultures that complement and support new work practices and change. As Morgan (*op. cit.*) says, for double-loop learning to occur, organisational culture must support change and risk-taking by developing a shared understanding or mental model of the environment through collective approaches to learning and change.

Culture change in the Rover Group

The influence of contemporary literature and management practices, most significantly that detailing the 'learning organisation' approach, is recognisable. Some managers in the case study organisations see this as a label that was tangential to the implementation and success of their own learning and change initiatives. The Rover Group, however, saw the development of the learning organisation as a pivotal initiative that would assist and demonstrate, both internally and externally, their commitment to people. The promotion of profound culture change was seen to be essential to maintaining organisational effectiveness within a competitive global arena. The company therefore reinforced its change programme with the creation of a separate business unit, Rover Learning Business (RLB), to plan and assist in the transference of knowledge and the development of people so that they would accept and accomplish change.

RLB's purpose was to transform relationships between management and employees and remove the 'them and us' culture that was symptomatic of traditional, hierarchical approaches prevalent in the 1970s and 1980s. By realigning internal relationships, the intention had been to create a more flexible, organic approach to work organisation that is responsive to a turbulent contextual environment (Burns and Stalker 1961). Furthermore, by recognising that new approaches to manufacturing have increased the complexity of work tasks and skills, the organisation made an investment in promoting employee initiative and providing greater discretion at work (Ashton and Felstead 1995). In this way, there have been attempts to realign 'tangible elements of culture' (Galpin *op. cit.*) so that a climate for double-loop learning and change is established.

The Rover Group's commitment to profound culture change was embodied in the launch of 'Rover Tomorrow – The New Deal'. This involved an attempt simultaneously to realign those elements of culture that can most readily be managed, such as rules and policies, customs and norms, rewards and recognition, management behaviour and communication (Galpin *op. cit.*). It incorporated:

- increased job security in return for a commitment from employees to continuous improvement and flexibility;
- an attempt to democratise the workplace, via the use of the term 'associates' to describe all Rover employees and the harmonisation of terms and conditions between white collar and blue collar employees;
- the transference of associates from administration to assembly lines when necessary with the expectation that white collar employees should be prepared to work on assembly lines;
- all employees, even directors, wearing the same overalls.

Embodied in these proposals was a clear attempt by the Rover Group, not to change people's behaviour *per se*, but rather to place people in a new organisational context that imposes new roles and relationships upon them. The intention is that new attitudes and behaviours may emerge.

Moreover, with the primary focus being the development of people, RLB became increasingly concerned with the relationship between learning and change management issues, and how these could contribute to the Rover Group's performance. Initially the key thrusts for Rover Learning Business were intended to complement the quality strategy that was in place in the Rover Group. Initiatives had an internal focus that involved the promotion of individual learning, energising and managing people so they were receptive to learning and change. Continuous corporate improvement was to be achieved through the promotion and integration of experiential workplace learning and self-development initiatives.

The company was attempting to develop its capacity to learn and change by tapping the internal capabilities of staff, in recognition of the strategic importance of developing human resources that in turn would ensure the long-term viability of the company. This demonstrates that Rover managers were aware that the future of an organisation might be determined by how effectively the component parts are integrated in responding to change (Emery 1969).

Impressions of RLB's contribution to assisting in culture change in the Rover Group appeared to be positive. Recognising that the process is lengthy and continuous reinforcement is needed, managers believe that the new culture will develop over time if 'sold' internally through action and communication (Nadler 1993). Indeed, people are conscious of a period of transition in the introduction of new work practices and systems that reinforce the culture change. Concerns focus on 'teething troubles' before new systems operate effectively, together with the need to refine methods when necessary through management and/or employee experience and suggestions for improvements. Indeed Jones (1992) comments that gradual change of this nature is likely to have more lasting results in terms of developing strategic learning.

One employee said in 1994 that RLB gave people the opportunity to be business-orientated and, as a result, he was piloting total productive maintenance (TPM) in his cell. Shift managers in turn said they had used the change-management system developed by RLB for large projects and recognised that 'it's difficult but good if used effectively and with help from members of RLB to guide us through it.' A shift manager on Discovery System 2 commented:

> people involved in manufacturing are usually very 'tasky' – they just get on with the job – the change process instigated by RLB forces them to plan the change project and it produces more effective and lasting results.

This would appear to indicate that the approach succeeded in developing people's capacity for 'systems thinking,' that is, to understand the 'whole' and to perceive the interrelationships or structures that underlie complex change situations.

Three shift managers interviewed claimed that Rover is seen as a world leader in people development and receptivity to change, both internally and externally, and this has been assisted by the influence of RLB. A team leader declared in 1995 that:

> RLB offers a new way of learning to Rover people through involvement and experience; you can learn at your own speed, there's good opportunities for secondment into other areas of the factory . . . there's no boundaries any more. Rover is seen as a place where people can learn and develop their skills.

Reflecting Rover Group's commitment to becoming a learning organisation, some people feel that it does indeed learn, by means of networking with other organisations, through a process of internal discovery, and by trying to be 'in the right place at the right time.' Rover continues to sustain a high profile as an organisation that has achieved significant culture change in its commitment to people, learning and development. A manager in RLB commented on the approach:

> There's a lot of nonsense written about culture change. It takes time and effort and there's two ways to do it. You can model a new way of doing things over a long period or you can make it impossible to do them the way they've always been done before, right away. We seem to have combined the two here.

Nevertheless, in promoting a culture for learning and continuous improvement, lies the problem of creating enthusiasm for development without expectation

(Legge 1995). Restructuring in Rover has created just seven grades of job through-out the organisation and only four levels of management, so the 'step change' or gap between levels is significant. It is unlikely that people find it an easy transition from a lower to a higher grade or that they expect such career progression in the long term. Learning and development interventions within the organisation (and indeed within all organisations that have reduced their structural tiers) may need to address these issues.

Volvo's approach

Volvo's approach to reorganising production systems and work practices, having evolved through five distinct phases (Kalmar, Torslanda, Uddevalla, Gent and Born), provides clear evidence of an organisational culture that supports double-loop learning and change. Significantly, the nature of the changes cannot be called unique to each plant, because many characteristics have become widespread and continue to be tested in different plants to varying degrees. Also there must be recognition that in the different plants will be a variety of sub-cultures that may assist or may prevent learning and change (Deal and Kennedy 1988, Denison 1990). Nevertheless, what is apparent within Volvo is a deliberate effort to develop a dominant organisational culture that promotes the transference of learning within and between plants, driven by internal and external change.

The promotion of a culture that is receptive to change was apparent at Volvo's Kalmar plant, a green-field site opened in 1974. Its significance was that it was the world's first auto-assembly plant without mechanically-driven assembly lines. Its design, incorporating dock assembly, was facilitated by what was intended to be a number of small factories within the large factory. The purpose of this was to ameliorate high labour turnover and absenteeism by providing an environment that would promote teamwork and a sense of joint production, so reducing the alienation associated with traditional forms of manufacture (Thompson and McHugh 1995).

The importance of understanding the culture that is to be changed is clearly recognised by Volvo. To effect this, factors seen as important to the individuals working in the traditional manufacturing environment (such as lighting, noise, heat, ergonomics, etc.) were addressed. Similarly, developing equipment geared to the needs of the individual was also seen as complementing the democratic, egalitarian nature of the national culture with the creation of an appropriate organisational culture. For example, individually controlled 'auto carriers', on which parts were assembled and transported around the factory, could be tilted and/or rotated by ninety per cent to facilitate work on the underbody and enable adjustment to the height of each individual worker. Workers could also stand on the moving carrier and perform tasks on parts that were in effect standing still relative to him or her. The layout at Kalmar also incorporated buffer stocks that enabled employees to have some degree of 'slack' or control over work pace. In these ways, there was a clear attempt to create a culture in which change not only became important to the organisation but also to individuals *per se* (Galpin *op. cit.*).

Similarly, innovations in building and work design became the basis for the development of a team culture and prospects for job rotation. The focus of the project was efficient production by motivated and capable co-workers who had developed a shared mental model and understanding of the current reality in which they were operating.

The significance of the innovations at Kalmar were that they were management led and driven, with involvement from unions, health and safety advisors, and job design consultants. Gaining wide involvement in the change process recognised the importance of testing opinions and potential areas of resistance prior to their implementation. Nevertheless, whilst changes were well received by workers, efficiency showed no significant improvement compared to other conventional plants, so refinements to the control of the pace of work were made. This indicated that, rather than becoming locked in a single-loop learning experience, managers were prepared to challenge existing norms and revise approaches, thereby demonstrating receptivity for double-loop learning and change. Although Kalmar was recognised as Volvo's 'best-practice' plant in Sweden, management was keen to stress the continuous improvement it anticipated through the development of an organisational culture that promotes innovation, experimentation and learning from mistakes. This is evident from the plurality of production concepts that have been instigated at the other plants in the Group.

Developments at Torslanda

Experimentation with alternative forms of production and work organisation at the Torslanda plant demonstrates the adoption, abandonment or refinement of approaches when necessary. This is indicative of the creation of a culture for change whereby change becomes part of the norm. For example, the use of dock assembly and autonomous work groups to assemble an entire vehicle was instigated, but within six months the approach was abandoned due to poor productivity, resulting from what was believed to be the workforce lacking sufficient skills to make the approach work. The learning and change solutions were to give increased attention to training and development within the company.

The most valuable change at Torslanda is judged by staff to be an increase in the amount and quality of information circulated. People say they are well informed of current developments, targets and performance, etc., which confirms that change is more easily accepted if those involved engage in open and active communication that incorporates genuine consultation. Regular meetings with group leaders assist in this process by passing information from management to the shopfloor and vice versa on a daily basis. The factory manager also speaks personally to all staff who, in turn, are welcome to present their views to her.

Similarly, in terms of the social organisation of production at the Uddevalla, Gent and Born plants, Volvo has clearly attempted to broaden employees' sense of ownership of, and involvement in, the whole task. Similarly, it has sought to develop a wider portfolio of skills in employees and to provide a work environment that is less stressful and more reflective. Through these efforts, a culture has developed in which people accept that change is not a planned linear event but is a process that emerges from learning from experimentation and, sometimes, mistakes.

The development of work organisation within Volvo over a twenty-five year period clearly demonstrates a plurality of production concepts introduced as a result of political, social and economic contexts in which the company has operated over time. They signify periods of interpreting and interacting with the environment, learning and instigating change processes, and learning from change *per se*. What is significant is that Volvo has created a culture and collective memory that regards learning and change as the norm, allowing the company to be experimental in its approach to work organisation. As a result, it has not always been inclined to follow mainstream practices if these were unlikely to be contextually or culturally sensitive. It has also been selective in exploiting practices with potential for further development but discarding those that failed or resulted in mistakes.

Conclusion

It is clear that developing a culture that supports change and risk taking is pivotal to the overall viability of organisations in the automotive sector. Volvo's trajectory over a twenty-five year period displays an organisation that has adopted a long-term, emergent strategy that incorporates radical approaches to production, facilitated by a culture that is accustomed to and comfortable with double-loop learning and change. For the Rover Group, there has been a clear intention to change the culture of the company over the past ten years in order to stimulate learning and facilitate change; the processes have therefore been more urgent and transformative in nature. It is important therefore to consider the fourth generic theme: how the approaches the companies employ impact upon individuals and groups within the organisations, and how people are encouraged to contribute to the learning and change processes.

(4) Promoting individual learning and development

In recognition that learning starts with the individual and the responsibility rests with the organisation to maximise the development of the people employed (Argyris 1957), both the Rover Group and Volvo have placed a premium on this activity. On the assumption that people are naturally learning while working, it is appropriate to examine the systems that have been developed in the organisations to assist in maximising the potential of this learning and how the organisations derive benefit from it.

The Rover Group

Whilst changes to structures and systems commenced in the 'Rover Tomorrow' initiative, effective double-loop learning involves how people think and how they use reasoning to define their actions (Argyris 1991). It was this understanding that formed the framework for the Rover Group's culture change. To encourage this, RLB launched two key products, Rover Employee Assisted Learning (REAL) and Personal Development Files (PDFs), both of which were intended to engender individual commitment to continuous development and double-loop learning.

The Rover Employee Assisted Learning (REAL) programme aimed to assist in the development of skills not necessarily directly connected with the individual's work at Rover. The intention was to promote a 'readiness' for individual learning, described by March and Olsen (1975) (see Figure 2.3 in Chapter 2) as the 'foundation stage'. Here the individual develops the skills needed to learn and experiences success and enhanced self-confidence in the activity. Rover also wanted to indicate to the workforce that responsibility for personal development rested with the individual rather than the organisation (Knowles 1984, Kolb *op. cit.*). By encouraging interest in new skills, it was hoped that people would be more creative and receptive to learning about innovative approaches to improving their performance at Rover, thereby promoting the simultaneous development of people and work. As one employee said, 'if people are given the opportunity to learn something they're interested in, it gives them confidence to try something new at work and that's what change is all about'. With regard to assisting culture change through the learning process, another employee commented 'it's good that Rover are keen to help achieve a few ambitions . . . it makes you think they're interested in the people . . . you're not just a nobody on the shopfloor'.

As management had intended, by 1991 some employees who undertook personal-interest courses opted to follow more academic avenues of study, or areas more closely linked with their work. This is indicative of the 'formation' stage of development (March and Olsen 1975) (see Figure 2.3 in Chapter 2) in which the individual takes responsibility for self-development and independent learning. Despite resource constraints from 1992 onwards, the initiative continues and any activities likely to promote skills useful for the shopfloor, such as leadership and team building, are usually supported by the organisation. This would appear to indicate that the company was responding to the individual development that was occurring within the organisation. Acknowledging that some people may have moved from dependency in their learning to a transitory phase, the company is continuing to provide opportunities to develop teamwork and experiential learning that may promote further learning. The continued commitment also signals the importance of the company's internal learning processes both internally and externally.

Indeed, some shift managers and team leaders confirmed that they took advantage of the REAL scheme and considered that the experiences had assisted in improving their work performance. These had also given them increased confidence in team situations, so they were able to challenge established practices and provide creative solutions for revised approaches to their work. Concerning uptake and impact of REAL in assisting work-related learning, however, a member of RLB expressed the view that there was no real evaluation of how REAL promoted the conversion from recreational learning experiences to academic or work-related study. One manager reported 'there appeared to be no difference between people involved in REAL and those not'. Whilst the REAL initiative is acknowledged to have created a learning environment that assisted in culture change, it would appear that the appropriate systems were not in place for the evaluation of learning interventions.

Traditional approaches to appraisal and performance review in the organisation were considered to be inadequate and, as a result, Personal Development Files (PDFs) were launched. PDFs were designed both to look at past performance and to measure individual learning objectives, matching these with overall business objectives for the coming year. Here, the Rover Group was attempting to link training and development interventions more closely to strategic planning within the organisation (Keep 1992). There would also appear to be recognition that adult receptivity to learning depends on individual interest in solving relevant problems (Knowles 1984). By engaging in this two-way process, it was intended that joint diagnosis of individual learning needs could be effected, while at the same time emphasising personal responsibility for learning and development.

Commitment from line managers is essential for the effective operation of the system and it is unclear how many people were regularly conversing with management on the topic. Interest from managers, team leaders and supervisors, in maintaining their own PDF appeared to be greater than that shown by shopfloor associates. One employee explained 'there's a bigger commitment from the company to training at management level anyway'. A manager considered that learning systems are more difficult to operate at the associate level because 'it's up to them'. This indicates that it is members of the organisation who are responsible for others and who display (or are given the opportunity to display) 'psychological maturity' (Argyris 1957) who are more likely to engage in dialogue with regard to the developmental process. Those who do not may be retained in the infancy stage (Argyris *op. cit.*) as a result of the continuation of 'traditional' approaches to training, development and management. For example, at the Landrover plant it was estimated that only 13 per cent of the distributed PDFs were actively used or 'live' in January 1995. One reason for this was the level of absenteeism; as one shift manager commented, 'releasing people for training at the associate level . . . with an absentee level of 5.3 per cent and only 3 per cent cover, it's pretty difficult to let them go on courses'.

In support of this statement, a cell manager confirmed that RLB was 'a bit remote from the action' in how far it understood organisational and shopfloor needs and that RLB was only one aspect of the opportunities available to employees within the Rover Group. He went on to stress that the Employee Development Centres (EDCs) in training and development departments at each site played an important role too. Open-learning facilities were available to all associates and it was claimed that these could usefully be extended to include a wider range of learning materials. In addition, subsidised college courses provided by external bodies were available for those who were interested in developing work-related skills. These, he confirmed, 'had no direct association with RLB in the minds of associates'. A criticism from an RLB employee, however, was that RLB had been effective in 'teaching Rover how to learn but not in enabling it to identify the specifics it needs to learn about'. He went on to suggest

> there is always a learning climate in organisations – the non-learning organisation/individual doesn't exist – the issue is how the best use of people is made by spreading learning throughout the organisation.

On the future direction of the organisation, he commented 'the problem is getting people to have confidence to do it and to get in touch. People would make more use of the opportunities if there were more time to release people. You can never stop learning – you're only hindered by lack of time and other resources.'

This would suggest a paradoxical situation that the organisations examined in the automotive sector encounter: whilst employees are now seen as assets to the organisation and worthy of investment and development, there is still the constant drive for cost reduction and productivity. Balancing the two factors through an imaginative approach to developing people would therefore appear to be a challenge that contemporary organisations must meet. In support of this, a manager stated that there is a continuing need 'to train producers to solve problems'. He continued, 'we also need to address the wider issue of mobility of labour and the transference of people from non-productive to productive work. . . . there is still the need to equip people with broader skills on a company-wide basis'. This suggests that systems and procedures that assist in learning from the consequences of actions and decisions have not been fully developed in the organisation, preventing people from maximising the learning opportunities available in the workplace.

An example is the use of the Group Learning Exchange Network (GLEN), which in the opinion of a member of RLB, has seen limited involvement of employees. However, the quality of information it could provide depended entirely upon employee commitment and enthusiasm to input data. The system would require a profound culture change to keep it up-dated and useful to the Group. It was thought that, in addition to GLEN, other sources of best practice were derived from the quality strategy within the Group and these could be shared more spontaneously through informal communication channels.

This confirms that imposed change involving the introduction of technology is unlikely to prove successful in terms of encouraging learning if the people involved do not understand the rationale for its implementation and/or have not been involved in the decision to adopt the system. Indeed, Martin (1988 cited in Scarborough and Corbett 1992) suggests that user participation in or exclusion from the technology process is likely significantly to impact upon its development within the organisation. In support of these views, interviews confirmed that few associates had tested the capability of GLEN. One manager felt it might be 'useful . . . perhaps I might use it for dealing with absence, sickness, Health and Safety, looking at what Nissan and JCB are doing?' He commented:

Much more information is gained from informal discussion during breaks and work-time, anyway. We've gone over to McDonald's or the pub to get away from the place and we come back with ideas about how to improve things . . . it just happens that way, sometimes. You can't make it too formal otherwise it gets to be expected by managers.

This would indicate that not enough attention has been paid to communicating the reason for the use of GLEN, with employees developing little understanding of the benefits it may offer. As Wilson (1992) suggests, the key to understanding change is individual cognition and interpretation, and if this is not recognised by management the tension between learning and control becomes apparent.

In 1995, employees in the Rover Group reckoned the company was moving through a transitional stage. There was still the need to create a real feeling that employees had two jobs – the one they are paid to do and the additional one of assessing how they can improve it by learning and development. This suggests that the culture change instigated by the Rover Group in the late 1980s was far from complete. As may be expected, profound change of this nature is likely to take considerable time, reinforcement and 'unlearning' of former behaviours if people are not to regress to old patterns (Nystrom and Starbuck 1984, Schein 1993). This requires nurturing an understanding of learning and change as integrated and reciprocally connected processes.

In view of RLB's objectives for Phase 3 (1994–1996), it was observed by a manager that some employees within RLB were influenced by contemporary management theorists on promoting individual learning and development. It was not clear how far the ideas were understood in RLB as a whole and, therefore, how effectively theoretical perspectives could be linked to the practical application. One manager asked 'they are just words but do they know what they mean?' He added that key issues for future consideration were assisting in developing learning processes for individuals and encouraging them onto 'the learning ladder'. On the development of a learning organisation, he commented:

I have difficulty with the learning organisation concept . . . it's difficult to define, it depends on what emphasis is placed upon it. Also the moral issues . . . who has the right to decide what people learn and how they do it? . . . helping people might destroy them in the end?

Conclusion

The creation of RLB was a clear indication of Rover's commitment to culture change. Over time, it acted as a catalyst to develop and reinforce the changes that were occurring in work practices and employment relationships. However, its existence created its own problems, which were exacerbated by the development of the business units as a whole. Besides, those who had embraced the changes appear to have found the existence of RLB unnecessary and unjustifiable. RLB's viability therefore began to be questioned so that by 1996, when confronted by a number of issues it was considered prudent to dissolve the company.

Individual learning and development at Volvo

Volvo's initiatives to develop individual learning have not been afforded high-profile documentation as in the case of the Rover Group. Nevertheless, whilst attention has been paid to the introduction of innovative production techniques, these require individuals who are skilled in maximising the potential of the systems in place. When it became clear to Volvo management at Torslanda in 1986 that some of the new production systems were failing to deliver increased levels of productivity, management instigated major changes that continue to be revised. Unions were involved from the outset with the intention of radically transforming the process of vehicle assembly. To achieve this, emphasis was placed on continuous training to develop workers' skills in effective teamwork and problem solving, together with the improvement of quality of working life within the plant. Communication between managers and employees was increased to encourage awareness of the specific learning needs that the external environment demanded from those employed in the organisation. These approaches clearly mirror Knowles' (1984) findings that adult learners benefit from active problem solving; they will learn if provoked by real-life events, and they will learn a skill that they can apply pragmatically to their immediate circumstances.

This would seem to demonstrate that Volvo, after the instigation of new forms of production processes in the manufacturing environment, was becoming concerned with 'mentofacture' or 'creation using the mind' (Burgoyne 1995a) and its capacity for double-loop learning and change. As a result, the critical means of production began to shift towards employees, giving them increased control over the pace of work and the ability to make continuous improvements to work tasks. For example, since 1986 the workforce has increased at the Torslanda plant and potential recruits must possess 'a good college education and demonstrate an ability to work well within a group environment' (a Volvo manager). Employees who are enthusiastic to increase their job-related skills are offered time-off with or without pay for further learning and development. Management judges the recruitment and retention rate for employees to be high, with absenteeism and staff turnover both low at only one per cent.

Whilst this may be attributed to current labour market and economic conditions (Karlsson 1996), work conditions (communication, production systems, culture, etc.) may also be interpreted by individuals as encouraging involvement and development. This may play a major part in attracting and retaining people, together with promoting receptivity for change. Moreover, change has been accepted as an established cultural pattern in Volvo over a twenty-five year period (Berggren 1992). This confirms Wilson's (1992) assertion that the extent to which changes conform to established change patterns in the operating environment will determine how it is helped or hindered in the organisation.

In the development of individual skills, Volvo has focused essentially on strategically integrating those that are work-related and likely to assist the long-term survival of the organisation. There are indications that the approach to individual development is pragmatic and driven by solving performance problems through multi-skilling and dialogue. The intention to multi-skill sits within the framework outlined by Ashton and Felstead (1995) insofar as Volvo see new production systems as increasing the complexity of work tasks and team inter-action. Therefore greater discretion and development must be offered to the individual in the workplace to address their learning needs. This is in tune with the views of Kolb *et al.* (1994), who suggest that adults learn best in situations where they are recognised as experts and equals – they need to teach as well as learn. This approach is reflected in the continuing introduction of robotics to remove what a manager described as 'the dirty, boring, monotonous, repetitive work from the equation, leaving the skilled and interesting work for the people to undertake'.

Whilst there is still some resistance by the Metal Workers' Union who wish to protect traditional demarcations, this has significantly declined since 1991. There is now recognition that multi-skilling and job rotation – some jobs are rotated every hour in some parts of the Torslanda plant – are neither a threat to individuals nor unions. Employees feel that their jobs are 'as secure as they can be within such a competitive sector'. Another commented 'it's good to see the plant recruiting for the production of the new model C70 [launched in August 1997] because it makes us feel that much safer.'

Conclusion

The automotive sector is a competitive and changing environment and organis-ations operating within it increasingly rely upon individuals who are motivated, flexible and capable of generating their own solutions to work problems. The Rover Group had to contend with a history of poor industrial relations, inferior product quality and reduced sales as a result of aggressive competition from Japanese producers. It commenced a profound culture change that had as its central focus the intention to become a 'learning organisation'. Volvo's approach to contending with a similar task but in a contextually unique environment was to embark upon a series of revolutionary changes in production systems that afforded an improved quality of working life for its employees.

Both the Rover Group and Volvo are attempting to equip people with the necessary skills and abilities to function effectively in this environment by offering development opportunities that reflect the importance to adults of the self-directed nature of the learning process. In the Rover Group there are clear indications that such approaches are enabling the organisation to move into a transitional phase (see Figure 2.3 in Chapter 2), with individuals prepared to take an increasing role in identifying and addressing their own development needs. In Volvo, approaches are well established and strategically integrated with organis-ational culture and systems. The emphasis is on process, whereby individuals are placed in an environment that encourages them to learn how to learn (double-loop learning) rather than just on skills and knowledge acquisition and application.

It is clear there are difficulties in isolating the crucial factors that contribute to an organisation's ability to remain effective and competitive in advanced industrial economies. Change remains a constant challenge which organisations in the automotive sector will continue to face. Both the Rover Group and Volvo have chosen to approach this challenge from a learning perspective that is directed not only at individual and organisational levels but also beyond the boundaries of the companies. As manufacturers and assemblers, they maintain positions of relative safety when compared to their component suppliers; to this extent, they are able to create their own environments by working closely with them, usually determining the terms on which the relationship is conducted. The discussion and analysis will now focus on the research findings from Creative Engineering and XZZ Components, two organisations operating as suppliers in the automotive sector, in order to explore their approaches to learning and change at the levels identified.

8 Discussion and analysis

Creative Engineering and XZZ Components

Summary

This chapter looks at the findings in the case studies of the two component suppliers in the automotive sector, Creative Engineering and XZZ Components, both of which supply to manufacturers such as the Rover Group, Ford, Nissan, Honda and Toyota. The destiny of those involved on the supplier side of the automotive sector is inextricably linked to, and largely determined by, their ability to meet the exacting standards of the manufacturers in quality, cost and delivery (Bratton 1992, Womack *et al.* 1990). Survival is dependent upon gaining a deep understanding of this environment; otherwise the manufacturers' choice of supplier can be changed. Given that change is a constant process in this sector, with 'best practice' often diffused between manufacturer and supplier, the approaches the supplier organisations adopt in order to capture the potential that such learning opportunities offer need to be examined.

The performance of the supplier side of this industrial sector has been a topic of much debate in recent years, 'with two reports in 1993 showing the European industry to be trailing its international counterparts' (Oliver *et al.* 1996: 85). Notwithstanding such concern, research undertaken in Creative Engineering and XZZ Components would appear to demonstrate that new work practices and systems that incorporate the 'lean' production approaches identified in Chapter six have resulted in improved levels of productivity and quality. For such change interventions to result in improved performance suggests that double-loop learning should be evident at individual and organisational levels. This expectation will be explored using the four themes identified in Chapter six: the performance of the organisations in monitoring and communicating environmental change; the promotion of emergent strategy-making and teamwork; the development of cultures that support these approaches; and the development and involvement of the individual to facilitate emergent strategy.

(1) **Monitoring and communicating environmental change**

Creative Engineering's approach

Creative Engineering is an example of an organisation that has placed considerable emphasis on scanning its environment. By monitoring changes and anticipating trends, it has been able to develop a competitive edge when faced with significant challenges and crises. At the same time, the company ensured that people in the organisation were developed to maximise the potential of new change in the form of systems and processes. In this way, Creative demonstrates an extensive and systemic understanding of the business environment in which it operates; it believes it can, to a large extent, identify the external drivers for change and can diagnose internal, cross-functional capability to respond in a systemic way (McCalman and Paton 1992).

Creative's ability to learn from its environment stems from the prevalent understanding in the company's senior management team that the automobile industry is at the leading edge of manufacturing initiatives. To maintain this position, it must innovate and strive for continuous improvement in performance. Indeed, throughout its history the company has been characterised by periods of evolution and crises over its future viability, and has therefore had to undergo profound change in order to survive. On occasions, as Morgan (1986) suggests can happen, this has meant completely changing the environment in which it operates. Learning from the experiences of these events, Creative has developed a proactive approach towards change to ensure its long-term survival. This has involved deliberately increasing the importance and intensity of individual and organisational learning interventions in periods of crisis and change.

Since the 1980s, Creative has constantly looked outside its own boundaries to monitor developments and changes in its operating environment. Senior management selected the automotive sector as the main focus of strategic direction. There was a clear understanding on their part that survival was dependent upon the company's rate of learning being equal to or greater than the rate of change in the environment, as identified by Revans (1982). Given that the greatest impetus for change at this time was the impact and influence of Japanese producers and the associated 'lean' production systems, Creative knew that its own systems and output must match or exceed its competitors. Over time, this challenge has enabled Creative to set itself two clear objectives: to exceed the performance of other suppliers, and to become the sole supplier of the components produced.

Accordingly, at director level all key members of the board have examined best practice in Japan, America, Germany and the United Kingdom, and have undertaken regular benchmarking exercises to increase their understanding of developments in the global automotive sector. Acting as 'learning agents' for the organisation, the directors have translated their reading of the environment into strategic approaches that have been experimental when necessary, whilst at the same time attempting to institutionalise innovation (Clegg *et al.* 1996) throughout the organisation. This external focus extends to Creative's major customers and suppliers, with the cultivation of close relationships that encourage sharing best practice. There is daily contact between Creative product group managers and their customers, particularly with regard to new product development. A manager on the Nissan product group commented:

> We have a positive relationship . . . the links are open and strong. Our supervisors visit monthly in order to understand their business and they come back with more understanding and knowledge which generates a greater effort to improve.

This demonstrates efforts to achieve the effective integration of sub-systems through the encouragement of 'boundary-spanning' that facilitates shared information and understanding.

In addition, Creative works closely with its own suppliers and is enthusiastic to learn from them, acknowledging that some are more innovative in changes to work practices than Creative itself. One, for example, is 'trialing' self-managing teams and it is hoped to benchmark from them in the future. The main concern is clearly to develop work systems that will allow greater stability and control of the environment in which the company operate. As one manager commented, 'the key will be when suppliers can choose who they supply to – we'll be looking at preferred customer status then, and maybe we can have more control'.

Creative is also involved in joint-industry projects with higher education and the Department of Trade and Industry, in connection with 'best-practice' approaches to cell manufacturing and *kaizen*, etc. One manager, however, remarked:

> They're good for cross-fertilisation of ideas but Creative is ahead in the field in many areas – robotics for example – we've got the most [robots] in Europe so there's not much training and development that's relevant – we're so far ahead of the rest at the moment.

This does not indicate complacency within Creative. The external focus is judged to be vital, so the organisation consistently anticipates and monitors changes in its operating environment. In 1997 for example, Creative Engineering and a United States company announced that they would build a world-class automotive chassis component plant in the United States. This serves to demonstrate the company's commitment to the support of the globalisation of the component industry and the needs of customers. By sharing the experiences of other organisations through such collaboration, it is anticipated that Creative can provide a combination of skills training and development, individual awareness and change interventions that will ensure that the organisation continues to understand and shape the environment in which it operates.

XZZ Components' approach

Like Creative, XZZ Components attempted to develop a good understanding of the external environment in which it operates following a series of crises in its development. As a traditional hierarchical organisation, the crises provoked by changes in the external environment were all the more significant and necessitated a transformation in approach at all levels in the company to encourage double-loop learning. By reflecting upon the experiences of these events and learning from them, XZZ Components has also developed a proactive approach to change. This recognises that not only is survival dependent on swift adaptation to a changing environment but also that the environment can be shaped by the organisation.

Strong links with the University of Central England have been established for the transference of academic and vocational learning, and close contact with the institution's liaison officer is maintained to monitor the performance of XZZ Components employees who have undertaken programmes of study. This shows the company's acknowledgement that new production approaches (such as team-work and quality systems) require an educated and socially skilled workforce if their potential is to be maximised (Thompson and Davidson 1995). An example is the graduate intake scheme, which is said to be 'difficult to get on'. Recruits embark upon a two-year project that might take them all over the world before they take a position on the first level of management. Mentors observe their progress throughout the process. This is again indicative of the company's commitment to acquiring information from its external environment in order to widen the scope of its learning beyond that of its immediate operating context.

To learn from the immediate operating environment and to develop close co-operation with customers, inter-departmental business units have been established within the organisation, comprising representatives from production, quality, engineering and sales. Each of the main customers was assigned to a unit with a view to increasing collaboration in the development of new models. This indicates that XZZ Components was implementing a proactive approach by learning from the immediate operating environment in order to reduce uncertainty.

Despite such interventions, the crisis of recalled parts for Nissan in 1992 (when it was stated that more than ten per cent of product output for the Micra had to be scrapped or re-worked before leaving the factory) provoked a further round of double-loop learning and change. The company was forced to re-examine its approach in the light of more fundamental realignments of systems and procedures than those previously undertaken, and it looked to Nissan to assist in the change process. The managing director reported that by developing close con-tact with its customers, XZZ Components became more familiar with Japanese manufacturing techniques, which then contributed substantially to the company's turnaround.

As a result, XZZ Components has now achieved close relationships with all its customers (Toyota, Nissan, Ford, Rover, Honda) and management claim that, as one of its first-tier suppliers, it has developed good working partnerships to exchange best practices. The company is scanning the external environment to understand system linkages and to reduce any unforeseen potential impacts on the organisation. For example, an XZZ engineer is permanently resident at the Nissan plant in Sunderland to ensure components meet required standards and to heighten customer confidence.

Developing this approach, XZZ now sees the onus as being on itself to promote such techniques with its own suppliers and customers. For example, XZZ's 'concern room' (in which solutions to production problems are explored) has been observed by representatives from Nissan with a view to its adoption by the company. This illustrates efforts to widen the scope and transference of its organisational learning capacity through the development of co-operative approaches that encourage collective learning from experience. On further learning and development interventions within the organisation, a manager commented that 'we need to consider developing a greater awareness of the external environment in the minds of people on the shopfloor so that the future does not seem frightening'. This external awareness is being developed through increased levels of upward and downward communication. Moreover, management is aware that access to knowledge is likely to encourage people to become life-long learners and so more able to tolerate change.

Conclusion

XZZ Components has sought to re-define organisational relationships and boundaries in order to encourage a multi-dimensional approach to change, so that perceived environmental instability can be reduced through learning and dialogue. In this way, the organisation is attempting to achieve a degree of control over its own environment by placing itself where it can identify environmental and market change quickly and opportunistically, and employees can translate this information into action. Whilst this understanding of the environment was initially perceived as a senior-management responsibility, there is increasing need in both XZZ Components and Creative Engineering for wider involvement in the process so that strategy emerges from bottom-up activity. How effectively this is achieved by both organisations may be determined largely by internal structures, systems and processes that afford individuals and teams the opportunity to challenge existing operating norms in the light of new information and change. The discussion will therefore continue with an examination of how far double-loop learning to encourage emergent strategic direction is promoted at the group and individual level.

(2) Emergent strategy and teamwork

When confronted by crises which threatened their existence, managers and directors in both XZZ Components and Creative Engineering were, in effect, forced to re-invent their organisations in order to survive. This involved establishing a strategic direction that has allowed them not only to regain their competitive position, but also to be awarded first-tier, preferred supplier status by industry partners. This seems to have been achieved by wider involvement in the planning process, by learning from the operating environment and stakeholders, and by the development of work systems that depend on the contribution of the team.

Creative's approach

Creative has sought to encourage a participative, emergent focus to planning through the development of approaches to work organisation that promote teamwork and dialogue amongst employees. Management claims this encourages the development of double-loop learning and change because people are placed in an environment in which the status quo can be challenged. The change to cellular manufacturing is said to have heightened the sense of belonging to specific teams in the organisation, together with generating an increased customer focus – the Ford team, the Rover cell, etc. According to a cell supervisor, 'cellular manufacturing is easier because it's tightly controlled but the control comes from the capability of the cell itself . . . people are only tools feeding the machines at the correct rate'.

He went on to suggest that the cell was 'driven by the customer and controlled by tightly scheduled deliveries'. The cellular approach also creates a sense of competition which, according to one production manager, 'is sometimes good and sometimes damaging'. Initially, training for new recruits occurs on the job within the cell. A product group manager stated:

> there has been a deliberate attempt to maintain a good team atmosphere throughout the period of expansion. This is helped by good communications and keeping team sizes down. We try to promote positive attitudes and turn people around to our way of thinking – that is, to adapt to change and be willing to learn – the two go hand in hand.

Suggestions or ideas for improvements are actively encouraged by managers who 'create an environment where people can speak freely about their ideas', but no rewards are offered. A director commented:

> We're against formal suggestion schemes because we want it to be an everyday part of the job to improve. We don't believe it's part of the culture if people are paid to come up with ideas . . . there are few really successful schemes of this type anyway.

Each cell has a facilitator for continuous improvement and a 'concern sheet' system is operated whereby improvements are highlighted by members. There is usually a quick response to the implementation of suggestions. However, some people suggested that the system is essentially 'related to the calibre of the supervisor . . . the more traditional ones may not act upon suggestions anyway . . . it is evolving though . . . but people are wary of forms and prefer it to be more spontaneous'.

To increase their skills and knowledge of such processes, supervisors are offered formal training programmes through college courses leading to National Examinations Board for Supervisory Management (NEBSM) and/or open learning opportunities, focusing on team-leading and coaching skills, etc. Within the framework of *kaizen*, the company is keen to promote training as being the responsibility of supervisors, to make it more spontaneous and to encourage 'enablement' rather than 'empowerment'. One manager stated that although not all supervisors are ready for this yet, 'ideas for improvement are always encouraged – what operators themselves can change even in a very small way means continuous development for people as well as continuous improvement for Creative'.

A cell manager confirmed that *kaizen* depends upon excellent supervision, and needs to be driven by supervisors if it is to succeed. In his opinion, it is the development of teamwork that closes the adversarial gap between managers and workers because the focus shifts to common ownership, productivity and profitability. The establishment of a Joint Consultative Group with representatives from management and shopfloor is also said to have significantly contributed towards aligning traditionally rival interest groups.

To increase and enhance the communication flows in Creative, an identified barrier was that of the traditional approach to wage bargaining. In the opinion of a director, 'although the role of union and shop steward had virtually disappeared with more direct communication and teamwork, wage bargaining was always a problem'. This was addressed with the establishment of the Joint Consultative Group, whose shopfloor members are elected by their peers. The Group is informed of and can discuss any anticipated changes and business developments on a monthly basis. The result of this opportunity for regular dialogue has been very positive, a manager suggested:

> it's the workers who are now dictating the pace of change . . . perhaps they are convinced that managers mean what they say? We are highly committed to training and development. We could be a learning organisation but we're not yet world class as far as quality, costs and delivery are concerned. So we've got to be careful – there's still quite a strong control needed so that we can address these issues.

In agreement, a cell manager said 'everyone has to think the same way . . . procedures have to be embedded as a way of life . . . the essence is control'.

Control in this context applies not only to individuals within Creative but to all other resources involved in the production processes. In a global environment where excellent levels of quality and performance are rapidly becoming the norm, organisations such as Creative must actively seek ways they can both reduce costs and differentiate themselves from the competition. There has been a concerted attempt by the company to explore contemporary best practice and then to adapt, modify and improve these processes to fit the people and the organisation so that ownership is created. One such example is the Creative approach to total productive maintenance (TPM).

Total Productive Maintenance (TPM)

TPM obviates the need for specialised maintenance staff (indirect workers) and transfers responsibility to operators (direct workers). The approach encourages preventative, autonomous maintenance, with faults identified by operators so that 'small losses are rectified in order to achieve the maintained "completeness" of the production process' (a cell manager). He observed 'it is the small, chronic losses that are more important than the sporadic ones. So you make sure that cleaning becomes checking.'

Operators are also focused to eliminate, rather than rectify, what are termed the six big losses: breakdown; set-up and adjustment; idling and minor stoppages; reduced speed; reduced yield; and defects in process and rework. According to a member of the training department, 'TPM's purpose is to increase operator skills and knowledge levels, to assist in culture change, and to establish cultural norms with new recruits'. A cell manager confirmed that he had seen how TPM training in Creative had helped people in creating interest in their work so that attitude and performance in terms of quality, cost and delivery were improved. He went on to argue that:

> There's not really any resistance to training . . . it's more change itself that people don't like. Sometimes they don't really understand the urgency for change. It's only the long-standing employees though, and when the aims are explained, then their resistance usually crumbles anyway.

Creative has developed extensive communication systems to ensure that the aims of TPM are fully understood by employees and that 'management connects with the shopfloor' (a director). This involves first a monthly core brief from senior level; a supervisor will then give a local brief that involves more depth and detail relating to systems and procedures; and finally there are frequent reinforcements of messages and aims by the training department who maintain a high profile within the company. A member of the training department claimed:

> TPM has had a direct influence on the culture of the company in terms of influencing change and reducing the productivity gap with world-class companies – it was developed by Creative for Creative and that's why it's been so well accepted so far.

A full-time instructor is employed to deliver the training and he reported that his role involves assisting 'an educative change process'. All operators are involved and are given five days 'off the job' for receiving training; Creative 'covers' by bringing in people on short-term contracts. Training is essentially geared to the requirements of specific cells, although some parts of the programme are generic. There are thirty-three modules to pass in becoming competent to complete them on the shopfloor, but re-tests are offered until competency is reached. According to one operator:

> TPM enables people to do a variety of tasks, it encourages problem solving and it makes work more interesting and challenging. It makes you feel that maybe you're increasing your job security too – nothing's forever any more but in Creative, maybe we're closer at looking at things in the long term than a lot of other organisations can be.

Creative's plans for the future expansion of the TPM process involve multi-skilling fitters to take on electrical work as well as robotic programmes. Despite some long-standing employees voicing their concerns over the threat to their skills and jobs, it is anticipated that in two years time, all apprentices will be multi-skilled and 'those employees, old or new, that aren't will leave' (a production manager).

XZZ Components' approach

XZZ Components' strategic initiative in response to loss of market share initially focused on the introduction of new technology to 'legitimise' proposed changes that would assist the company's bid for survival (Scarborough and Corbett 1992). From 1989 the strategy involved the selection of forty people from the shopfloor to be trained in the use of computer-aided machinery. This approach has since been criticised by members of the shopfloor, one of whom stated:

> People were brainwashed into believing they were going to be the 'elite'. They wore different overalls and worked in a special area called 'the slab'. They were the hand-picked ones and it generated a lot of resentment from the rest of the workforce.

This statement indicates that the approach resulted in feelings of fear among those excluded from the change intervention due to perceptions of loss of control of old, established systems and procedures (Scarborough and Corbett *op. cit.*). New technology has, however, been fully integrated into the production processes. Most staff are familiar with its use. A group leader who has worked for the company for nineteen years and who was one of the forty selected to introduce the new processes, commented:

> It was sold as being the future of XZZ. To stay in business we needed to adopt new ideas and approaches. Once people realised their jobs were safe they welcomed it. We were given a lot of information so I saw it as a good career move.

As the investment in new technology grew it became clear that more people were required to be trained in its use and were able to achieve the same standards of performance. This would suggest that change of this nature is a lengthy process that needs to be reinforced over time by an educational approach (Hendry 1995).

A further strategic initiative is the establishment of cellular manufacturing together with Targets for Operational Performance (TOPS), which set annual targets that the workforce should strive to achieve in the work group environment. They are not financial targets as such, but are linked to individual and group performance of the workforce. They include customer satisfaction, scrap, costs, energy, process capability, overtime, accidents and attendance; each target is set and monitored by the team.

The development of teamwork in XZZ Components provides a further platform for participative and emergent strategy formulation. Commentators (Anderson *et al.* 1994, Brown and Duguid 1991, Hendry *op. cit.*, Stacey 1996) suggest that the use of the team for stabilising and reinforcing change interventions will gather momentum as organisations adapt their structures in this way. Creating environments that promote group learning through dialogue and socialisation provides opportunities for participative planning approaches to emerge and is likely to become a rich source of research for the future.

In this context, employees are empowered to make decisions and to solve problems associated with their work tasks. The learning interventions, identified earlier in the chapter, seek to equip the individual and team so that they can perform effectively in such an environment. The managing director observed:

> Teams can change the standards with agreement with their managers but it's important that empowerment is disciplined and not just an excuse for management avoiding the responsibility they should take themselves. I suppose you could say that what we operate here is 'tramline' empowerment – clear boundaries are defined.

This confirms the claims of theorists that empowerment does not always involve any significant sharing of power or authority (Coopey 1996, Cunningham *et al.* 1995). The level of management and self-control is clearly defined in the perception of the individuals working within the cell. An operator of twenty-eight years' experience remarked:

> Cells work with the right people in them . . . it depends on their attitude. I don't think peer pressure works because people won't use it . . . they'll complain but they will always remain loyal to their co-workers and 'carry' them sometimes. I'm motivated by managers who lead by example but this isn't always done.

This is an indicator of the depth of culture change that has occurred within the organisation so far. Re-defined control mechanisms are recognised but at the same time there is an understanding that new work regimes remain subject to achieving a balance of control and consent between managers and employees.

Conclusion

From the discussion, it would appear that a number of common themes emerge that have been addressed by Creative Engineering and XZZ Components. First, both companies have achieved a substantial shift towards the development of people and the strategic integration of approaches to human resource management. Second, whilst the learning organisation as a concept does not receive a high profile in the organisations, it is deemed worth attaining by seeking to provide an environment where it becomes a possibility. To achieve this in any organisation, it would appear necessary to remove the real and imagined cultural barriers that prevent a meaningful investment in development. This must be an ongoing process at all levels of the organisation. As a member of the human resource team at XZZ Components observed:

> There is a need to move development to a strategic level in organisations because then it becomes a very powerful tool. If it's under-represented at board level then its strategic potential is undervalued. XZZ is not typical . . . development is represented directly into the Board and is fully supported by all.

Third, the emphasis on new work structures established through teamwork encourages dialogue and creativity by placing people in re-defined organisational contexts that impose a new employment relationship upon them. Whilst this appears to offer empowerment to individuals and teams, the reality is that management control remains intact but on a revised basis, under the display of the 'softer' side of human resource management approaches (Legge 1995, Storey 1992). Nevertheless, whilst people working within the organisations are aware of this, they are ready to commit themselves to the new approaches in return for improved work conditions and the likelihood of increased job security if they continually up-date their skills and are prepared to learn and change.

As a result of these changes, both XZZ Components and Creative Engineering have achieved a turnaround in the performance and effectiveness of their organisations. The culture change that has occurred is a third theme for discussion here. In both companies, it can be attributed to the commitment of both management and workers to re-invent and re-establish the companies in a highly competitive global environment.

(3) Creating cultures that challenge

Both Creative and XZZ Components are examples of organisations that were characterised by traditional approaches to work structures and organisation. They incorporated bureaucratic regimes, hierarchical structures and approaches to managing people that ensured that they were the passive recipients of organisational training and change interventions. The environmental turbulence that both companies encountered throughout the 1970s and 1980s meant the measures they had to undertake to survive were profound; they involved not just change but complete transformation of systems and processes, in tandem with gaining the commitment of employees to make these changes work.

Acknowledging that such change was necessary was the first stage in the long and continuing process of double-loop learning the organisations embarked upon. How they approached this task focused on the development of systems that allow established norms to be challenged, hence enabling double-loop learning to occur. At an organisational level, developing a culture that promotes questioning and challenging established norms and practices would appear to be fundamental to success. At the individual level, this involves equipping people with the skills, knowledge, ability and confidence to question and challenge the status quo. On this basis, the approaches of the two companies to promoting a culture for learning and change, and how the individual is developed to cope, will now be explored.

Creative Engineering's approach

As a result of the series of crises that Creative had to contend with in the past, people within the organisation now regard change as part of the culture. Notwithstanding this, they are also aware that the change that the company has experienced since 1990 is slow and incomplete, confirming that it is essentially a cultural and cognitive phenomena that management must understand if change is to succeed (Johnson cited in Mabey and Mayon-White 1993). Management in Creative is aware of the potential to innovate and to learn in the organisation, and accept that success in a dynamic environment is achieved through the consent of the people. For these reasons, Creative has invested substantially in developing communication, training and learning interventions that seek to translate the forces of the external environment into internal levers for change (Clarke 1994, Dawson 1994). This has been achieved through production systems and processes that attempt to create a work environment in which people feel motivated, receptive to continuous improvement and change. According to one manager:

> Creative has good managers who are committed, well-developed and believe in what the company is doing. But there always has to be something substantial behind training. People have to know why, where will it take them and the organisation.

This comment reflects the approach that has been undertaken in Creative to developing a culture for change. Key players in the organisation have been instrumental in ensuring people understand the momentum for change and what will be involved in the process. They have done this by increasing two-way communication channels, creating flatter organisational structures in the form of cellular groups that do not obstruct the process of double-loop learning, and developing a customer-oriented approach. Internal barriers have been removed and managers appear to have developed an understanding of the emotional and intellectual processes that dictate whether change is accepted or resisted.

Similarly, by managing other tangible elements of organisational culture, such as the physical environment and recruitment and selection, change may be implemented and sustained more effectively (Galpin *op. cit.*). For example, Creative is aware that it is becoming more important to recruit the 'right' people for the organisation, that is, those who are capable of working effectively in the systems and who will be sufficiently interested in improving them. This implies that people are selected solely on the basis of their potential ability to fit the organisation's culture, rather than on skills and knowledge possessed. As a product manager indicated:

> Selection techniques are better, the interview is more in-depth now. We give people a clearer picture of how nasty it can all be because of customer demands. It puts pressure on people to do overtime and to put forward ideas – the conditions aren't brilliant – freezing in the winter and boiling hot in summer. But it's better than it was.

Most significant has been the introduction of cellular manufacturing and team-work, together with a system of total productive maintenance (TPM). The aim is to reduce the ratio of direct to indirect employees – Creative had 200 indirects in 1996 and reckons it needs to reduce this to 50 by developing multi-skilling approaches and reducing or eliminating such recruitment in the future. The company does not provide traditional job descriptions because, as one production manager remarked, 'we'd be continually having to up-date them – the jobs change so fast – but people know their main accountabilities'. This recognises the need for heightened levels of flexibility and a participative approach to the diagnosis of business problems in the management of change.

Over time, Creative has gained a local reputation as an employer with potential for growth and expansion in the future, together with a commitment to an investment in training and developing people. Internally, it can be argued that the company has succeeded in creating what Senge (*op. cit.*) describes as a source of meanings and superordinate goals for its employees, by placing people in a new organisational context that imposes new roles, relationships and responsibilities upon them. This has encouraged new attitudes and behaviours to develop that have been instrumental in promoting and sustaining change. The company has embarked upon a culture change that has enabled new values and beliefs to emerge and become accepted.

XZZ Components' approach

Technology and work systems were the primary vehicles for promoting change at XZZ Components until 1994, when managers realised that these alone were insufficient to secure employee commitment. As a result, 'Partnership for Change' was launched, requiring a profound culture change and including the development of team work, increased communication systems and participative management approaches. Since then, those interviewed report there has been a substantial improvement in relationships between management and the shopfloor, despite a number of setbacks. A member of the human resource team suggested:

> The culture change that the company has been instigating has only gained momentum in the past three years when it became clear to long-standing managers and employees that autocratic behaviour was just not going to be rewarded anymore.

This indicates that culture involves the accumulation of prior learning based on prior success. Unless and until people understand the need for change, the tendency is to repeat or regress to former behaviours until it becomes clear that these are dysfunctional to the individual and the organisation (Schein 1993). Nevertheless, despite attempts to increase involvement and participation, controls over the workforce remain tight, in the opinion of some shopfloor staff. An operator who has worked for XZZ Components for eighteen years commented: 'you always have to have a manager but people do tend to make more decisions about their work now. The barriers have been broken but there's always a bit of doubt about how far you can trust them [managers].'

Some employees consider that cellular manufacture and the unremitting pace of 'just-in-time' demand that this is so, confirming the views of commentators who suggest that lean production systems decentralise tactical responsibility but result in increased centralised control mechanisms and work intensification (Sewell and Wilkinson 1992b, Thompson and Davidson 1996). In connection with the new employment relationship and culture XZZ Components are seeking to create, a fitter of thirty years experience agreed:

> There has to be a division between workers and managers. Workers feel uncomfortable and lose respect for managers if there isn't. The approach is different though – it's 'arm around' rather than bullying now, but it's still all about scare tactics.

So despite a less confrontational stance, it seems that the approach to the employment relationship is still perceived as dominated by management control mechanisms, but that the control is inner, focusing on loyalty, beliefs and values, rather than outer and dictated by rules and regulations (Burgoyne 1995a, Legge *op. cit.*). 'Scare tactics' tended to focus on the continuing circulation of information regarding the competition in the environment and perceptions of job security. Again, this is indicative of the simultaneous increase in workers' knowledge and management control that intensifies the insecurity of those in subordinate positions (Jermier *et al.* 1994). Wilson (1992) however, suggests that learning and change are precipitated by making impending crises real to everyone in the organisation. Indeed, throughout the company, the over-riding feeling was that no worker in the automotive sector was safe anymore, but if people were responsive to change they were more likely to safeguard their jobs than if they were not.

Notwithstanding these observations, shopfloor staff agreed that the most significant changes that had occurred were beneficial and focused on improved work conditions (housekeeping, safety, etc.), better communication, job security, equality of pay, quality of products manufactured, and training opportunities for the individual. This indicates that XZZ Components, like Creative, has made efforts to manage the tangible aspects of culture to promote and sustain culture change.

Conclusion

Despite the clear turnaround of both organisations, it would appear that attempts to change culture are slow and often problematic processes. Creative Engineering has managed the change process by the development of people through the introduction of new work systems dependent on flexibility, teamwork and continuous improvement, so that change is slowly becoming accepted as part of organisational culture. Following the successful introduction of teamwork, managers are investigating further refinements that involve a greater degree of self-management. Moreover, by manipulating the tangible elements of organis-ational culture, management appears to have assisted in developing people's understanding of the current organisational reality in order to create joint meaning and collective action that they hope will promote survival in the future.

In XZZ Components, despite the profound transformation the company has undergone so far, some managers consider that the attitude and ethos of the work-force remains poor compared to their European counterparts. A manager observed:

> If you were to benchmark against the Spanish and Germans (who will virtually work all day), the British rate as a third-world supplier in comparison. Our productivity is not good so we can't afford to offer top wages. The UK has the ability to be world leader but hasn't got the right mental attitude.

He attributes this to the difficulties in eroding long-standing 'them and us' cultures and the poor receptivity of hourly-paid workers to change. He continued:

> The problem is they've never really known any pain at XZZ – they've never had the feeling that there is a real need to give more than you take when you're at work. People don't understand it's in their own interests, not just the organisation's.

These comments reveal that a traditional outlook on the employment relationship still exists within parts of the organisation. People in the company have clearly known the pain of job losses and fundamental changes to work practices that have called for further training and development, but such comments tend to disregard these factors. Similarly, workers in XZZ Components appear more sceptical of management actions than in Creative Engineering, demonstrating a higher level of resignation to, rather than enthusiasm for, the new approaches.

Nevertheless, XZZ Components has made considerable efforts to begin the transformation of a traditional culture into one that may facilitate the processes of learning and change more readily. Given that culture is an accumulation of past behaviours and successes, it is inevitable that this cannot be accomplished on a short timescale. Nevertheless, the organisation has removed many of the traditional hierarchical systems and barriers that prevent double-loop learning, and has replaced them with approaches that are more conducive to the contemporary environment in which it operates. Though the culture change programme is still in its early stages, the achievements so far are considerable.

This chapter will now consider the final theme that emerges from the literature and the research: how individuals and groups are developed in the organisations so that they can contribute to the change process.

(4) Individual learning and development

Associated with creating a dominant culture that supports learning and change is the issue of how far individuals in the organisation are developed and encouraged to challenge existing norms and procedures so that double-loop learning and change occurs. The approaches of the case studies will therefore be examined in order to transfer the analysis from the institutional to the individual level. Continuous improvement, quality and flexibility are required in contemporary production systems in the automotive sector, and this demands that the individual is responsive to double-loop learning and change. This represents a departure from traditional manufacturing methods that involved numerous job classifications with limited mobility of labour. What is becoming increasingly evident in the automotive sector is that companies are operating in environments in which they cannot guarantee or foresee what skills, knowledge and abilities they may need in individuals in the future. To overcome this difficulty, attention is being directed to ensuring that people can learn to learn (double-loop learning) so they can contribute to this climate of change in a productive way.

Creative Engineering's approach

Creative places a strong emphasis on developing individuals in the organisation, believing the workforce to be a vital source of innovation and creativity. To harness the potential of the individual, a focused approach to learning is offered that incorporates industry-related skills training and knowledge acquisition. The Employee Development Scheme, for example, aims to promote the simultaneous development of people and work through strategic interventions by:

- aligning individual objectives with organisational objectives;
- providing regular feedback on performance;
- identifying employees' strengths and weaknesses;
- constructing training and development plans for twelve-month periods.

All apprentices on the shopfloor follow the National Vocational Qualifications (NVQ) route with the opportunity to take HNC/HND and part-time degrees, and/or professional qualifications if they desire. Despite the criticisms of the 'past' and 'present' orientation of NVQs, rather than developing skills the individual may need in the future (Iles and Salaman 1995), some managers at Creative claim the system does provide an effective framework to encourage people to learn. Day-release for training is available, although one manager commented on the difficulties of this in a production environment when he observed 'there's not a lot of manoeuvrability with this – it's better now that local FE colleges are offering half-day and evening courses especially for industry'.

For these reasons, training mainly occurs on-site and is run internally, although specialists are sometimes brought in to 'provide exactly what's needed'. For example, the introduction of cellular manufacturing and teamwork within Creative has been achieved by an approach developed to meet the specific needs of individuals and the organisation. It is clear from this that people in the organisation are seen as proactive contributors to the production process and are deemed capable of development and collaboration. Nevertheless, findings also appear to confirm Gill's (1995) suggestion that contemporary organisations are essentially concerned with solving performance problems in order to ensure that continuous improvement is achieved, rather than developing wider learning *per se*. However, given that adult learning crucially depends on individual interest in solving relevant problems (Knowles 1984), Creative's approach appears to fulfil the needs of both the individual and the organisation. Furthermore, this is evidence of an organisation that has passed the foundation stage of learning, and is promoting a basic readiness for individual learning through success and self-confidence (March and Olsen 1975) (see Figure 2.3 in Chapter 2).

Creative's long-term commitment to promoting wider learning opportunities is manifested in the Employee Development Centre opened in 1996. This indicates that the organisation is moving towards the formation stage, which focuses on wider issues of self-development and teamwork (March and Olsen *op. cit.*). The Centre offers to all members of the organisation a wide selection of open-learning materials and skills training that focuses on industry-specific topics. Its purpose is to encourage people to take responsibility for their own learning by undertaking learning projects with the help of a facilitator within the centre. However a number of employees had not visited the centre, due to 'lack of time', 'too many family commitments', 'don't know much about it yet', and some managers expressed disappointment at the lack of enthusiasm displayed.

Despite such initiatives, the central focus for development is based upon problem-solving and best-practice routines. This recognises that adult learners are motivated to learn by situations that require new or additional knowledge or skills

(Knowles *op. cit.*). The practices are usually benchmarked from within and beyond the automotive industry and then developed or 'Creativeised' so that people in the organisation have 'ownership' of them. In this way, the systems themselves, together with their customisation, make a significant contribution to individual learning and change management.

At management level, Creative offers full sponsorship to individuals who undertake development activities (internal or external) that are directly linked to business objectives. These may include Open University courses, Master of Business Administration (MBA), Post-Graduate Diploma in Management Studies, etc., or any training that is linked to professional development such as the Institute of Personnel Development. If the development is deemed only indirectly linked, sponsorship is for fifty per cent of the total cost. As one person said, 'anyone can apply – it's not really publicised but it's determined as a result of progress review or if supervisors are approached. Most of those who apply succeed in gaining sponsorship.'

XZZ Components' approach

XZZ Components commenced the transformation of the company by employing both political and educative approaches to change. A manager recalled that 'in 1989 the attitude of the 1,950 people employed on the shopfloor was terrible – their behaviour was poor, there was a low work ethos and people had no ownership of their jobs'. In view of the changes the company intended to implement in order to recapture competitive advantage, it was clear these issues had to be addressed. An assessment of workforce abilities indicated that standards of literacy and numeracy were low so an intensive, focused programme of shopfloor education and training was commenced in 1990 to address individual needs. This involved on-the-job training for shopfloor staff, together with management and director training and development interventions. This suggests that XZZ Components was embarking on the foundation stage identified by March and Olsen (*op. cit.*) (see Figure 2.3 in Chapter 2), in order to develop the confidence of individuals about learning.

In tandem were continued efforts to improve upward communication and to encourage people to contribute suggestions for improvements to work practices by creating a climate in which experimentation was welcomed and mistakes tolerated. However, it is acknowledged that change is occurring only slowly. This is linked with the persistence of traditional culture and employment relationships, which mean that there are inevitable tendencies to regress to existing behaviours.

A member of the human resource development department suggested that the reality of achieving production targets in a manufacturing industry often means that the development of people is neglected. This results in the under-utilisation of the workforce and for him implies that 'we are still a long way from being a learning organisation . . . perhaps we need to get beyond the labels, which are never useful anyway?' If the underlying motives for XZZ Components' investment in learning and development are not focused on becoming a learning organisation as such, they are based upon ensuring that people will accept change as a constant process. A manager commented: 'people are more responsive to change if the development initiatives are right. You can't have change without development but whether this requires training is debatable. We just need to become better at learning.'

This suggests not only a recognition of the relationship between learning and change but also the inadequacies of traditional approaches that assume the learner is the passive recipient of training. If people are expected to be flexible and innovative in contemporary manufacturing environments then equipping them with the necessary skills and abilities must also reflect self-directing approaches. Furthermore, only by developing an approach to individual development that encourages double-loop learning will enable change to occur.

Internal and external development programmes are available, although the company tries to provide its own training in-house and 'buy in' as little as possible. For example, the apprentice scheme provides off-the-job, on-site training for thirteen candidates in a newly refurbished training workshop that matches the work environment as closely as possible. Two instructors have been recruited to operate the workshop on the basis that 'external training provision seldom under-stands or meets the requirements of the organisation' (member of human resource team). As suggested by managers at Creative, this is symptomatic of the fast pace of change in the industry and the inability of the education system to keep pace with what is needed.

Whilst there is open access to development opportunities at any level within the organisation, there are clear requirements that they are evaluated and justified against the business 'bottom line'. A member of the human resource department commented:

> We need to be satisfied that courses are in line with the needs of the business but we try to be as flexible as possible in providing help with fees, time off etc. The hourly paid workers are encouraged to take FE courses – the only barriers erected are from them.

Approaches that ensure that the financial investment in learning is used in the most cost-effective way are evident throughout the organisation. For example, with regard to recruitment for the apprentice scheme, a manager stated 'we try to target those people not likely to get university degrees because they are very expensive and people might move on. We really want to train just for XZZ.'

This is indicative of the drive to ensure that both people and the organisation are simultaneously developed, but with an emphasis on solving performance problems individuals are likely to encounter in the workplace (Gill 1995). The continuous drive to improve quality levels has seen the establishment of a 'concern management room' on the shopfloor. Workers are encouraged to enter the room whenever they have any concerns about their own work or that of their colleagues. Problems have to be tackled within twenty-four hours and a solution found within five days. Since its inception in 1994, customer complaints have reduced by fifty per cent and representatives from other organisations have observed the process.

Line manager involvement at XZZ Components

The company is seeking to generate greater involvement in the training process from line managers by encouraging them to initiate feedback from their teams on courses of study and training interventions. Whilst this is recognised to be a difficult change for many, the system is gradually becoming accepted by most line managers in the organisation. A group leader in the 'tulip factory' commented:

> Training is driven from the shopfloor now, whether this is on-the-job or otherwise. It's up to the team leaders to fit training around production requirements. It can be difficult but we achieved eighty per cent of the target in 1995.

Shopfloor employees agreed there was now a significant interest and investment in training and developing the individual. In accord with the claim that adults are competence based learners (Knowles *op. cit.*), a fitter with thirty years experience at XZZ Components observed:

> The bulk of all learning happens on-the-job anyway. You can only learn the foibles of the machines when you operate them yourself. Another point is that the workforce is so reduced that there is no surplus anymore so it's difficult to release people for training.

In the light of this observation, a significant initiative introduced to the organisation is the National Vocational Qualifications (NVQ) programme, in which all shopfloor workers are involved. A member of the human resource team reported:

> It gives people recognition for the skills and competences they hold already. It's good for external relations and it gets people into the development cycle. There are no resource constraints at present and we are training our own assessors from the shopfloor so that we can cascade the process down. The NVQ system is so successful that we have people from other companies coming to see what we're doing here.

An NVQ assessor remarked on the importance of the inherent learning that occurs on an informal and continuous basis. This can be recognised through the NVQ system, thereby promoting confidence and success in the foundation stage of learning (March and Olsen *op. cit.*, Stacey *op. cit.*). He thought his role was pivotal in developing people's confidence in the NVQ system and training because 'the turning point is when it's one of their own that introduces them to the benefits of training . . . they trust me and they know I'm not giving them any bullshit.'

This indicates the importance of the informal organisation (Brown and Duguid 1991) in aiding the learning and change processes, in so far as they are both also processes of socialisation. Hendry (1996) claims that the way people attach meaning and their strategies for action are inevitably associated with values developed in social or interpersonal situations. If their peers are convinced that an approach is useful and effective, they are likely to be convinced to try it themselves. As an example, some members of the shopfloor have undertaken courses in presentation skills within the NVQ framework, and have delivered presentations to members of the board of directors to demonstrate their learning from the programme of study. An NVQ assessor commented: 'training gives confidence, it opens the mind and it never ends, it just becomes different'.

An appraisal system operates for managers and staff (though not shopfloor employees). This is seen as the primary vehicle for the identification of development needs, and opportunities for academic and professional courses of study are available. The company utilises a succession planning committee, which involves directors and managers in the identification of those employees with potential to move on; development plans are produced for their continued performance within the framework of a group management development programme. The company also operates a 'fast-track' management/leadership programme whose purpose is 'to identify managers with super potential to be directors' (a member of the human resource team). Interventions have also taken place with the Board of Directors (considered by managers to be operationally and strategically active) on such topics as motivation, communication, problem solving and change management. Key areas for further development have been identified as coaching, mentoring and stress management, together with raising awareness of team roles and functions.

Conclusion

It is apparent that Creative Engineering and XZZ Components place considerable emphasis on the development of individuals at all levels of the organisation. In their efforts to maintain their positions in the sector in which they operate, management see investment in this function is unavoidable, not only because of expectation from industry partners, but also to remain competitive and innovative so their organisations survive and grow. There is also a clear indication that the companies are pragmatic in their approaches to development, ensuring that people with attitudes that 'fit' the goals and cultures of the organisations are recruited before any investment is made. Both companies are keen to ensure that their investment in learning and development remains within the organisation. In tandem has been an increase in upward and downward communication, with people reporting they are more informed of their organisation's activities and performance. In XZZ Components, however, some employees interpret increased information as a subtle management tactic to scare and control workers. Nevertheless, both companies have experienced profound changes to culture, work practices and the social organisation of production since the late 1980s and that these aspects continue to evolve.

It is clear that in both organisations the transformation is incomplete. In Creative Engineering, where teamwork has become established within the organisation, training and development assumes a higher profile, with more encouragement of interventions that promote creativity and problem solving. In XZZ Components, which retains a more traditional structure in which teams are only beginning to be established, team and individual learning to complement the more structured training interventions based around national industrial schemes are gradually assuming a greater significance. Nevertheless, in both companies there are concerns surrounding the difficulties of releasing people for training in a manufacturing environment. Further attention will need to be directed to ensuring that new (and future) manufacturing methods are accompanied by complementary human resource management approaches. These need to continue to encourage self-directed and integrative double-loop learning so that individuals are equipped with the skills and abilities to manage future change.

The final chapter that follows summarises the literature and research findings on the key themes discussed and identifies conclusions that can be drawn from the study as a whole. In so doing, the limitations of the present study, together with areas that merit future research in the sector and beyond, are also explored.

9   Summary and conclusions

The purpose of the book has been to examine the robustness of organisational learning and the learning organisation concepts in assisting organisations in the automotive sector to manage change. The context of enquiry was selected on the basis that the automotive sector is recognised by theorists and practitioners alike as not only dynamic in nature but also influential in establishing new forms of work organisation that impact beyond the sector. The study first examined the development and nature of the changes that are specific to the research sector. Second, the literature on organisational learning and the learning organisation was reviewed. In tandem with that review, the literature surrounding approaches to managing change was explored in order to identify the connections with and reciprocal nature of the relationship between learning and change. Finally, the study reported and compared the experiences of four case studies of organisations that accept that change is most effectively accomplished by the adoption of an educational, learning approach.

This chapter revisits the key themes that emerge from the literature and the empirical research. These are: the ability of senior managers to understand and articulate the nature of environmental change; the involvement and contribution of individuals and teams so that existing orthodoxy is challenged and emergent strategy occurs; the development of cultures that support this phenomenon; and lastly, the learning and development of individuals so that they have the skills and knowledge to challenge. The discussion continues with an evaluation and comparison of the performance of the case study organisations in terms of their progress towards developing a learning approach to change. The chapter concludes by identifying some of the limitations of the study and potential areas for further research.

The literature

It is clear from the wealth of literature that has and continues to be generated on the topics that organisational learning and the learning organisation are concepts that have become increasingly attractive to management since the mid-1980s (Dixon 1994, Garratt 1987, Pearn *et al.* 1995, Senge 1990). Given that competition and globalisation have intensified the need for organisations to manage change effectively, it would appear that organisational learning has gained wide acceptance by offering an approach that matches and indeed is required by the new forms of work organisation that have emerged in the automotive sector.

If organisational learning is positioned in its historical and evolutionary context, it is apparent that when the task and contextual environment was perceived as stable by managers, work organisation essentially followed the established classical, mechanistic approach (Fayol, Taylor, Weber). Developing individuals in the organisation was therefore systematic and formal, with the individual regarded as a passive learner of discrete and clearly defined tasks in a training event or experience. These training interventions were identified and controlled by management because, as Ashton and Felstead (1995) indicate, mass production systems give management control over the skill formation process.

As a result of disruption in the global environment in the 1970s (oil crises, inflation, Japanese competition, industrial unrest in traditional manufacturing industries, etc.) however, it became clear to managers that they had to respond more effectively to environmental instability. Mechanistic approaches to work organisation depend not only upon environmental stability but also, as Morgan (1997: 27) suggests, 'when the human "machine" parts are compliant and behave as they have been designed to do'. Given that at this time people were becoming increasingly vocal in expressing their dissatisfaction with the traditional work environment in the automotive sector, it was clear that management had to re-address the issues if it was to re-establish control over both the people and the environment in which it operated.

Accordingly, within a framework of organisational development work tasks began to be used more as opportunities for learning and developing the individual, in an effort to increase productivity, to encourage responsiveness to change and to improve the quality of working life (Thompson 1983). Various writers (Keep 1989, Legge 1995, Wood 1988) have commented upon the emergence in the 1980s of human resource management (HRM) as an ideological framework. This approach, *inter alia*, recognised the significance of the simultaneous development of people and work, and how these aspects could be broadly and strategically, linked to the performance of the organisation.

Concomitant in the 1980s was the influence of Japanese organisations and their economic success in specific industries such as the automotive sector (Bratton 1992, Pascale and Athos 1982). The linkages between Japan's success and the culture–excellence debate (Peters and Waterman 1982), together with the subsequent belief in the transferability of their 'lean' work practices, were profoundly influential as a catalyst for change in Western industrial practice. Moss Kanter (1989), Handy (1989) and Pedler *et al.* (1991) identify the new organisational form that emerged from these developments as based upon collaboration rather than competition and flexibility, with openness and trust across and between companies. Learning at all levels was seen by theorists as essential to achieve and maintain high levels of quality, and thus organisational effectiveness and survival. Again, these characteristics were evident in Japanese practices in the automotive sector, particularly in the nature of work and relationships between buyers and suppliers.

The shamrock organisation identified by Handy (1993) for example, provides a simple framework for the Japanese 'lean' approach as described by Womack *et al.* (1990). Handy suggests that the organisation should comprise a core of essential workers, supported by outside contractors and part-time or temporary assistance when required. Storey (1994) develops this model and locates the lean approach in a framework of 'new wave manufacturing' that places emphasis on teamwork and flattened hierarchies, with quality, creativity, flexibility and continuous improvement seen as the responsibility of the individual. In this framework, flexibility and non-standard forms of employment are identified by theorists as rapidly growing aspects of work organisation from 1985 to 1995 (Ashton and Felstead 1995, Atkinson 1984, Daley and McCann 1992). In such a dynamic environment, training and development may well be deemed essential but treated *ad hoc* or often prove difficult to achieve. Research findings suggest that people believe that their skill levels in work have increased, more want to be trained, and more are willing to pay for training themselves (Gallie and White 1995). How organisational learning assists in the change process has become an important consideration.

Organisational learning and change

The nature of the environment that organisations operate in is identified by contemporary writers as one that may be understood and managed from the perspectives of chaos and complexity theories (Morgan 1997, Senge 1990, Stacey 1996). This sees organisations as open learning systems characterised by non-linear interaction that is both ordered and chaotic, but that spontaneous self-organisation emerges from this activity. This implies that management must create a milieu in which appropriate forms of self-organisation can occur so there is greater control of and stability and choice in, the environment (Burnes 1996).

Burdett (1994), Hodgetts *et al.* (1994), McGill and Slocum (1993) regard organisational learning as providing the basic platform from which change and self-organisation can occur. They warn, however, that this requires transformation of traditional core paradigms so that revised approaches to managing people can emerge. This view is endorsed by Burgoyne (1992 and 1995), Cook and Yanow (1996) and Hendry (1996), who note that new organisational forms focus more upon collective learning and interaction rather than individual approaches. Learning is identified as a social, interactive process that is dependent upon effective dialogue within and between various individuals, departments and cultures if the creation of shared meanings is to be accomplished. Whilst the contribution of the formal organisation is acknowledged, the social nature of the learning process – may often occur spontaneously in a team environment in contemporary workplaces – demands growing recognition of the contribution of the informal organisation (Brown and Duguid 1991, Fisher and Torbert 1995, Stacey *op. cit.*). The development of learning communities of practice (Brown and Duguid *op. cit.*) therefore offers opportunities to promote mutual support, together with common commitment to shared goals.

Blackler (1995), Burgoyne (1995a), Drucker (1992), Nonaka (1991), however, identify knowledge creation and making this new knowledge available to the organisation as essential factors in promoting organisational learning. Lean or human-centred work practices and team environments, for example, see continuous improvement as the basis for the creation of new knowledge; hence changes and improvements to systems are likely to emerge. The key to this, Burgoyne (*op. cit.*) contends, is personal commitment to the organisation and identification with its culture, values and beliefs; these, he claims, have become the primary vehicles for implementing contemporary organisational change programmes.

Continuous improvement and change are dependent upon the depth of learning that results, so it is important, as Bateson (1972) and Argyris and Schon (1978) note, that double-loop learning occurs. This enables existing systems and procedures to be challenged and revised by those closest to the point of activity, allowing new strategies to emerge that are more appropriate for changed contexts. If organisations remain locked in single-loop learning modes, however, they will repeat the same procedures regardless of their usefulness in changed contexts. Hence they will suffer because their rate of learning will not be equal to or greater than the rate of change in the environment (Bateson *op. cit.*).

Whether they do or not will be dependent on the organisation providing a framework that supports individual and collective development initiatives that enable people to challenge and change the status quo so that strategy can emerge (Morgan *op. cit.*). It also requires the development of approaches to managing people that are based more upon participation and facilitation than positional and hierarchical power structures. Senge (*op. cit.*) suggests that in a learning environment the manager becomes steward and leader rather than the authoritarian figure recognised in traditional organisational arrangements.

Moreover, in a learning environment it is clear that greater attention must be given to how individuals and groups learn most effectively. Knowles (1984), Kolb (1984), Reynolds (1997) and Zemke and Zemke (1995) argue that adult learners are pragmatic in their approach and prefer problem-solving and experiential activities. Similarly, Holman *et al.* (1997) and Revans (1982) identify the importance of practical argumentation with oneself and others as factors that stimulate learning and change. Whilst the new-wave, team-based manufacturing environment that Storey (*op. cit.*) describes provides opportunities for the promotion of learning and change, the traditional barriers still remain for organisations to overcome before a learning approach to change can achieve its goals.

Barriers to learning and change

Traditional organisations are recognised as having inherent barriers to double-loop learning and change. Argyris (1992), Morgan (1986), Pearns *et al.* (1995) and Schein (1993) argue that these barriers exist at both individual and organisational levels, and can be evident in characteristics of bureaucratic regimes, 'them and us' cultures and management attitudes. Barriers are likely to be manifested in approaches to such issues as change management, decision-making, training and development, communication and external relationships. Interventions that maintain the barriers are characterised by lack of involvement of the wider organisation, close direction and supervision by management, poor levels of communication, and a short-term, inward-focused perspective. Additionally, individuals may be actively discouraged from participating and experimenting because of political activities that seek to preserve positional power or because mistakes are not tolerated. Hence opportunities for double-loop learning and change are non-existent or limited.

It is generally accepted that a learning approach to change requires a paradigm shift in outlook and beliefs for traditional companies. Such approaches may be incomplete and take time to become embedded as part of organisational culture. Whilst Galpin (1996) and Johnson (1993) accept that management may seek to change the tangible elements of culture (communications, removal of key individuals from the 'old regime', work environment, etc.), but they stress that considerable reinforcement of new approaches is required over time to prevent regression.

It is useful when considering the issues surrounding the promotion of a learning approach to change to revisit March and Olsen's (1975) model (see Figure 2.3 in Chapter 2). This sets out the progress of individual learning, from a foundation stage in which there is a basic readiness to learn, to the formation stage in which the individual becomes a more independent learner, and then to the continuation stage in which there is more autonomy, challenging and group inter-action. Hendry *et al.* (1995) identify corresponding interventions that organisations can offer to promote this development. It would appear that it is only when individual and team learning ability is established in the continuation stage, and the organisation demonstrates appropriate support mechanisms that encourage new and improved practices to replace existing theory-in-use, that double-loop learning and change will occur. That this level is not evident at a given point in time may indicate that the organisation has not yet reached that stage in its development, rather than it never will.

Despite the barriers to developing learning and change, many theorists and practitioners alike endorse the approach (Dawson 1994, Dixon *op. cit.*, Stewart 1996). Moving beyond the practical advantages and limitations, theorists are beginning to explore the more complex levels on which organisational learning might occur, and critically to evaluate the implications of the phenomenon. Hawkins (1994), for example, suggests that organisational learning and change occur on a spiritual level that is instrumental in creating the current reality for the company. In support of this point, Argyris (1987) identifies the organisations most likely to survive in the future as those that become adaptive to environmental change and vary their strategy and structure according to the choices they face.

Commentators (Jermier *et al.* 1994, Sewell and Wilkinson 1992, Thompson and Wallace 1996) however, critique the so-called 'new employment relationship' embodied in the new wave manufacturing environment. They suggest that practices that purport to encourage organisational learning (teamwork, devolved responsibility, empowerment, etc.) serve to reinforce managerial control and favour those formally appointed as managers. They argue that teamwork provides increased opportunities for control to be exerted by both management and peers, while production systems demand tight controls simply because they are lean, with no margins for error. Similarly, Cunningham *et al.* (1996) contend that if empowerment and autonomy exist, they operate within parameters that are defined by management.

What emerges in the literature from the 1980s onwards is the importance of developing an increased awareness of the external environment and how organisations, as open learning systems, can be proactive in managing the change process and thereby create their own destinies. The new organisational forms and work practices based upon teamwork in lean manufacturing and human-centred contexts ostensibly offer opportunities to interact more closely with the individuals and the environment and to engage in dialogue and learning. Moreover, they are dependent on the creation of cultures in which meaning, values and impressions of the current reality are understood and shared by members of the organisation. They require that self-development, experiential and action learning approaches to achieve quality, continuous improvement and involvement are promoted. These are seen as viable constructs to assist the individual and organisation to engage in double-loop learning, in order to interact effectively with the environment and to understand and manage the process of change.

In contemporary work environments, whilst management would appear to be offering greater levels of autonomy and involvement to individuals and teams, it remains possible that the approach requires recognition of the importance of managing paradox and dialectical tension rather than just resistance to change. The paradox here is that while the lean system and the human-centred approaches afford individuals and teams the opportunity for empowerment, management still needs to exert some form of control over employees so that disparate learning initiatives are co-ordinated and channelled to achieve organisational goals. This control, Burgoyne (1995a) and Legge (*op. cit.*) suggest, is more subtle than that evident in traditional organisational arrangements, involving alignment of beliefs, values and images rather than the imposition of rules and formal procedures.

The discussion will now look at the empirical research findings in the case study organisations in order to assess their contribution to the academic and theoretical debate outlined above. The key themes that emerge from the literature and the empirical research will be revisited in determining the significance and limitations of the study. Areas of further research that may enhance future analyses will then be identified.

The case studies: generic issues

At the outset, it is important to consider the limitations of the research reported in this book and the drawbacks of the qualitative, case-study approach it adopted. First, the sample selected was limited and biased towards those organisations in the automotive sector already established in the development of learning and change.

Their relevance is that they provide a field of interpretive investigation that may inform future studies in a wider sample and different organisational settings. Second, there are general considerations to do with the limitations of qualitative research, focusing on issues of reliability and accuracy of method. Given the nature of the methods used for the generation of qualitative data in the case study approach (interview, observation, etc.), these are often deemed less standardised and less precise than quantitative methods. Accordingly, they may be considered subjective, because assessments are not made in terms of established standards and data is defined by the subject rather than structured in advance by the researcher.

Similarly, the subsequent recording and analysis of findings are likely to be more interpretive, exploratory and concerned with meanings and impressions rather than the measurable and quantifiable. In the framework of this research, however, concerted efforts were made throughout to ensure that the generation of data was consistent and appropriate to the investigation. Similar efforts were made to ensure that data recording and analysis were thorough and accurate, and represented the interviewees' views fairly and consistent with their meanings.

A further general consideration to do with qualitative research concerns the validity of the data analysis and the interpretation on which it is based. It is important to demonstrate how the interpretation was reached. The objectives of the empirical research here have been to examine the approaches to developing organisational learning and how this impacts on the management of change in four organisations operating in the automotive sector. From the findings presented and compared in Chapters seven and eight it is evident that the impact of organisational learning on the management of change is dependent on a range of factors that are both generic and specific to the organisations. Generic factors involve issues central to the industry sector and focus on instability in the external environment that determines change in the case study organisations. Specific factors relate to the nature of the internal environment and how far structures, systems and processes exist, or are developed, to encourage double-loop learning and change to occur.

As manufacturers and component suppliers, the Rover Group and Volvo, and Creative Engineering and XZZ Components were confronted with generic factors to do with profound change and instability in the automotive sector from the 1960s onwards. Change was characterised by mature product markets and industrial unrest as a result of the inadequacies of, and dissatisfaction with the Taylorist–Fordist paradigm. Theorists (Atkinson 1984, Bratton *op. cit.*, Womack *et al. op. cit.*) suggest that alternative approaches to managing people were beginning to emerge. Meanwhile, increased competition from Japan and the consequent enthusiasm for the adoption of lean manufacturing approaches in the West added to the instability of the organisations. The industrial reality becoming evident, therefore, was that established forms of work organisation were no longer viable and profound change was essential in order to survive. Whilst there was recognition by all of the case studies of these generic changes in the background environment, the nature of internal change and the approaches they adopted are specific to the individual organisations.

Approaches to change

For the Rover Group, significant crises from the late 1970s to the mid 1980s involving industrial unrest and union militancy, poor-quality products and financial problems forced management to undertake drastic action to bring about the recovery of the organisation. After this uncertain period, from 1989 onwards, and with assistance from Honda, there were concerted efforts to revamp products, work practices and employment relations. Management was forced to reconsider its traditional approaches to manufacturing and the employment relationship in order to regain control of the production process and the environment in which it was operating. Factors influencing the Rover Group's recovery include:

(1) Senior management was aware of the changing environment and came to believe that the traditional approach to the employment relationship was no longer appropriate. There was a need to establish a form of authority and control over workers and the production process that was less confrontational and 'them and us' in style.

(2) Recognition that once control had been re-established, the lean work practices that were increasingly driving the pace of change in the automotive sector required more involvement from the workforce and that people's initiatives, skills and abilities were the essential ingredients for the recovery of the company. If the organisation was to establish the team approach the new manufacturing environment demanded, then it needed to gain both the commitment and consent of workers. It concluded that only by demonstrating that investment in people was a critical success factor could it hope to change attitudes.

(3) To ensure these factors were fully developed, the company declared its commitment to become a learning organisation, and created a separate business unit, Rover Learning Business (RLB), to demonstrate the distinctive approach it was pursuing both within the organisation and beyond. This was an innovative strategy that distinguished the company from others in the sector. It did much to earn it a convincing reputation for learning and change externally, if not throughout the Rover Group as a whole. Though RLB has since been dissolved, it served to integrate the disparate learning initiatives the company was pursuing by providing a focused platform for change. Given that culture change of this nature cannot be achieved quickly, its dissolution may well indicate that some success in the promotion of a learning culture within the organisation has been achieved.

By comparison, Volvo's response from the 1960s onwards was to break away from traditional Fordist manufacturing principles by redesigning work tasks, enlarging and rotating jobs, and establishing teamwork as the norm throughout the organisation. Innovative and experimental approaches have subsequently become embedded in organisational culture and from this has emerged a plurality of production concepts that continue to develop, many of which allow teams the autonomy to determine the pace of work themselves. This approach enabled Volvo to remain untouched by the fervour for Japanisation in the 1980s, having established the foundations for innovative approaches within their own socio-technical framework that continues to evolve.

Volvo's approach emerged from a number of different sites, with experimentation and refinements occurring over a long period. The specific factors that have influenced its development include:

(1) The environment was such that issues of absenteeism and high labour turnover could not be resolvede by traditional approaches to managing the employment relationship. The company therefore had to consider more human-centred approaches to work that addressed the monotony and boredom that was the cause of these problems. This intervention also reflected the more egalitarian and democratic nature of the host society, evidenced by public pressure and considerable involvement of unions in many of the refinements to work organisation.

(2) There was a simultaneous move to give management greater control of individual sites, creating opportunities for autonomy and experimentation with different approaches to work organisation. This can be seen from developments at Uddevalla, which were considered too radical by some managers in the wider organisation but which have nevertheless formed the basis for further development at other sites.

(3) Given that developments have occurred over time and at different sites, it is significant that any knowledge, learning and experience gained as a result has been transferred and adapted throughout the organisation. The capacity for facilitating and diffusing organisational learning seems to be the key to Volvo's ability to change and maintain an innovative approach to work organisation. This is apparent in the Born plant in Belgium, the site of the collaborative venture with Mitsubishi, with work organisation based on a combination of the work approaches of the two companies. Whilst the alliance enabled Volvo to enter volume markets, employing work organisation approaches containing elements of Mitsubishi's 'lean' system, Volvo's work practices also ensure a greater degree of team autonomy and incorporate what are considered to be more humanistic work practices than those found in a totally lean environment. The alliance may therefore also be indicative of Mitsubishi's recognition of the shortcomings of the lean systems and that they may now need adaptation to give them a more human-centred focus.

Volvo's experiences in developing radical approaches to work organisation have been influenced by a number of factors that are specific to its task and contextual environments. Moreover, management in the organisation from the 1960s onwards appears to be committed to maintaining an innovative approach to work organisation that is continually prepared to challenge dominant paradigms in the industry. This proactive approach has ensured that a culture for learning and change has been established.

From 1955 to 1980, when Creative Engineering had no distinctive product or customer base, there was increasing concern over the viability of the organisation. A proactive approach was then adopted by senior management to understand the changes in the external environment. It recognised the need to identify the industry in which it should seek to operate (the automotive sector) and what approaches to work organisation would best fit this environment. The company accomplished this by exploring both Japanese lean systems and German methods of manufacturing. Management then conveyed the urgency of the need for change to the workforce, and most significantly, recognised that change could be achieved only if the workforce was developed to ensure the continuous improvement the automotive sector demanded. Factors influencing Creative Engineering's approach to change therefore include:

(1) A long-term strategy to adapt and differentiate both products and processes in order to achieve competitive advantage. Having succeeded in gaining business from Ford and Rover in the early 1980s, its objective was to become the single-source supplier for the components manufactured. Throughout the 1980s Creative Engineering introduced production approaches including just-in-time manufacturing and statistical process control, which enabled strong partnerships to be forged with manufacturers with whom preferred supplier status could be achieved.

(2) Management recognised that whilst management itself is important in identifying change in the external environment, there is also a need for involvement from the workforce in order to achieve quality and continuous improvement. In 1986, involvement was encouraged through the introduction of cellular manufacturing and teamwork. In this environment, people were actively encouraged critically to evaluate their jobs with a view to improving their work organisation and practices, so they could contribute to the planning process.

(3) The effective operation of cellular manufacturing and teamwork was recognised by managers as being slow to establish. More importantly, it was recognised that it required an investment in training and developing team leaders, multi-skilling the workforce and shifting the balance of power towards the teams so they possessed the skills and information needed to perform their tasks. Over the ten-year period, this initiative has been most significant in achieving a culture change within the entire organisation, promoting changes in attitudes, behaviour and performance that are now based upon co-operation and discussion rather than individualism and reactivity.

Creative Engineering has also widened its business portfolio and continues to develop a global reputation for both the quality of products and the commitment of the workforce to innovate and develop new work practices. Teams are an established part of the organisational structure and suggestions for improvements from the workforce emerge as spontaneous contributions that are inevitable rather than unusual.

Like the Rover Group, the component supplier XZZ Components experienced significant problems associated with quality, delivery and productivity in the 1980s. In the 1960s and 1970s it had been one if the most successful component plants in the United Kingdom and had become complacent and resistant to change. Managers communicated to the shopfloor through powerful, full-time trade union officials, while the organisational structure was confused and hierarchical with practices that reflected traditional Fordist approaches. In view of the profound changes that were occurring in the environment from the 1970s onwards, it was clear that the company would need to embark upon radical change itself if it was to survive. The factors that were influential for XZZ Components' change of fortune in the 1990s include:

(1) The failure of piecemeal changes in the late 1980s (e.g. the introduction of robotics) led to management recognition that more fundamental changes to work practices and processes, such as communication and decision making, needed to be addressed simultaneously with changes to work organisation.

(2) In tandem was the need to develop the workforce to operate effectively in this changed environment. This began with increasing upward and downward communication; introducing a harmonisation policy; developing greater customer focus in the organisation; and introducing cellular manufacturing.

(3) Problems with quality persisted despite these interventions. The company was forced to undertake more radical action that involved increased commitment to improving communication. To achieve this, a layer of management was removed so that the distance between management and the shopfloor was reduced. Learning and benchmarking from manufacturers, particularly Nissan, was instigated. Finally, introducing more flexible manufacturing techniques across the organisation led to staffing being reduced from 2,000 to 1,000, and further investments in training and developing both management and the workforce were made to enable them to perform effectively in the new work environment. These interventions include development in change skills and leadership for all members of management and shopfloor. The move to cellular manufacturing and team-work has clearly been a painful process that has only gathered momentum since 1993, and there remain those who are reluctant to change. Despite this, the company has moved significantly away from its traditional past and is in the process of a transformation that will assist its future survival.

Generic environmental instability in the automotive sector had significant implications for all the case study organisations, each having developed specific responses in order to survive and manage change. Volvo appears the most innovative and proactive in its approach, moving away from the traditional Fordist regime and establishing a reputation for imaginative approaches to work organis-ation. The company has developed a plurality of production concepts based upon teamwork, learning and employee involvement that have continued to evolve from the 1970s onwards.

The Rover Group, however, faced a series of crises that threatened its viability and it was only when forced to respond to these crises that radical change was undertaken. At first these addressed products and work organisation, but when this did not achieve the changes required, harnessing and developing the skills and talents of people became the focus. The creation of Rover Learning Business established a unique framework for the Rover Group to distinguish itself in its environment as a learning organisation with a clear investment in people. As a result, the company's culture change continues to evolve, given the traditional foundations on which it was established. Despite the comparatively short period, it has achieved significant improvements in both the performance and attitude of the workforce.

In Creative Engineering, management has been more skilful and quicker than the Rover Group in anticipating, understanding and coping with environmental change. It concentrated on developing a proactive strategy for change that involved people, systems and work organisation simultaneously. Consequently, teamwork, flexibility and continuous improvement are practices that appear well embedded in work practices, indicating that the company has achieved considerable culture change since 1986. Importantly, both management and shopfloor workers recognise that there is still much more that can be achieved given the pace of change in the environment and are aware that complacency may lead to loss of market share.

Like the Rover Group, management in XZZ Components was preoccupied with the internal environment in the 1970s and 1980s and had not anticipated or understood the significance of external changes until it was almost too late. Managers admit they had grown complacent and were unaware of the impending threats to their survival. Again like the Rover Group, their strategy involved changing work organisation and then recognising that changing the way people were managed and developed were equally important factors in the equation. If people are given opportunities for development, they will gain understanding of the business environment, contribute ideas for continuous improvement, and perform effectively in teams.

Key themes in the case studies and the literature

Key interrelated themes apparent in the literature and the experiences of the four organisations are as follows.

(1) Understanding changes in the external environment and communicating these to the organisation

In monitoring the environment, deemed fundamental in developing a learning approach to change, the case-study organisations display differing levels of expertise and responsiveness. If managers have a good understanding of their environment and can translate this into vision and action, there is greater opportunity for a proactive approach and choice in determining the future of the organisation rather than having to react to crises. Commentators have identified the importance of systems thinking in understanding complex change situations as patterns of events, and developing such thinking appears to be an essential prerequisite for learning and change. Management in Volvo, for example, observed and understood the nature of environmental change and challenged established orthodoxy in the late 1960s, which was earliest of the four organisations. The company then established a pattern of experimentation with work organisation that has continued to evolve, characterised by adaptation and refinement and hence double-loop learning and change. The company succeeded in becoming proactive, in creating its own environment rather than having to respond to external environmental change and uncertainty.

The Rover Group demonstrated high levels of reactivity in monitoring environmental change from the 1960s to the mid-1980s. It was only when faced with significant crises that it began to take a proactive approach. This was manifested through collaborative ventures with Honda and management intervention in the creation of a separate business unit to assist the company in becoming a 'learning organisation'. This latter intervention indicates management awareness of the expanding literature on and increasing importance of the topic of organisational learning from the mid-1980s onwards, and in itself provides evidence that double-loop learning was occurring. Whether this was most effectively achieved by a commitment to become a learning organisation *per se* is debatable. Nevertheless, there is evidence to show that the Rover Group recognises the importance of monitoring the external environment more closely and that it continues to develop links with external bodies in the automotive industry and beyond, together with educational and learning establishments.

Creative Engineering, like Volvo, has placed considerable emphasis on monitoring the external environment. The determination of senior management from the beginning of the 1980s onwards to ensure that patterns of change were anticipated has enabled the company to be proactive in its choice of approaches to change. The company has developed close links with other suppliers and manufacturers in order to share and develop best practice. It has also developed links with educational establishments. Management continues to regard external interaction as vital to maintaining competitive advantage and monitoring the global environment as a concern that cannot be over-stated.

XZZ Components' approach to environmental change is similar to that of the Rover Group. It was only when the viability of the company was challenged that it appeared important to look beyond the organisational boundaries and to learn. Consequently, the company was forced to embark upon a period of catching up with competitors before its recovery was secured and it could adopt a more proactive stance. Management has since embarked upon an approach that recognises the importance of understanding the environment and shaping it in accordance with the needs of the organisation. Like the other organisations, this is evident in the links that have been forged with manufacturers and educational establishments.

Monitoring the external environment can provide senior management with a vision of the future of the organisation and the basis on which strategic planning can proceed. In the initial stages, senior management must supply the main impetus for learning and change; it does this in order to bring stability into an otherwise unstable world. The role of management leadership and its ability to engage in double-loop learning is therefore crucial and influential in determining the success of an organisation. This aspect was not examined in depth in the present study, and so is a subject for research in the future.

What is also apparent in the four organisations is recognition that involvement of the wider organisation is needed to establish learning and change once the initial thrust has been generated. Nonaka (1991) argues that the only reliable source of competitive advantage is knowledge and that successful strategies are integrally linked to knowledge creation. Recognition of the need to create knowledge from within via the contribution of the wider organisation is a second theme common to the literature and the case studies.

(2) Emergent strategy formulation and the contribution of individuals and teams

To greater and lesser degrees, the case-study organisations have developed a learning approach to strategy that recognises the importance of the contribution of the wider organisation. Senior management have created, or is attempting to create, an environment in which accepted and articulated ways of doing things and the mental models on which they rest can be challenged by individuals, thereby creating a buffer between the organisation and the environment. For their part, theorists (Ohmae 1986, Pascale 1990, Stacey 1996) have argued that planning is determined by inquiry-driven action, which can provide a foundation on which double-loop learning and change can occur, with strategy emerging from the learning process.

In Volvo, a well-established team-based environment is apparent, in which individuals are encouraged to experiment and innovate. This has enabled double-loop learning and change to occur through the transference and adaptation of practices within and between plants. Senior management and shopfloor workers demonstrate increased levels of autonomy and this is also contributory to learning and change. This illustrates the development of what Grundy (1994) describes as strategic islands of learning that spread throughout the organisation to provide a critical mass of learning. As a result, the company is not only responsive to change but also has the ability to influence and shape the environment in its favour.

In the Rover Group, a learning approach to strategy making is gradually developing, with greater involvement from individuals and teams. People are encouraged to contribute suggestions and ideas for improving the performance of the organisation and hence maintaining competitive advantage. The success of such initiatives is dependent on the enthusiasm and involvement of both individuals and line managers, and whilst there is no evidence to suggest that people resisted or obstructed the process, there were those who were apathetic and/or disinterested. Given the traditional nature of the employment relationship in the Rover Group, the company has made considerable progress in developing this aspect, but needs to reinforce the approach so that over time it can become established practice throughout the organisation.

Like Volvo, Creative Engineering has moved towards a team-based structure, in which people contribute ideas for improvement as a matter of course. In an environment in which there are increased levels of autonomy, teams generate their own ideas for improvements and these are quickly communicated to management. This indicates that the distance between management and the shopfloor has been reduced and that there is greater commitment from team leaders to encouraging the process. The level of shopfloor interest in improving work practices was higher than in the Rover Group, indicating greater involvement in the process.

In XZZ Components, the contribution of individuals is beginning to take a more significant role in the organisation but it would appear that this is more difficult to establish than in the other organisations. As in the Rover Group, the approach is dependent on commitment from individuals and line managers. Among those who are familiar with traditional arrangements, long-standing conceptions of the employment relationship and the responsibilities of manage-ment and the shopfloor in this context remain in operation. Also, management motives for developing the approach are interpreted by some employees as more suspect and coercive than in the other organisations. The centrality of organis-ational culture and the length of time that elapses before change occurs is thus still recognised. This brings the discussion to the third theme – the creation of cultures that challenge established norms.

(3) The creation of cultures that encourage established norms to be challenged by individuals and teams

Established norms can be challenged only in cultures that support and encourage the practice. Given that culture is an accumulation of past knowledge and experience, memory and learning (Huber 1991, Schein 1993) change is neither simple nor quick to accomplish. Commentators suggest this involves unlearning past behaviour and managing the more tangible elements of culture (work environment, structures, training and development, etc.) to achieve the desired outcomes. In essence, the desired culture within a learning approach is one that tolerates mistakes, has open channels of information and communication, and allows individuals and teams levels of autonomy and responsibility that reflect investment by the organisation in learning and development.

In Volvo, a culture of this nature has been developing since the 1960s, so challenging the status quo has become an accepted facet of organisational life. This is supported by the team-based structure that enables experimentation and flexibility. The Rover Group, having introduced a learning approach in the late 1980s, does not yet seem to have firmly embedded this in organisational culture; management stresses the need to convince people they have two jobs – the second being how they can improve.

Creative Engineering, however, does seem to have mobilised commitment to challenging established procedures. Like Volvo, this may be attributed to the team-based environment in which it operates and where there is greater opportunity for dialogue and experimentation. On the whole, people consider that the culture evident in 1997 shows a marked change to that of ten years ago and that individuals are seen as valued contributors to the production process and the destiny of the organisation.

In XZZ Components, whilst management recognise that the company has moved forward significantly, there is still much that can be accomplished by culture change. Attitudes and behaviours of both management and the shopfloor, developed over considerable time, still reflect the traditional culture and conceptions of the employment relationship in some areas of the organisation. Nevertheless, for many people the culture has changed from 'us and them' to understanding that change is a normal ongoing process that requires the involvement of all employees. As a result, it is said that mistakes are tolerated more than in earlier times and that it is recognised how it is vital to remove people's fear of change. This constitutes the final theme to be discussed: how and to what degree people are encouraged to view change from an educational, learning perspective.

(4) Promoting individual learning and involvement.

It is clear that individual learning and involvement are promoted in all the case-study organisations and that there has been a deliberate strategy to encourage its development, to demonstrate managerial commitment to the workforce and to assist in the process of change. If the performance of the organisations is considered in terms of the models of March and Olsen (*op. cit.*) and Hendry *et al.* (1995) (see Figure 2.3 in Chapter 2), the following conclusions can be drawn.

(1) Individual learning ability in Volvo has reached the continuation stage, in which individuals are self-motivated, questioning and display high levels of autonomy at group and individual levels. In response, the organisation offers a broad commitment to maintain and increase work group autonomy and continues to experiment with work approaches that ensure learning is developed.

(2) Individual learning ability in the Rover Group and XZZ Components remains at the formation stage, in which individuals show a general interest in self-development and teamwork. In response, the organisation offers opportunities for teamwork and experiential learning, together with wider industry training. In XZZ Components, training is more formal and structured than in the Rover Group, which is indicative of the early formation stage.

(3) Individual learning ability in Creative Engineering, whilst demonstrating many of the characteristics of the formation stage, appears to be more advanced than the Rover Group and XZZ Components and is approaching the continuation stage. Management do not think all individuals have become independent learners in the organisation, but recognise that many are prepared to assume a greater role in determining their own learning needs and those of the organisation, and are more autonomous in addressing these issues.

Conclusion

The argument has been developed that the effective management of change is dependent upon organisational learning that challenges the status quo. The key themes that emerge from the literature and the case-study research as influential in encouraging organisational learning and change may be listed as: understanding changes in the external environment and articulating these effectively to the organisation; emergent strategy through the contribution of individuals and teams; the promotion of cultures that encourage individuals and teams to challenge established norms; the promotion of individual learning and involvement in the organisation.

Exploring these themes shows that the organisational environment in the automotive sector is characterised by change, uncertainty and instability. However, there is much that managers can do to exercise choice and control in that environment, and so influence future survival and success. By understanding the reciprocal nature of learning and change, and developing these processes at all levels in the organisation, it is more likely that a proactive stance can be maintained.

At the first level, it is important to remove the barriers between the organisation and the environment. Patterns of events can then be detected and understood, appropriate responses developed or anticipated. This requires that leaders and managers have the capacity to engage in double-loop learning and to challenge the status quo, so that new forms of action can emerge. This may well apply to the fundamental principles upon which the organisation is founded and involve the creation of a new vision for the future of the organisation. Essentially, however, it is indicative of management's need to re-establish some form of control over an unstable environment, and requires creativity and a capacity for systems thinking and perceiving the whole. Moreover, it is important that managers are able to provide a conceptual framework that assists employees to understand the new reality to be achieved.

Second, accurate interpretation of external change together with internal implementation of organisational responses cannot be confined to leaders but has to be seen as the responsibility of the wider organisation. This occurs in what commentators such as Hancke and Rubinstein (1995) and Storey (*op. cit.*) identify as a new social organisation of car production that involves teamwork, commitment, training and development. This locates the issue in the framework of human resource management, clearly increasing the importance of human resources whereby individuals and teams act as buffers for, and champions of, change strategies. This does not, however, imply that management perceives their role as diluted. Rather, by offering individuals and teams the opportunity to contribute, the knowledge base of the organisation, together with the commitment and motivation of the individuals, are increased. Whilst some individuals may find this uncomfortable, again it is evidence of management attempting to exert greater control by adopting an approach that includes, rather than excludes, wider learning and involvement.

That this form of control is more subtle than that in traditional work arrangements is indicative of the more participatory nature of the employment relationship managers believe is required to maintain competitive advantage. In this relationship, the distance between the employee and the environment is reduced. Increased information, greater involvement in work organisation, and the expectation that individuals and teams will contribute to improve performance are seen to effect the process. Nevertheless, this contribution is made within parameters defined by management and this, in turn, influences the depth and extent of learning that can or is likely to occur. In organisations where traditional approaches to managing people remain in operation, the opportunities for transferring learning within the organisation are limited or denied by failure fully to exploit the process.

This points to the third theme: how far organisational cultures encourage individuals and teams to challenge established norms. For traditional organisations this represents a significant shift in approach that affects both management and workers. Whilst people in the organisations researched are offered more opportunities to question and debate work organisation, and are more willing to contribute suggestions for improvement, there is little evidence to suggest that management control has been reduced or replaced. What is apparent is that management makes more use of the informal organisation embedded in the social interaction and team learning that occurs in the workplace, and that this is interpreted by workers both negatively and positively.

On the negative interpretation, there is little overt resistance from workers, who may well subscribe to the fundamental principles of developing organisational learning in order to manage change but believe it is yet another management tactic to control and exploit the individual. On the positive interpretation, there are managers and workers who perceive the employment relationship to have profoundly changed, having been re-established on more democratic terms. In both cases, people in the organisations are increasingly aware that change is an ongoing process that cannot be resisted. Rather, there is a greater capacity to manage paradox and dialectical tension not just by management but throughout the organisation.

The final theme relates to the development of individuals so that they can contribute effectively to the performance of the organisation. The case-study research suggests that people in the organisations are keen to learn and recognise that by increasing their skill levels and involvement they will contribute more effectively to the organisation. However, whilst for some individuals this represents a genuine interest in and involvement with the organisation, for many it is pragmatic and borne out of feelings of job insecurity and uncertainty for their futures if they do not comply. Given precarious economic and labour-market conditions in the manufacturing sector, management clearly has control over the terms on which people are recruited to and retained by the organisation and can therefore insist that selected forms of learning and development are placed high on the agenda.

What can be concluded is that organisational learning has emerged as a dominant theme in the 1990s and is being employed by organisations in the automotive sector to encourage people to contribute their knowledge, skills and creativity to innovate and achieve competitive advantage. It is clear that the approach takes time to establish in organisations because it challenges the traditional nature of work and organisational life and requires culture change to support its development. How far this provides a foundation for a new theory of management, however, is debatable because whilst people are encouraged to challenge established practices, management control must remain intact to co-ordinate the disparate learning initiatives that emerge. Nevertheless, promoting learning can assist in the achievement of competitive success. Learning can occur at different levels and at identifiable stages in the life cycle of the organisations, and management can employ deliberate strategies and interventions to encourage the process.

Future research

There has been a dearth of empirical research on organisational learning and its impact on the change process. This study has sought to remedy this by identifying and analysing the approaches adopted in selected case-study companies in the automotive sector, and evaluating their significance in achieving and sustaining organisational success. Identifying the different levels at which the organisations can maximise their potential to capture learning opportunities offers a framework for further investigation and analysis. However, the use of case-study research methodology in one sector raises questions about generalisability, about how far the research findings can be applied to other sectors and situations.

There are many issues that require further investigation and the limitations of the present research reveals other aspects that would provide a deeper understanding of organisational learning and change and their impact in contemporary organisations. A significant limitation of this study is that it was confined to four organisations in a sector noted for innovative work practices, and that, to varying degrees, the companies have made progress in developing learning approaches to manage change. How far these findings apply outside the sector studied is debatable. It would therefore be valuable to research the issues beyond the sector, particularly in smaller organisations that have limited knowledge or understanding of organisational learning *per se*.

With respect both to the literature explored and the empirical research undertaken for the study, further examination of the informal organisation and its implications for future work arrangements would provide a greater depth of understanding. This may be significant, given what appears to be a drift toward what some might see as a more social organisation of production. It would be useful to examine and research contemporary analyses of the experiential learning process and how it can be further developed in the team and workplace environment. The case-study research suggests specific aspects that may provide scope for future development, such as the significance of leadership in the organisations and how far leaders are instrumental in establishing or preventing impetus and continuity for learning and change. Similarly, the ability of leaders to communicate and translate the need for change and to establish new organisational realities may provide a rich source for future research. Finally, at the shopfloor level, it is clear that 'post-lean' developments that are occurring in the automotive sector are worthy of further exploration. They may have significant impact on the design of work, the relationships within and between organisations, and the skills and competencies individuals will require for employability and organisational success in the future.

Bibliography

Abo, T. (1995) Comparison of Japanese hybrid factories in US, Europe and Asia, *Management International Review*, vol. 35, pp. 79–94.

Abodaher, D. (1986) *Iacocca: The Most Dynamic Businessman of Our Time*, London: W. H. Allen.

Ackoff, R. (1989) The circular organization, *Academy of Management Executive*, vol. 3, part 1, pp. 11–16.

Ackroyd, S., Burrell, G., Hughes, M. and Whitaker, A. (1988) The Japanization of British industry, *Industrial Relations Journal*, pp. 11–23.

Adler, P. S. and Cole, R. E. (1993) Designed for learning: a tale of two auto plants, *Sloan Management Review*, Spring, pp. 85–94.

Allaire, Y. and Firsirotou, M. E. (1984) Theories of organizational culture, *Organization Studies*, vol. 5, no. 3, pp. 193–226.

Allaire, P. (1993) The new productivity, *Executive Excellence*, January, pp. 3–4.

Altmann, N. (1995) Japanese work policy: opportunity, challenge or threat, in A. Sandberg (ed.) *Enriching Production*, Aldershot: Avebury.

Anderson, N., Hardy, G. and West, M. (1994) Innovative teams at work, in C. Mabey and P. Iles (eds) *Managing Learning*, London: Routledge.

Arkin, A. (1993) An education in training, *Personnel Management*, December, pp. 42–5.

Argyris, C. (1957) *Personality and Organization*, New York: Harper and Row.

Argyris, C. (1985) *Strategy, Change and Defensive Routines*, New York: Pitman.

Argyris, C. (1987) *Social Science Approaches to Business Behaviour*, New York: Garland Publishing Inc.

Argyris, C. (1990) *Overcoming Organizational Defenses: Facilitating Organizational Learning*, New Jersey: Prentice-Hall.

Argyris, C. (1992) *On Organizational Learning*, Oxford: Blackwell.

Argyris, C. (1977) Double-loop learning in organizations, *Harvard Business Review*, September–October, pp. 115–25.

Argyris, C. (1991) Teaching smart people how to learn, *Harvard Business Review*, May–June, pp. 99–109.

Argyris, C. (1995) Action science and organizational learning, *Journal of Managerial Psychology*, vol. 10, no. 6, pp. 20–7.

Argyris, C. and Schon, D. (1978) *Organizational Learning*, Reading, Mass: Addison-Wesley.

Ashby, W. R. (1960) *An Introduction to Cybernetics*, London: Chapman and Hall.

Ashley, S. (1993) The making of an effective manager, *Mechanical Engineering*, January pp. 61–3.

Ashton, D. and Felstead, A. (1995) Training and development, in J. Storey (ed.) *Human Resource Management: A Critical Text*, London: Routledge.

Atkinson, J. (1984) Manpower strategies for flexible organizations, *Personnel Management*, vol. 16, issue 8, pp. 28–31.

Atkinson, J. and Meager, N. (1986) *Changing Working Patterns: How Companies Achieve Flexibility to Meet New Needs*, London: NEDO.

Atkinson, J. (1987) Flexibility or fragmentation? The United Kingdom labour market in the Eighties, *Labour and Society*, vol. 12, no. 1, pp. 87–105.

Auer, P. (1995) Lean production: the micro-macro dimension, employment and the welfare state, in A. Sandberg (ed.) *Enriching Production*, Aldershot: Avebury.

Bailey, J. (1993) *Managing People and Technological Change*, London: Pitman.

Barnard, C. (1938) *The Functions of the Executive*, Cambridge, MA: Harvard University Press.

Barrow, M. J. and Loughlin, H. M. (1992) Towards a learning organization, *Industrial and Commercial Training*, vol. 24, no. 1, pp. 3–7.

Bateson, G. (1972) *Steps to an Ecology of Mind*, New York: Ballantine.

Bayley, S. (1999) Swede smell of success, *The Guardian*, 1 February, p. 15.

Baylin, L. (1993) Patterned chaos in human resource management, *Sloan Management Review*, Winter, pp. 77–83.

Beard, D. (1993) Learning to change organizations, *Personnel Management*, January, pp. 32–5.

Beer, M., Eisensat, R. A. and Spector, B. (1993) Why change programmes don't produce change, in C. Mabey and B. Mayon-White (eds) *Managing Change*, London: Paul Chapman Publishing (2nd ed.).

Beer, M. and Eisenstat, R. A. (1996) Developing an organization capable of implementing strategy and learning, *Human Relations*, vol. 49, no. 5, pp. 597–620.

Benders, J. (1995) Leaving lean? Contemporary developments in Japanese car factories, unpublished paper, 13th Labour Process Conference, 5–7 April, Blackpool.

Benjamin, G. and Mabey, C. (1993) Facilitating radical change, in C. Mabey and B. Mayon-White (eds) *Managing Change*, London: Paul Chapman Publishing (2nd ed.).

Bennet, J. K. and O'Brien, M. J. (1994) The building blocks of the learning organization, *Training*, vol. 31, issue 5, pp. 41–9.

Benson, T. (1993) The learning organization: heading towards places unimaginable, *Industry Week*, January 4, pp. 35–8.

Berggren, C. (1992) *The Volvo Experience*, London: Macmillan.

Berggren, C. (1995) Japan as number two: competitive problems and the future of alliance capitalism after the burst of the bubble boom, *Work, Employment and Society*, vol. 9, no. 1, pp. 53–95.

Blackler, F. (1993) Knowledge and the theory of organizations: organizations as activity systems and the re-framing of management, *Journal of Management Studies*, vol. 30, no. 6, November, pp. 863–84.

Blackler, F. (1995) Knowledge, knowledge work and organizations: an overview and interpretation, *Organization Studies*, vol. 16, no. 6, pp. 1021–47.

Blackler, F., Reed, M. and Whitaker, A. (1993) Knowledge workers and contemporary organizations, *Journal of Management Studies*, vol. 30, no. 6, November, pp. 851–62.

Blagg, N., Lewis, R. and Ballinger, M. (1994) Thinking and learning at work, *Employment Department Research Series*, no. 23, February.

Blyton, P. and Turnbull, P. (1992) (eds) *Reassessing Human Resource Management*, London: Sage Publications.

Boddy, D. and Buchanan, D. (1992) *The Expertise of the Change Agent*, London: Prentice-Hall.

Boer, H. (1994) Flexible manufacturing systems, in J. Storey (ed.) *New Wave Manufacturing Strategies*, London: Paul Chapman Publishing.

Bohm, D. (1980) *Wholeness and the Implicate Order*, New York: Ark Paperbacks.

Bohm, D. (1993) For truth try dialogue, *Resurgence*, January–February, issue 156, pp. 10–13.

Bower, D. G. (1993) The learning organization: a Rover perspective, *Executive Development UK*, vol. 6, part 2, pp. 3–6.

Brandon, L. G. (1993) Learning organizations hold the key to success, *National Underwriter*, vol. 27, issue 43, pp. 22 and 43.

Bratton, J. (1992) *Japanization at Work*, Basingstoke: Macmillan Press.

Braverman, H. (1974) *Labour and Monopoly Capital*, New York: Monthly Review Press.

Brierley, D. (1996) How BMW put the driving force back into Rover, *The European*, 28 March, no. 307, p. 21.

Briggs, P. (1988) The Japanese at work: illusions of the ideal, *Industrial Relations Journal*, vol. 19, no. 1, pp. 24–30.

Brown, J. S. and Duguid, P. (1991) Organizational learning and communities of practice; towards a unified view of working, learning and innovation, *Organization Science*, vol. 2, no. 1, pp. 40–57.

Brunson, N. and Olsen, J. P. (1993) *The Reforming Organization*, London: Routledge.

Bryman, A. and Burgess, R. G. (1994) *Analyzing Qualitative Data*, London: Routledge.

Buchanan, D. and Boddy, D. (1992) *Take the Lead: Interpersonal Skills for Change Agents*, London: Prentice-Hall.

Buchanan, D. and Huczynski, A. (1997) *Organisational Behaviour: An Introductory Text*, London: Prentice Hall (3rd ed.).

Burdett, J. O. (1993) Managing in the age of discontinuity, *Management Decision*, vol. 31, no. 1, pp. 10–17.

Burdett, J. O. (1994) The magic of alignment, *Management Decision*, vol. 32, no. 2, pp. 59–63.

Burgoyne, J. (1988) Management development for the individual and the organization, *Personnel Management*, June, pp. 40–4.

Burgoyne, J. (1992) Creating a learning organization, *Royal Society of Arts* paper, April, pp. 321–32.

Burgoyne, J. (1994) Managing by learning, *Management Learning*, vol. 25, no. 1, pp. 35–55.

Burgoyne, J. (1995) Learning from experience: from individual discovery to meta-dialogue via the evolution of transitional myths, *Personnel Review*, vol. 24, no. 6, pp. 61–73.

Burgoyne, J. (1995a) Feeding minds to grow the business, *People Management*, vol. 1, no. 19, pp. 22–6.

Burgoyne, J., Pedler, M. and Boydell, T. (1994) *Towards the Learning Company*, London: McGraw-Hill.

Burnes, B. (1996) *Managing Change*, London: Pitman (2nd ed.).

Burnes, B. (1991) Managerial competence and new technology, *Behaviour and Information Technology*, vol. 10, no. 2, pp. 91–109.

Burnes, B. (1993) Structure and culture: putting the human dimension of CIM in perspective, *International Journal of Human Factors in Manufacturing*, vol. 3, no. 2, pp. 183–91.

Burnes, B. and New, S. (1996) Understanding supply chain improvement, *European Journal of Purchasing and Supply Management*, vol. 2, no. 1, pp. 21–30.

Burns, T. and Stalker, G. M. (1961) *The Management of Innovation*, New York: Tavistock.

Burrell, G. (1997) *Pandemonium*, London: Sage.

Bushe, G. and Shani, A. (1991) *Parallel Learning Structures*, New York: Addison-Wesley.

Calvert, G., Mobley, S. and Marshall, L. (1994) Grasping the learning organization, *Training and Development*, vol. 48, issue 6, pp. 38–43.

Camuffo, A. and Costa, G. (1993) Strategic human resource management – Italian style, *Sloan Management Review*, Winter, pp. 59–66.

Capra, F. (1992) A systems view of the world, *Resurgence*, no. 151, pp. 34–7.

Carnall, C. A. (1990) *Managing Change in Organizations*, London: Prentice-Hall.

Carr, F. (1994) Introducing teamworking – a motor industry case study, *Industrial Relations Journal*, vol. 25, no. 3, pp. 199–209.

Carter, R., Martin, J., Mayblin, R. and Munday, J. (1984) *Systems, Management and Change*, London: Paul Chapman Publishing.

Cassell, C. and Symon, G. (1995) (eds) *Qualitative Methods in Organizational Research*, London: Sage.

Chen, M. (1995) *Asian Management Systems*, London: Routledge.

Clark, J. (1993) (ed.) *Human Resource Management and Technical Change*, London: Sage Publications.

Clark, K. B. and Fujimoto, T. (1991) *Product Development Performance: Strategy, Organisation and Management in the World Auto Industry*, Boston, Mass: Harvard Business School Press.

Clarke, L. (1994) *The Essence of Change*, London: Prentice-Hall.

Clegg, C. (1986) Trip to Japan: A synergistic approach to managing human resources, *Personnel Management*, August, pp. 35–9.

Clegg, S. and Palmer, G. (1996) (eds) *The Politics of Management Knowledge*, London: Sage.

Clegg, S., Barrett, M., Clarke, T., Dwyer, L., Gray, J., Kemp, S. and Marceau, J. (1996) Management knowledge for the future, in S. Clegg and G. Palmer (eds) *The Politics of Management Knowledge*, London: Sage.

Cole, R. E. (1980) Learning from the Japanese: prospects and pitfalls, *Management Review*, September, pp. 22–43.

Cook, S. D. and Yanow, D. (1993) Culture and organizational learning, *Journal of Management Inquiry*, vol. 2, no. 4, pp. 373–90.

Cook, S. D. and Yanow, D. (1996) Culture and organizational learning, in M. D. Cohen and L. Sproull (eds) *Organizational Learning*, California: Sage Publications.

Coopey, J. (1996) Crucial gaps in the learning organization: power, politics and ideology, in K. Starkey (ed.) *How Organizations Learn*, London: Thomson Business Press.

Coughlan, D. (1993) In defence of process consultation, in C. Mabey and B. Mayon-White (eds) *Managing Change*, London: Paul Chapman Publishing (2nd ed.).

Coulson-Thomas, C. (1990) The responsive organization, *Journal of General Management*, Summer, vol. 15, no. 4, pp. 21–31.

Cressey, P. (1996) Enriching production: perspectives on Volvo's Uddevalla plant as an alternative to lean production, *Industrial Relations Journal*, vol. 27, no. 1, pp. 77–80.

Crossan, M. M. and Inkpen, A. (1995) The subtle art of learning through alliances, *Business Quarterly*, vol. 60, no. 2, pp. 68–77.

Crowther, S. and Garrahan, P. (1988) Invitation to Sunderland: corporate power and the local economy, *Industrial Relations Journal*, vol. 19, no. 1, pp. 51–9.

Cummings, T. G. (1989) Self-designing organizations, *Organization Development and Change*, West Publishing Company: University of Southern California.

Cummings, T. G. and Huse, E. F. (1989) *Organization Development and Change*, St Paul, USA: West Publishing Company.

Cunningham, I. (1994) *The Wisdom of Strategic Learning: The Self-Managed Learning Solution*, Maidenhead: McGraw-Hill.

Cunningham, I., Hyman, J. and Baldry, C. (1996) Empowerment: the power to do what? *Industrial Relations Journal*, vol. 27, no. 2, pp. 143–54.

Dale, M. (1994) Learning organizations, in C. Mabey and P. Iles (eds) *Managing Learning*, London, Routledge.

Daley, M. and McCann, A. (1992) How many small firms? *Employment Gazette*, February, pp. 47–51.

Darlington, R. (1994) Shop stewards' organization in Halewood: from Beynon to today, *Industrial Relations Journal*, vol. 25, no. 2, pp. 136–49.

Davies, J. (1989) *The Challenge to Western Management Development*, London: Routledge.

Davies, J. and Easterby-Smith, M. (1984) Learning and developing from managerial work experiences, *Journal of Management Studies*, vol. 21, part 2, pp. 169–83.

Dawson, P. (1994) *Organizational Change: A Processual Approach*, London: Paul Chapman Publishing.

Dawson, P. and Webb, J. (1989) New production arrangements: the totally flexible cage? *Work, Employment and Society*, vol. 3, no. 2, pp. 221–38.

de Geus, A. (1988) Planning as learning, *Harvard Business Review*, March–April, pp. 70–4.

de Saint-Amboise, R. (1992) The east wind: personal competence and the learning company, *Management Education and Development*, vol. 23, part 1, pp. 3–5.

Deal, T. and Kennedy, A. (1988) *Corporate Cultures: The Rites and Rituals of Corporate Life*, Harmondsworth: Penguin.

Delbridge, R., Turnbull, P. and Wilkinson, B. (1992) Pushing back the frontiers: management control under JIT/TQM factory regimes, *New Technology, Work and Employment*, vol. 7, no. 2, pp. 97–106.

Delbridge, R., Lowe, J. and Oliver, N. (1995) The process of benchmarking: a study from the automotive industry, *International Journal of Operations and Production Management*, vol. 15, no. 4, pp. 50–64.

Denison, D. R. (1990) *Corporate Culture and Organizational Effectiveness*, New York: J. Wiley and Sons.

Denton, K. D. and Wisdom, B. L. (1991) The learning organization involves the entire workforce, *Quality Progress*, December, pp. 69–72.

Denzin, N. K. (1989) Interpretive interactionism, in G. Morgan (ed.) *Beyond Method: Strategies for Social Research*, London: Sage.

Dichter, S. F. (1991) The organization of the '90s, *The McKinsey Quarterly*, no. 1, pp. 145–55.

Dixon, N. (1994) *The Organizational Learning Cycle: How We Can Learn Collectively*, Maidenhead: McGraw-Hill.

Donegan, J. (1990) The learning organization: lessons from British Petroleum, *European Management Journal*, vol. 8, no. 3, pp. 302–12.

Doyle, M. (1995) Organizational transformation and renewal: a case for re-framing management development? *Personnel Review*, vol. 24, no. 6, pp. 6–19.

Drucker, P. (1959) *Landmarks of Tomorrow*, New York: Harper.

Drucker, P. (1968) *The Age of Discontinuity*, New York: Harper and Row.

Drucker, P. (1989) *The New Realities*, New York: Heinemann.

Drucker, P. (1992) *Managing for the Future*, New York: Butterworth Heinemann.

Drucker, P. (1971) What can we learn from Japanese management?, *Harvard Business Review*, March–April, pp. 110–22.

Drucker, P. (1981) Behind Japan's success, *Harvard Business Review*, January–February, pp. 83–90.

Drucker, P. (1992) The new society of organizations, *Harvard Business Review*, September–October, pp. 95–104.

Easterby-Smith, M. (1990) Creating a learning organization, *Personnel Review*, vol. 19, no. 5, pp. 24–8.

Easterby-Smith, M., Burgoyne, J. and Araujo, L. (1999) (eds) *Organisational Learning and the Learning Organisation*, London: Sage.

Elger, T. (1990) Technical innovation and work re-organization in British manufacturing in the 1980s: continuity, intensification or transformation? *Work, Employment and Society*, Special Issue, pp. 67–101.

Elger, T. and Smith, C. (1996) The problematical management of labour and the patterning of workplace relations in Japanese manufacturing transplants in Britain, Employment Research Unit Conference, Manufacturing Matters: Organisation and Employee Relations in Modern Manufacturing, Cardiff Business School, 18–19 September.

Ellegard, K., Jonsson, D., Engstrom, T., Johansson, M., Medbo, L. and Johansson, B. (1992) Reflective production in the final assembly of motor vehicles – an emerging Swedish challenge, *International Journal of Operation and Production Management*, vol. 12, nos. 7/8, pp. 117–33.

Ellegard, K. (1995) The creation of a new production system at the Volvo automobile plant in Uddevalla, Sweden, in A. Sandberg (ed.) *Enriching Production*, Aldershot: Avebury.

Emery, F. E. (1969) *Systems Thinking*, Harmondsworth: Penguin.

Emery, F. and Trist, E. (1965) The causal texture of organizational environments, *Human Relations*, vol. 18, no. 1, pp. 21–32.

Emmott, B. (1992) *Japan's Global Reach*, London: Century.

Evans, P. (1991) International management development and the balance between generalism and professionalism, *Personnel Management*, December, pp. 46–50.

Fenton-O'Creevy, M. and Nicholson, N. (1994) Middle managers: their contribution to employee involvement, *Employment Department Research Series*, no. 28, June.

Festinger, L. (1957) *The Theory of Cognitive Dissonance*, Stanford, California: Stanford University Press.

Fiol, M. C. and Lyles, M. A. (1985) Organizational learning, *Academy of Management Review*, vol. 10, no. 4, pp. 803–13.

Fisher, D. and Torbert, W. (1995) *Personal and Organizational Transformations: The True Challenge of Continual Quality Improvement*, Maidenhead: McGraw-Hill.

French, R. and Grey, C. (1996) *Rethinking Management Education*, London: Sage.

Friedlander, F. (1984) Patterns of individual and organisational learning, in Srivastava, S. and Associates, *The Executive Mind – New Insights on Managerial Thoughts and Actions*, San Francisco: Jossey Bass.

Fucini, J. J. and Fucini, S. (1990) *Working for the Japanese: Inside Mazda's American Plant*, New York: The Free Press.

Fulmer, R. M. (1984) A model for changing the way organizations learn, *Planning Review*, vol. 22, issue 3, pp. 20–4.

Galer, G. and van der Heijden, K. (1992) The learning organization, *Marketing Intelligence and Planning*, vol. 10, part 6, pp. 5–12.

Galiardi, P. (1986) The creation and change of organizational cultures, *Organization Studies*, vol. 7, part 2, pp. 117–34.

Gallie, D. and White, M. (1995) Employee commitment and the skills revolution, in J. Storey (ed.) *Human Resource Management: A Critical Text*, London: Routledge.

Galpin, T. (1996) Connecting culture to organizational change, *HRM Magazine*, vol. 41, no. 3, pp. 84–90.

Garrahan, P. and Stewart, P. (1992) *The Nissan Enigma: Flexibility at Work in a Local Economy*, London: Mansell Publishing Ltd.

Garratt, B. (1987) *The Learning Organization*, London: Fontana.

Garratt, B. (1990) *Learning to Lead*, London: Fontana.

Garratt, B. (1990) The short-sighted rhinoceros, *Director*, April, pp. 92–8.

Garratt, B. (1993) The learning board, *Director*, May, pp. 62–6.

Garratt, B. (1995) The learning organization: an old idea that has come of age, *People Management*, vol. 1, no. 19, pp. 25–8.

Garvin, D. A. (1993) Building a learning organization, *Harvard Business Review*, July–August, pp. 78–91.

Gill, S. J. (1995) Shifting gears for high performance, *Training and Development*, May, vol. 49, no. 5, pp. 24–31.

Glaser, S. (1991) A note on corporate culture, *Management Decision*, vol. 29, no. 2, pp. 6–8.

Gleick, J. (1988) *Chaos: Making a New Science*, London: Heinemann.

Godet, M. (1987) Ten unfashionable and controversial findings on Japan, *Futures*, August, pp. 371–84.

Golder, J. D. and Lei, D. (1991) The shape of 21st century global manufacturing, *Journal of Business Strategy*, March–April, vol. 12, pp. 37–41.

Gordon , J. (1992) Performance technology: blueprint for a learning organization, *Training*, May, pp. 27–36.

Goshal, S. (1992) The Kao Corporation case study, *European Management Journal*, vol. 10, no. 2, pp. 179–92.

Graham, H. T. (1986) *Human Resources Management*, London: Pitman (5th ed.).

Graham, I. (1988) Japanization as mythology, *Industrial Relations Journal*, vol. 19, no. 1, pp. 69–75.

Greiner, L. E. (1972) Evolution and revolution as organisations grow, *Harvard Business Review*, July–August, pp. 37–46.

Groggins, B. and Millar, I. (1992) Change – an all-employee programme, *Industrial and Commercial Training*, vol. 24, no. 1, pp. 8–11.

Grundy, T. (1994) *Strategic Learning in Action: How to Accelerate and Sustain Business Change*, Maidenhead: McGraw-Hill.

Guest, D. (1992) Right enough to be dangerously wrong, in G. Salaman (ed.) *Human Resource Strategies*, London: Sage.

Guest, D. (1989) Personnel and HRM: can you tell the difference? *Personnel Management*, January, pp. 48–51.

Guglilmino, P. J. (1991) The self-directed learner, *Sundridge Park Management Review*, vol. 5, part 4, pp. 32–8.

Hakim, C. (1992) *Research Design: Strategies and Choices in the Design of Social Research*, London: Routledge.

Hampden-Turner, C. (1990) *Charting the Corporate Mind*, New York: The Free Press.

Hancke, B. and Rubinstein, S. (1995) Limits to innovation in work organisation? in A. Sandberg (ed.) *Enriching Production*, Aldershot: Avebury.

Hand, A., Gambles, J. and Cooper, E. (1994) Individual commitment to learning, *Employment Department Research Series*, no. 42, November.

Handy, C. (1976) *Understanding Organizations*, London: Penguin.

Handy, C. (1977) Is this the way to the future? *Management Education and Development*, vol. 8, pp. 57–62.

Handy, C. (1989) *The Age of Unreason*, London: Arrow Books.

Handy, C. (1993) *The Empty Raincoat*, London: Hutchinson.

Harrison, A. (1994) Just-in-time manufacturing, in J. Storey (ed.) *New Wave Manufacturing Strategies*, London: Paul Chapman Publishing.

Harrison, A. and Storey, J. (1996) New wave manufacturing strategies: operational, organizational and human dimensions, *International Journal of Operations and Production Management*, vol. 16, no. 2, pp. 63–77.

Hartley, J. F. (1994) Case studies in organisational research, in C. Cassell and G. Symon (eds) *Qualitative Methods in Organisational Research*, London: Sage.

Hassard, J. and Parker, M. (1994) (eds) *Towards a New Theory of Organizations*, London: Routledge.

Hatcher, T. G. (1997) An interview with Malcolm Knowles, *Training and Development*, vol. 51, no. 2, pp. 37–8.

Hatvany, N. and Pucik, V. (1984) An integrated management system: lessons from the Japanese experience, *Academy of Management Review*, vol. 6, pp. 469–79.

Hawkins, P. (1991) The spiritual dimension of the learning organization, *Management Education and Development*, vol. 22, no. 3, pp. 172–87.

Hawkins, P. (1994) Organizational learning, *Management Learning*, vol. 25, no. 1, pp. 71–82.

Hawkins, P. (1994) The changing view of learning, in J. Burgoyne, M. Pedler and T. Boydell (eds) *Towards the Learning Company: Concepts and Practices*, London: McGraw-Hill.

Hayes, R. H. (1981) Why Japanese factories work, *Harvard Business Review*, July–August, pp. 57–66.

Hedberg, B. (1981) How organizations learn and unlearn, in P. Nystrom and W. Starbuck (ed.) *Handbook of Organizational Design*, vol. 1, pp. 8–27, Oxford: Oxford University Press.

Hedberg, B., Nystrom, P. and Starbuck, W. (1976) Camping on seesaws: prescriptions for a self-designing organization, *Administrative Science Quarterly*, vol. 21, part 1, pp. 41–65.

Hendry, C., Pettigrew, A. and Sparrow, P. (1988) Changing patterns of human resource management, *Personnel Management*, November, pp. 37–41.

Hendry, C., Arthur, B. and Jones, A. (1995) *Strategy Through People*, London: Routledge.

Hendry, C. (1996) Understanding and creating whole organizational change through learning, *Human Relations*, vol. 49, no. 5, May, pp. 621–41.

Henry, J. (1991) *Creative Management*, London: Sage.

Henry, J. and Walker, D. (1991) *Managing Innovation*, London: Sage.

Herriot, P. and Pemberton, C. (1995) *Competitive Advantage Through Diversity: Organizational Learning Through Difference*, London: Sage.

Herzberg, F. (1968) One more time: How do you motivate employees? *Harvard Business Review*, 46, pp. 53–62.

Heyes, J. (1993) Training provision and workplace institutions: an investigation, *Industrial Relations Journal*, vol. 24, no. 4, pp. 296–307.

Hill, S. (1991) Why quality circles failed but total quality might succeed, *British Journal of Industrial Relations*, vol. 29, no. 4, pp. 541–68.

Hinton, R. W. and Londo, E. (1992) Learning to manage strategically: prescriptions for a changing world? *Journal of Management Development*, vol. 11, no. 6, pp. 13–24.

Hirschorn, L. and Gilmore, T. (1992) The new boundaries of the boundaryless company, *Harvard Business Review*, May–June, pp. 104–15.

Hodgetts, R. M., Luthans, F. and Lee, S. (1994) New paradigm organizations, *Organizational Dynamics*, vol. 22, no. 3, pp. 5–19.

Hodgson, G. (1995) *People's Century*, London: BBC Books.

Holberton, S. (1991) Two routes that lead to the same goal, *Financial Times*, 6 February.

Holloway, J. (1987) The red rose of Nissan, *Capital and Class*, vol. 32, pp. 142–64.

Holman, D., Pavlica, K. and Thorpe, T. (1997) Rethinking Kolb's theory of experiential learning in management education, *Management Learning*, vol. 28 (2), pp. 135–48.

Holt, J. (1983) *How Children Learn*, New York: Delacorte.

Holti, R. and Norris, M. (1991) The search for innovation and learning in organizations, *The Tavistock Institute Review*, pp. 17–21.

Hommen, J. and Tijmstra, S. (1990) New challenges for management development, *European Management Journal*, vol. 8, no. 3, pp. 328–32.

Honey, P. (1991) The learning organization simplified, *Training and Development*, July, pp. 30–3.

Honey, P. and Mumford, A. (1992) *Manual of Learning Styles*, London: Peter Honey (3rd ed.).

Honold, L. (1991) The power of learning at Johnsonville Foods, *Training*, vol. 28, pp. 54–8.

Horsley, W. and Buckley, R. (1990) *Nippon: New Superpower, Japan Since 1945*, London: BBC Books.

Hsieh, Tsun-Yan, (1992) The road to renewal, *The McKinsey Quarterly*, no. 3, pp. 28–36.

Huber, G. P. (1991) Organizational learning: the contributing processes and the literatures, *Organization Science*, February, pp. 88–115.

Hyden, H. (1991) Winning organizations, *Executive Excellence*, vol. 8, p. 20.

Iles, P, and Salaman, G. (1995) Recruitment, selection and assessment, in J. Storey (ed.) *Human Resource Management: A Critical Text*, London: Routledge.

Jackson, C. (1991) Career development: The challenge for organizations, *International Journal of Career Management*, vol. 3, no. 3, pp. 17–25.

James, P. (1996) Employee development programmes: the US auto approach, *Personnel Review*, vol. 25, no. 2, pp. 35–49.

Jermier, J. M., Knights, D. and Nord, W. R. (1994) *Resistance and Power in Organizations*, London: Routledge.

Johnson, G. (1993) Processes of managing strategic change, in Mabey, C. and Mayon-White, B. (eds) *Managing Change*, London: Paul Chapman Publishing (2nd ed.).

Johnson, G. and Scholes, K. (1997) *Exploring Corporate Strategy*, London: Prentice Hall (2nd ed.).

Jones, D. T. (1981) Maturity and crisis in the European car industry: structural change and public policy, *Sussex European Papers*, no. 8, Sussex European Research Centre, University of Sussex, Brighton.

Jones, D. T. (1983) Technology and the UK auto industry, *Lloyds Bank Review*, no. 148, April, pp. 14–27.

Jones, D. T. (1985) The import threat to the UK car industry, *Science Policy Research Unit*, University of Sussex, Brighton.

Jones, K. K. (1992) Competing to learn in Japan, *The McKinsey Quarterly*, no. 1, pp. 45–57.

Jonsson, D. (1995) Lean production in the automobile industry, in A. Sandberg (ed.) *Enriching Production*, Aldershot: Avebury.

Kakabadse, A., Ludlow, R. and Vinnicombe, S. (1988) *Working in Organizations*, London: Penguin.

Kamata, S. (1973) *Japan in the Passing Lane: An Insider's Account of Life in a Japanese Auto Factory*, New York: Pantheon.

Karlsson, C. (1996) Radically new production systems, *International Journal of Operations and Production Management*, vol. 16, no. 11, pp. 8–19.

Karlsson, C. and Ahlstrom, P. (1996) Assessing changes towards lean production, *International Journal of Operations and Production Management*, vol. 16, no. 2, pp. 24–43.

Katayama, H. and Bennett, D. (1996) Lean production in a changing competitive world, *International Journal of Operations and Production Management*, vol. 16, no. 2, pp. 8–24.

Keep, E. (1992) Corporate training strategies: the vital component? in G. Salaman (ed.) *Human Resource Strategies*, London: Sage.

Kendal, G. (1989) Effective learning, *Employment Gazette*, October, pp. 521–5.

Kenney, M. and Florida, R. (1993) *Beyond Mass Production*, Oxford: Oxford University Press.

Keys, J. B. and Miller, T. (1986) The Japanese management theory jungle, *The Management of Organizations*, pp. 337–49.

King, N. (1994) The qualitative research interview, in C. Cassell and G. Symons (eds) *Qualitative Methods in Organisational Research*, London: Sage.

Knowles, M. S. (1984) *The Adult Learner: A Neglected Species*, New York: Gulf Publishing (3rd ed.).

Kolb, D. A. (1984) *Experiential Learning*, Englewood Cliffs, New Jersey: Prentice-Hall.

Kolb, D. A. (1989) Strategic management development: experiential learning and managerial competencies in G. Morgan (ed.) *Beyond Method: Strategies for Social Research*, London: Sage.

Kolb, D., Lublin, S., Spoth, J. and Baker, R. (1994) Strategic management development; using experiential learning theory to assess and develop managerial competencies, in C. Mabey and P. Iles (eds) *Managing Learning*, London: Routledge.

Kraar, L. (1995) Korea's auto-makers take on the world, *Fortune*, vol. 131, no. 4, pp. 152–8.

Kramlinger, T. (1992) Training's role in a learning organization, *Training*, July, pp. 46–51.

Kuhn, T. B. (1962) *The Structure of Scientific Revolutions*, Chicago: University of Chicago Press.

Lathrope, K. (1985) Stop your workforce standing still, *Personnel Management*, October, pp. 50–3.

Lawler, E. E. (1994) Ten new realities, *Executive Excellence*, vol. 10, issue 3, pp. 18–19.

Lawrence, P. R. and Lorsch, J. W. (1967) *Organization and Environment*, Boston: Harvard University Press.

Laycock, M. (1994) *Tallent Engineering Limited*, Henley Management College, MBA Modules in Managing Strategic Change.

Leary, M. (1992) Making a difference, integration consciousness, *Industrial and Commercial Training*, vol. 24, no. 1, pp. 22–8.

Legge, K. (1995) *Human Resource Management: Rhetorics and Realities*, London: Macmillan Business.

Leicester, C. (1989) The key role of the line manager in employee development, *Personnel Management*, March, pp. 53–7.

Leijon, S. and Lofstrom, M. (1993) The good work in Sweden – twilight time? An analysis of the debate following the closure of alternative car production in Sweden, paper presented to the Labour Process Conference, 31 March–2 April, Blackpool.

Leonard-Barton, D. (1992) The factory as a learning laboratory, *Sloan Management Review*, Fall, pp. 23–38.

Lessem, R. (1989) *Global Management Principles*, London: Prentice-Hall.

Lessem, R. (1990) *Developmental Management, Principles of Holistic Business*, Oxford: Blackwell.

Lessem, R. (1991) *Total Quality Learning*, Oxford: Blackwell.

Lessem, R. (1993) *Business as a Learning Community*, Maidenhead, England: McGraw-Hill.

Lewin, K. (1952) *Field Theory in Social Sciences*, London: Harper and Row.

Lewin, T. (1995) Car-makers find crumbs of comfort, *The European*, June 30, p. 28.

Lichstein, H. (1991) Innovation, *Executive Speeches*, vol. 5, issue 9, pp. 7–11.

Lillrank, P. (1995) The transfer of management innovations from Japan, *Organisation Studies*, vol. 16, no. 6, pp. 971–91.

Lillrank, P. (1995) Social preconditions for lean manufacture and its further development, in A. Sandberg (ed.) *Enriching Production*, Aldershot: Avebury.

Lindgren, A. (1993) Dualism and labour markets: the case of Volvo, Saab and Renault, paper presented to the Labour Process Conference, 31 March–2 April, Blackpool.

Lippitt, G. (1987) *Implementing Organizational Change*, New York: Jossey Bass.

Lorenz, A. (1994) The British car is dead; long live the British car, *Management Today*, August, pp. 36–42.

Lundberg, C. (1991) Creating and managing a vanguard organization, *Human Resource Management*, vol. 30, issue 1, pp. 89–112.

Lyles, M. A., Near, J. P. and Enz, C. (1992) A simulation for teaching skills relating to organization self renewal, *Journal of Management Development*, vol. 11, no. 7, pp. 39–47.

Lynch, R. (1997) *Corporate Strategy*, London: Pitman.

Lynn-Meek, V. (1988) Organizational culture: origins and weaknesses, *Organization Studies*, vol. 9, no. 4, pp. 453–73.

Mabey, C. and Mayon-White, B. (1993) *Managing Change*, London: Paul Chapman Publishing (2nd ed.).

Mabey, C. and Iles, P. (1994) *Managing Learning*, London: Routledge.

Maccoby, M. (1993) What should learning organizations learn? *Research Technology Management*, May–June, pp. 49–52.

Malerba, F. (1992) Learning by firms and incremental technical change, *The Economic Journal*, July, pp. 845–59.

March, J. G. and Olsen, J. P. (1975) The uncertainty of the past; organizational learning under ambiguity, *European Journal of Political Research*, vol. 3, pp. 147–71.

Marchington, M. and Parker, P. (1988) Japanization: A lack of chemical reaction, *Industrial Relations Journal*, vol. 19, no. 4, pp. 272–85.

Marchington, M., Goodman, G., Wilkinson, A. and Ackers, P. (1992) New developments in employee involvement, *Employment Department Research Series*, no. 2, May.

Marginson, P. (1989) Employment flexibility in large companies: change and continuity, *Industrial Relations Journal*, vol. 20, no. 2, pp. 101–9.

Maslow, A. H. (1943) A theory of human motivation, *Psychological Review*, vol. 50, pp. 370–96.

Mason, D. H. (1994) Scenario-based planning, *Planning Review*, vol. 22, part 2, pp. 6–11.

Mason, J. (1996) *Qualitative Researching*, London: Sage.

Maul, G. P. and Gillard, J. S. (1993) Training today's managers to effectively use TQM, *Industrial Engineering*, January, pp. 49–50.

Mayo, A. and Lank, E. (1994) *The Power of Learning*, London: IPD.

Mayo, A. and Lank, E. (1995) Changing the soil spurs new growth, *People Management*, November, pp. 26–8.

Mayon-White, B. (1993) Problem solving in small groups: team members as agents of change, in C. Mabey and B. Mayon-White (eds) *Managing Change*, London: Paul Chapman Publishing (2nd ed.).

McCalman, J. and Paton, R. A. (1992) *Change Management: A Guide to Effective Implementation*, London: Paul Chapman Publishing.

McCarthy, M. (1990) Ancient wisdom: the new science – towards a philosophy of change, *Management Education and Development*, vol. 21, part 1, pp. 22–9.

McCollum, A. and Calder, J. (1995) Learning effectiveness of open and flexible learning in vocational education, *Employment Department Research Series*, no. 57, August.

McGill, I. and Beatty, L. (1992) *Action Learning*, London: Kogan Page.

McGill, M. E. (1992) Management practices in learning organizations, *Organizational Dynamics*, vol. 20, pp. 5–17.

McGill, M. E. and Slocum, J. (1993) Unlearning the organization, *Organizational Dynamics*, vol. 22, issue 2, pp. 67–79.

McGuire, M., McGuire, S. and Felstead, A. (1993) Factors influencing individual commitment to lifetime learning, *Employment Department Research Series*, no. 20, December.

McIntosh, S. S. (1994) A remedy for complacency, *HRM Magazine*, vol. 39, July, p. 89.

McKinlay, A. and Starkey, K. (1994) After Henry: continuity and change in Ford Motor Company, *Business History*, vol. 36, no. 1, pp. 184–206.

Mercer, D. (ed.) (1992) *Managing the External Environment: A Strategic Perspective*, London: Sage.

Metcalfe, H., Waling, H. and Fogarty, M. (1994) Individual commitment to learning: employers attitudes, *Employment Department Research Series*, no. 40, November.

Miles, R. E. and Snow, C. C. (1995) The new network firm: A spherical structure built on a human investment philosophy, *Organizational Dynamics*, vol. 23, no. 4, pp. 4–19.

Miller, D. (1996) A preliminary typology of organisational learning: synthesising the literature, *Journal of Management*, vol. 22, no. 3, pp. 485–506.

Miller, J. and Glassner, B. (1997) The 'inside' and the 'outside': finding realities in interviews, in D. Silverman (ed.) *Qualitative Research: Theory, Method and Practice*, London: Sage.

Mintzberg, H. (1994) *The Rise and Fall of Strategic Planning*, Hemel Hempstead: Prentice Hall.

Mitroff, I. I. and Bennis, W. (1993) *The Unreality Industry: The Deliberate Manufacture of Falsehood and What it is Doing to our Lives*, Oxford: Oxford University Press.

Morgan, G. (1986) *Images of Organization*, London: Sage.

Morgan, G. (1988) *Riding the Waves of Change: Developing Managerial Competencies for a Changing World*, London: Jossey Bass.

Morgan, G. (1989) *Beyond Method: Strategies for Social Research*, London: Sage.

Morgan, G. (1989) *Creative Organizational Theory*, London: Sage.

Morgan, G. (1993) *Imaginization*, London: Sage.

Morgan, G. (1997) *Images of Organization*, London: Sage (2nd ed.).

Morris, J. (1988) The who, why and where of Japanese manufacturing investment in the UK, *Industrial Relations Journal*, vol. 19, no. 1, pp. 31–40.

Morris, J. (1989) The clenched fist and the open hand, *Association for Management Development*, unpublished paper.

Moss Jones, J. (1992) The learning organization, The Open University, Centre for Technology Strategy, unpublished paper.

Moss Kanter, R. (1985) *The Change Masters*, New York: Unwin.

Moss Kanter, R. (1989) *When Giants Learn to Dance*, New York: Unwin.

Mumford, A. (1986) Learning to learn for managers, *Journal of European Industrial Training*, vol. 10, no. 2, pp. 3–28.

Mumford, A. (1989) *Management Development, Strategies for Action*, London: IPM.

Mumford, A. (1991) Learning in action, *Personnel Management*, July, pp. 34–7.

Mumford, A. (1992) Individual and organizational learning: the pursuit of change, *Management Decision*, vol. 30, no. 6, pp. 143–8.

Mumford, A. (1993) *How Managers Can Develop Managers*, Aldershot: Gower.

Mumford, A. (1994) Individual and organisational learning, in C. Mabey and P. Iles (eds), *Managing Learning*, London: Routledge.

Murakami, M. (1995) Introducing team working – a motor industry case study from Germany, *Industrial Relations Journal*, vol. 26, no. 4, pp. 293–305.

Murata, K. and Harrison, A. (1991) *How to Make Japanese Management Methods Work in the West*, London: Gower.

Nadler, D. A. (1993) Concepts for the management of strategic change, in C. Mabey and B. Mayon-White (eds) *Managing Change*, London: Paul Chapman Publishing (2nd ed.).

Naisbitt, J. (1994) *Global Paradox*, London: Nicholas Brealy Publishing.

Naylor, P. (1991) Bringing home the lessons, *Personnel Management*, August, pp. 34–7.

Nevis, E. C., Dibella, A. and Gould, J. M. (1995) Understanding organizations as learning systems, *Sloan Management Review*, Winter, vol. 36, no. 2, pp. 73–85.

Nicolini, D., Meznar, M., Stewart, G., Manz, C. and Klein, R. (1995) The social construction of organizational learning, *Human Relations*, vol. 48, no. 7, pp. 727–48.

Niimi, A. (1993) Assembly line automation at Toyota, in J. Benders (1995) *Leaving Lean? Contemporary Developments in Japanese Car Factories*, unpublished paper, 13th Labour Process Conference, 5–7 April, Blackpool.

Nishiguchi, T. (1994) *Strategic Industrial Sourcing – The Japanese Advantage*, New York: Oxford University Press.

Noel, J. L. and Charan, R. (1992) GE brings global thinking to Light, *Training and Development*, July, pp. 29–33.

Nohria, N. and Eccles, R. G. (1992) (eds) *Networks and Organizations*, Boston: Harvard Business School Press.

Nonaka, I. and Johanssen, J. (1985) Japanese management: what about the hard skills? *Academy of Management Review*, vol. 10, no. 4, pp. 181–91.

Nonaka, I. (1988) Towards middle-up-down-management: accelerating information creation, *Sloan Management Review*, Spring, pp. 9–18.

Nonaka, I. (1991) The knowledge creating company, *Harvard Business Review*, November–December, pp. 96–104.

Nurmi, R. (1992) Corporate transformation, *Leadership and Organizational Development*, vol. 13, issue 5, pp. 1–111.

Nystrom, P. and Starbuck, W. H. (1984) To avoid organizational crises, unlearn, *Organizational Dynamics*, Spring, pp. 53–65.

Ohmae, K. (1982) *The Mind of the Strategist*, New York: Penguin.

Ogbonna, E. (1992) Organization culture and human resource management: dilemmas and contradictions, in P. Blyton and P. Turnbull (eds) *Reassessing Human Resource Management*, London: Sage.

Oliver, N. and Wilkinson, B. (1989) Japanese manufacturing techniques and personnel and industrial relations practice in Britain, *British Journal of Industrial Relations*, March, pp. 73–91.

Oliver, N. and Wilkinson, B. (1992) *The Japanization of British Industry*, London: Blackwell (2nd ed.).

Oliver, N., Delbridge, R. and Lowe, J. (1996) The European auto components industry: manufacturing performance and practice, *International Journal of Operations and Production Management*, vol. 16, no. 11, pp. 85–97.

Osbaldeston, M. and Barham, K. (1992) Using management development for competitive advantage, *Long Range Planning*, vol. 25, no. 6, pp. 18–24.

Ouchi, W. (1981) Theory Z: How Japan gets the most from its workers, extract taken from *San Francisco Chronicle*, June.

Owen, H. (1987) *Spirit: Transformation and Development in Organizations*, New York: Abbot Publishing.

Palmer, G. (1996) Circumventing quality and control: a perspective from the Japanese shopfloor in Britain, paper presented to the Globalisation of Production and the Regulation of Labour Conference, 11–13 September, Warwick University.

Palmer, G. (1996) Reviving resistance: the Japanese factory floor in Britain, *Industrial Relations Journal*, vol. 27, no. 2, pp. 129–44.

Park, A. (1994) Individual commitment to learning: individuals' attitudes, *Employment Department Research Series*, no. 32, July.

Parker, M. and Slaughter, J. (1988) *Choosing Sides*, Boston: South End Press.

Parkhe, A. (1991) Interfirm diversity: organizational learning and longevity in global strategic alliances, *Journal of International Business Studies*, fourth quarter, pp. 579–601.

Pascale, R. and Athos, A. (1982) *The Art of Japanese Management*, London: Penguin.

Pascale, R. (1990) *Managing on the Edge*, London: Penguin.

Pascale, R. (1993) Management fads under attack, *Personnel Management*, December, p. 17.

Pascale, R. (1994) Intentional breakdowns and conflict by design, *Planning Review*, vol. 22, part 3, pp. 12–19.

Payne, R. (1991) Taking stock of corporate culture, *Personnel Management*, July, pp. 26–9.

Pearn, M., Roderick, C. and Mulrooney, M. (1995) *Learning Organizations in Practice*, Maidenhead, England: McGraw-Hill.

Pedlar, N. (1991) The man who gave Japan the quality edge, *Japan Digest*, January, pp. 8–12.

Pedler, M. (1983) *Action Learning in Practice*, London: Gower.

Pedler, M. and Boydell, T. (1985) *Managing Yourself*, London: Gower.

Pedler, M., Burgoyne, J. and Boydell, T. (1978) *A Managers Guide to Self-Development*, London: McGraw-Hill.

Pedler, M., Burgoyne, J. and Boydell, T. (1987/88) *The Learning Company Project Report*, London: Manpower Services Commission.

Pedler, M., Burgoyne, J. and Boydell, T. (1989) Towards the learning company, *Management Education and Development*, vol. 20, part 1, pp. 1–8.

Pedler, M., Burgoyne, J. and Boydell, T. (1991) *The Learning Company*, London: McGraw-Hill.

Perrow, C. (1970) *Organizational Analysis: A Sociological View*, London: Tavistock Publications.

Perrow, C. (1989) The short and glorious history of organizational theory, in G. Morgan (ed.) *Beyond Method: Strategies for Social Research*, London: Sage.

Peters, T. (1987) *Thriving on Chaos*, New York: Macmillan.

Peters, T. (1988) Facing up to the need for a management revolution, *California Management Review*, Winter, pp. 7–38.

Peters, T. (1989) New products, new markets, new competition, new thinking, *The Economist*, March pp. 27–30.

Peters, T. (1992) *Liberation Management*, New York: Macmillan.

Peters, T. and Waterman, R. (1982) *In Search of Excellence*, New York: Harper and Row.

Pettigrew, A. and Whipp, R. (1993) Understanding the environment, in C. Mabey and B. Mayon-White (eds) *Managing Change*, London: Paul Chapman Publishing (2nd ed.).

Piore, M. and Sabel, C. (1984) *The Second Industrial Divide*, New York: Basic Books.

Pilkington, A. (1996) Learning from joint venture: the Rover–Honda relationship, *Business History*, vol. 38, no. 1, pp. 90–115.

Pitman, B. (1994) How to build a learning culture to cope with rapid change, *Journal of Systems Management*, vol. 45, no. 7, pp. 27–8.

Pollert, A. (1988) Dismantling flexibility, *Capital and Class*, vol. 34, Spring, pp. 42–75.

Pollit, C. (1990) *Managerialism in the Public Services*, London: Blackwell.

Prigogine, I. and Stengers, I. (1984) *Order Out of Chaos*, Glasgow: Fontana.

Pugh, D. (1993) Understanding and managing organizational change, in C. Mabey and B. Mayon-White (eds) *Managing Change*, London: Paul Chapman Publishing (2nd ed.).

Quinn, J. B. (1993) Managing strategic change, in C. Mabey and B. Mayon-White (eds) *Managing Change*, London: Paul Chapman Publishing (2nd ed.).

Quinn Mills, D. and Friesen, B. (1992) The learning organization, *European Management Journal*, vol. 10, no. 2, pp. 146–56.

Reed, M. (1991) Scripting scenarios for a new organization theory and practice, *Work, Employment and Society*, vol. 5, no. 1, pp. 119–32.

Reed, M. and Hughes, M. (1992) *Rethinking Organizations*, London: Sage.

Rehder, R. R. (1981) What American and Japanese managers are learning from each other, *Business Horizons*, February, pp. 63–70.

Rehder, R. R. (1992) Building cars as if people mattered: the Japanese lean system vs. Volvo's Uddevalla system, *Columbia Journal of World Business*, vol. 27, no. 2, pp. 56–70.

Rehder, R. R. (1994) Saturn, Uddevalla and the Japanese lean systems: paradoxical prototypes for the 21st century, *International Journal for Human Resource Management*, vol. 5, no. 1, pp. 1–31.

Revans, R. (1982) T*he Origins and Growth of Action Learning*, England: Chartwell Bratt.

Reynolds, M. (1997) Learning styles: a critique, *Management Learning*, vol. 28, no. 2, pp. 115–33.

Ritzer, G. (1995) *The McDonaldization of Society*, London: Sage (revised ed.).

Roddick, A. (1992) *Body and Soul*, London: Vermilion.

Rogers, C. (1989) *The Carl Rogers Reader*, London: Constable.

Rogers, E., Metlay, W., Kaplan, I. and Shapiro, T. (1995) Self-managing work teams: do they really work? *Human Resource Planning*, vol. 18, no. 2, pp. 53–9.

Roth, V. A., Marucheck, A. S., Kemp, A. and Trimble, D. (1994) The knowledge factory for accelerated learning, *Planning Review*, vol. 22, part 3, pp. 26–46.

Salaman, G. (1992) (ed.) *Human Resource Strategies*, London: Sage.

Salaman, G. and Butler, J. (1994) Why managers won't learn, in C. Mabey and P. Iles (eds) *Managing Learning*, London: Routledge.

Sandberg, A. (1995) (ed.) *Enriching Production*, Aldershot: Avebury.

Sandkull, B. (1996) Lean production: the myth which changes the world? in S. Clegg and G. Palmer (eds) *The Politics of Management Knowledge*, London: Sage.

Sayer, A. (1992) *Method in Social Science: A Realist Approach*, London: Routledge.

Savage, P. (1988) Energising organizations through employee participation, *Personnel Management*, July, pp. 35–9.

Scarborough, H. and Corbett, M. (1992) *Technology and Organization: Power, Meaning and Design*, London: Routledge.

Schein, E. H. (1985) *Organizational Culture and Leadership*, London: Jossey-Bass.

Schein, E. H. (1993) How can organizations learn faster? *Sloan Management Review*, Winter, pp. 85–92.

Schon, D. A. (1983) *The Reflective Practitioner*, New York: Basic Books.

Schon, D. A. (1989) Organisational learning, in G. Morgan (ed.), *Beyond Method: Strategies for Social Research*, London: Sage.

Schonberger, R. (1982) *Japanese Manufacturing Techniques*, New York: Free Press.

Schuring, R. (1996) Operational autonomy explains the value of group work in both lean and reflective production, *International Journal of Operations and Production Management*, vol. 16, no. 2, pp. 171–83.

Senge, P. (1990) *The Fifth Discipline: The Art and Practice of the Learning Organization*, New York: Century Business.

Senge, P. (1991) The learning organization made plain, *Training and Development*, October, pp. 37–44.

Senge, P. (1992) Building learning organizations, *Journal for Quality and Participation*, March, pp. 30–8.

Senge, P. (1994) Personal transformation, *Executive Excellence*, vol. 11, issue 1, pp. 17–18.

Sewell, G. and Wilkinson, B. (1992a) Empowerment or emasculation? Shopfloor surveillance in a total quality organization, in P. Blyton and P. Turnbull (eds) *Reassessing Human Resource Management*, London: Sage.

Sewell, G. and Wilkinson, B. (1992b) Someone to watch over me – surveillance, discipline and the just-in-time labour process, *Sociology*, May, pp. 271–89.

Sheridan, J. H. (1996) Where's the agility game plan? *Industry Week*, vol. 245, no. 14, 14 July, pp. 50–2.

Silverman, D. (1993) *Interpreting Qualitative Data: Methods for Analysing Talk, Text and Interaction*, London: Sage.

Sinclair, J. and Collins, D. (1991) Training and development's worst enemies – you and management, *Journal of European Industrial Training*, vol. 16, no. 5, pp. 21–5.

Sisson, K. and Storey, J. (1988) Developing effective managers: a review of the issues and an agenda for research, *Personnel Review*, vol. 17, part 4, pp. 3–8.

Slaughter, J. (1987) The team concept in the US auto industry: implications for unions, paper given at ERU Conference on the Japanization of British Industry, 20–22 September, UWIST, Cardiff.

Sloan, A. P. (1986) *My Years at General Motors*, Harmondsworth, England: Penguin.

Smith, D. (1988) The Japanese example in south west Birmingham, *Industrial Relations Journal*, vol. 19, no. 1, pp. 41–50.

Smitka, M. (1991) *Competitive Ties: Subcontracting in the Japanese Auto Industry*, New York: Columbia University Press.

Snow, C., Miles, R. and Coleman, B. (1993) Managing 21st century network organizations, in C. Mabey and B. Mayon-White (eds) *Managing Change*, London: Paul Chapman Publishing (2nd ed.).

Soloman, C. M. (1994) HR facilitates the learning organisation concept, *Personnel Journal*, vol. 73, no. 11, pp. 56–65.

Sorensen, C. (1956) *My Forty Years with Ford*, New York: W. W. Norton.

Sorum Brown, J. (1993) The quest for quality, *Leadership*, pp. 25–9.

Srivastava, S., Bilimoria, D., Cooperrider, D. L. and Fry, R. E. (1995) Management and organisation learning for positive global change, *Management Learning*, vol. 26, no. 1, pp. 37–54.

Stacey, R. D. (1992) *Managing Chaos*, London: Kogan Page.

Stacey, R. D. (1996) *Strategic Management and Organizational Dynamics*, London: Pitman (2nd ed.).

Starkey, K. (1996) (ed.) *How Organizations Learn*, London: Thompson Business Press.

Stata, R. (1989) Organizational learning – the key to management innovation, *Sloan Management Review*, Spring, pp. 63–74.

Stead, V. and Easterby-Smith, M. (1995) Evaluation oils the wheels of industry, *People Management*, vol. 1, no. 24, pp. 28–31.

Stephenson, J. and Weil, S. (1992) *Quality in Learning*, London: Kogan Page.

Stewart, P. and Garrahan, P. (1995) Employee responses to new management techniques in the auto industry, *Work, Employment and Society*, vol. 9, no. 3, pp. 517–36.

Stewart, J. (1996) *Managing Change Through Training and Development*, London: Kogan Page (2nd ed.).

Stewart, J. (1999) *Employee Development Practice*, London: Financial Times Pitman Publishing.

Stewart, T. A. (1996) The invisible key to success: communities of practice, *Fortune*, vol. 134, no. 3, pp. 173–7.

Storey, J. (1989) Management development: a literature review and implications for future research, *Personnel Review*, vol. 18, no. 6, pp. 3–19.

Storey, J (1994) (ed.) *New Wave Manufacturing Strategies*, London: Paul Chapman Publishing.

Storey, J. (1995) (ed.) *Human Resource Management: A Critical Text*, London: Routledge.

Sullivan, K. (1991) Inventing the future, *Employment Relations Today*, vol. 18, issue 4, pp. 417–24.

Taylor, A. (1994) The new golden age of autos, *Fortune*, vol. 129, no. 7, pp. 50–61.

Taylor, A. (1996) It's the slow lane for auto makers, *Fortune*, vol. 133, no. 6, pp. 59–61.

Taylor, F. W. (1911) *Principles of Scientific Management*, New York: Harper and Row.

Taylor, S. (1992) Managing a learning environment, *Personnel Management*, October, pp. 54–7.

Teresko, J. (1994) Japan: reengineering versus tradition, *Industry Week*, vol. 243, no. 16, pp. 62–8.

Thomas, C. W. (1994) Learning from imagining the years ahead, *Planning Review*, vol. 22, part 3, pp. 6–11.

Thompson, J. D. (1967) *Organizations in Action*, New York: McGraw-Hill.

Thompson, P. (1983) *The Nature of Work*, London: Macmillan.

Thompson, P. and McHugh, D. (1995) *Work Organizations*, London: Macmillan Business (2nd ed.).

Thompson, P. and Davidson, J. A. (1995) The continuity of discontinuity: Managerial rhetoric in turbulent times (the rhetoric and culture of HRM) *Personnel Review*, June, vol. 24, no. 4, pp. 17–33.

Thompson, P. and Ackroyd, S. (1995) All quiet on the workplace front? A critique of recent trends in British industrial sociology, *Sociology*, vol. 29, no. 4, pp. 615–33.

Thompson, P., Wallace, T., Flecker, J. and Ahlstrand, R. (1995) It ain't what you do it's the way that you do it; production organization and skill utilization in commercial vehicles, *Work, Employment and Society*, vol. 9, no. 4, pp. 719–42.

Thompson, P. and Wallace, T. (1996) Redesigning production through teamworking: case studies from the Volvo truck corporation, *International Journal of Operations and Production Management*, vol. 16, no. 2, pp. 103–18.

Thompson, J. K. and Rehder, R. R. (1995) Nissan UK: A worker's paradox, *Business Horizons*, vol. 38, no. 1, pp. 48–58.

Thornhill, A., Lewis, P., Millmore, M. and Saunders, M. (2000) *Managing Change: A Human Resource Approach*, London: Financial Times Pitman Publishing.

Thurow, L. (1993) *Head to Head*, London: Nicholas Brealy Publishing.

Toffler, A. (1971) *Future Shock*, London: Pan Books.

Toffler, A. (1981) *The Third Wave*, London: Pan Books.

Tomkins, J. A. (1993) Team based continuous improvement, *Material Handling Engineering*, January, pp. 73–6.

Torrington, D., Hall, L. and Myers, J. (1998) *Human Resource Management*, London: Prentice Hall (4th ed.).

Torrington, D., Hall, L. and Myers, J. (1998) *The Human Resource Function*, London: Financial Times Pitman Publishing.

Tosey, P. (1994) Energies of organization and change, in J. Burgoyne *et al.* (eds), *Towards the Learning Company: Concepts and Practices*, London: McGraw-Hill.

Tsang, E. (1997) Organisational learning and the learning organisation: a dichotomy between descriptive and prescriptive research, *Human Relations*, vol. 50, no. 1, pp. 73–89.

Turnbull, P. J. (1986) The Japanization of production and industrial relations at Lucas Electrical, *Industrial Relations Journal*, vol. 17, no. 3, pp. 193–206.

Turnbull, P. J. (1988) The limits to Japanization – just-in-time, labour relations and the UK automotive industry, *New Technology, Work and Employment*, vol. 3, no. 1, pp. 7–20.

Udagawa, M. (1995) The development of production management at the Toyota Motor Corporation, *Business History*, vol. 37, no. 2, pp. 107–20.

Vaill, P. B. (1989) *Managing as a Performing Art*, San Francisco: Jossey Bass.

Vance, C. M. (1991) Formalising storytelling in organizations: a key agenda for the design of training, *Journal of Organizational Change Management*, vol. 4, no. 3, pp. 52–8.

Vicere, A. A. (1991) The changing paradigm of executive development, *Journal of Management Development*, vol. 4, no. 3, pp. 44–7.

Vince, R. (1996) Experiential management education as the practice of change, in R. French and C. Grey (eds), *Rethinking Management Education*, London: Sage.

Vogel, E. (1979) *Japan as Number One*, New York: Harvard University Press.

Voss, C. A. and Robinson, S. J. (1987) Application of just-in-time manufacturing techniques in the United Kingdom, *International Journal of Operations and Production Management*, vol. 7, no. 4, pp. 46–52.

Vowles, A. (1993) Gaining competitive advantage through organizational learning, *CMA Magazine*, April, pp. 12–14.

Wack, P. (1985) Scenarios: uncharted waters ahead, *Harvard Business Review*, September–October, pp. 73–89.

Wagstyl, S. (1996) Evolution not revolution, *Financial Times*, 25 March, p. 11.

Watson, T. J. (1994) *In Search of Management: Culture, Chaos and Control in Managerial Work*, London: Routledge.

Watson, T. J. (1995) In search of HRM: the rhetoric and culture of HRM, *Personnel Review*, vol. 24, no. 4, pp. 6–17.

Weber, M. (1947) *The Theory of Social and Economic Organization*, London: Oxford University Press.

Weick, K. E. (1977) Organisation design: organisations as self-designing systems, *Organisational Dynamics*, Autumn, pp. 31–46.

Weisbord, M. (1987) *Productive Workplaces: Organizing and Managing for Dignity, Meaning and Community*, New York: Jossey-Bass.

Werner, M. (1992) The great paradox, responsibility without empowerment, *Business Horizons*, September–October, pp. 55–8.

West, P. (1994a) The concept of the learning organization, *Journal of European Industrial Training*, vol. 18, no. 1, pp. 15–21.

West, P. (1994b) The learning organization: losing the luggage in transit, *Journal of European Industrial Training*, vol. 18, no. 11, pp. 30–8.

West, P. (1995) Infinity goes on trial: the imperatives for a sustainable reality, *Leadership and Organization Development Journal*, vol. 16, no. 8, pp. 10–16.

Wheelwright, S. C. (1981) Japan – where operations really are strategic, *Harvard Business Review*, July–August, pp. 67–74.

Whitehill, A. M. (1991) *Japanese Management: Tradition and Transition*, London: Routledge.

Whittaker, D. H. (1990) The end of Japanese style employment? *Work, Employment and Society*, vol. 4, no. 3, pp. 321–47.

Whittington, R. (1993) *What is Strategy and Does it Matter?* London: Routledge.

Whittle, S., Smith, S., Tranfield. D. and Foster, M. (1992) Implementing total quality, *International Journal of Technology Management*, vol. 7, pp. 235–43.

Wickens, P. (1992) Management development is dead! *Management Development Review*, vol. 5, no. 5, pp. 3–7.

Wickens, P. (1993) Lean production and beyond: the system, its critics and the future, *Human Resource Management Journal*, vol. 3, no. 4, pp. 75–89.

Wiener, N. (1961) *Cybernetics*, Cambridge, MA: MIT Press.

Wilkinson, E. (1990) *Japan versus the West*, London: Penguin.

Wilkinson, A. and Willmott, H. (1995) *Making Quality Critical: New Perspectives on Organizational Change*, London: Routledge.

Williams, A. (1989) *Changing Culture*, London: IPM.

Williams, K., Haslam, C. and Haslam, J. (1992) Ford versus 'Fordism': the beginning of mass production? *Work, Employment and Society*, vol. 6, no. 4, pp. 517–55.

Williams, K., Haslam, C. and Johal, S. (1995) Fait accompli? A Machiavellian interpretation of the Renault–Volvo merger in Sandberg, A. (ed.) *Enriching Production*, Aldershot: Avebury.

Willmott, H. (1993) Strength is ignorance, slavery is freedom: managing culture in modern organizations, *Journal of Management Studies*, vol. 30, pp. 515–52.

Willmott, H. (1994) Management education, provocations to a debate, *Management Learning*, vol. 25, no. 1, pp. 105–36.

Willmott, H. (1995) The odd couple? Reengineering business processes, managing human resources, *Manchester School of Management*, UMIST, unpublished paper.

Wills, G. (1992) Enabling managerial growth and ownership succession, *Management Decision*, vol. 30, part 1, pp. 10–26.

Wilson, D. C. (1992) *A Strategy of Change*, London: Routledge.

Winfield, I. and Kerrin, M. (1994) Toyota and management change in the East Midlands, *Journal of Managerial Psychology*, vol. 9, no. 1, pp. 3–6.

Womack, J. P., Jones, D. T. and Roos, D. (1990) *The Machine that Changed the World*, New York: Macmillan.

Wood, S. (1988) *Continuous Development: The Path to Improved Performance*, London: IPM.

Wood, S. (1989) The Japanese management model, *Work and Occupations*, vol. 2, pp. 27–38.

Wood, S. (1991) Japanization and/or Toyotaism? *Work, Employment and Society*, vol. 5, no. 4, pp. 567–600.

Woodward, J. (1965) *Industrial Organization: Theory and Practice*, Oxford: Oxford University Press.

Zemke, R. and Zemke, S. (1995) Adult learning: what do we know for sure? *Training*, June, vol. 32, no. 6, pp. 31–7.

Zuboff, S. (1988) *In the Age of the Smart Machine*, New York: Basic Books.

Index